THE ARCHAEOLOGY OF

BOKERLEY DYKE

FRONTISPIECE   The country behind Bokerley Dyke: Ackling Dyke, a Roman road, strikes north east across Oakley Down, with barrows just masked by smoke, continuing as the modern road and pointing into the major settlement Pentridge (15) at 'Bokerley Junction'. (NMR BB71/2649)

ROYAL COMMISSION ON THE HISTORICAL MONUMENTS OF ENGLAND

THE ARCHAEOLOGY OF
BOKERLEY DYKE

H C Bowen

Edited by B N Eagles

LONDON: HMSO

ISBN 0 11 300019 7

British Library Cataloguing in
Publication Data
A CIP catalogue record for this book is
available from the British Library

Printed in the United Kingdom for HMSO
Dd. 240087, 6/90, C5, GP 3385/2, CCN 16268

CONTENTS

Part III: Area Plans

Part IV: A review of monuments east and west of Bokerley Dyke

Summary

Part V: Inventory

Bibliography

Index

LIST OF ILLUSTRATIONS

AREA PLANS

PREFACE

This volume is different in character and treatment from previous Royal Commission works and its origins are given in some detail in the first and second chapters of the book. Essentially, it derives from an awareness that some monuments present problems requiring particularly critical analysis. In the case of Bokerley Dyke, lying between Dorset and Hampshire on a line now established as prehistoric, the emergence of a variety of new information and the interest in linear ditch systems, especially, springing from a preliminary review of field archaeology in Hampshire, combined both to justify and to shape the volume here offered. The subject is reviewed in some depth and, by reason of wide landscape considerations, in breadth.

The work has involved additions and certain modifications to the content of the Royal Commission's later Dorset inventories, some of which were anticipated by Commissioners when, in the fifth volume, they noted that Bokerley could only be adequately studied if looked at from Hampshire as well as from Dorset. Some of the hypotheses advanced are inevitably tentative but it is hoped that the reasons for them are adequately clear. It has been necessary, however, in the interests of economic publication, to assemble much tabulated inventory data in a separate supplementary cover, available to readers at cost, as explained in the Editorial Notes.

To this factual description of *The Archaeology of Bokerley Dyke*, the Royal Commission wishes to add its particular appreciation of the author. Collin Bowen, for many years head of the Royal Commission's Salisbury Office, has played a crucial part in shaping our country's post-war progress in agrarian archaeology and interpretative fieldwork. The archaeological content of the Dorset inventories, much of which was compiled under his immediate direction, records a largely vanished prehistory in rare detail, and is buttressed by a range of papers in national and county journals and, above all, by his immensely influential book *Ancient Fields*. It is a matter of record that public awareness of, and response to, the post-war scale of destruction of archaeological monuments was much influenced by the Royal Commission's *A Matter of Time* (1960) and that the formation of the pressure group RESCUE in 1971 arose in large part from the detailed statistics of such rural destruction in Dorset. It is less well known that Collin Bowen was a prime mover in this phase, providing irrefutable evidence from the field and allowing others to take the limelight. His greatest contribution to archaeology has been to train, by precept and by long association, a generation of fieldworkers within and beyond the Royal Commission; in so doing, he provided a style, laid down standards and widened personal horizons in a manner that few such practical teachers can hope to match.

The Archaeology of Bokerley Dyke is the work of one who writes, with profound authority, of a prehistoric Wessex landscape that he knows, comprehends and has done his best to preserve for the rest of us. In publishing it, the Royal Commission would emphasise — from Commissioners and staff alike — the deep respect, gratitude and affection in which this former colleague is held.

CHARLES THOMAS *Acting Chairman*

COMMISSIONERS

EDITORIAL NOTES

Throughout this volume, the variant spelling of 'Bokerley' has been used, although, of course, General Pitt-Rivers' use of the form 'Bokerly' has been retained in extracts quoted from his work.

Monuments discussed in this volume have been referenced according to the parish in which they occur; thus, they are prefixed by the full parish name (eg, Pentridge) or, in Part V, by the initial letter of the parish name (eg, P). In all cases, this reference is followed by a number (eg, P (16)); monuments have mostly been allocated numbers according to their location within the parish, in sequence from west to east, following normal Royal Commission practice. Some monument references have a third element, such as A, B or C (eg, Martin (80) A or P (16) B), which denotes an identifiable feature within the principal monument. Monuments in Dorset which are described in this volume and are additional to those published in the Royal Commission's Dorset inventories are prefixed by 'a' (eg, Gussage St Michael (a 36)).

Plans and sections have been prepared for this publication using a variety of scales, details of which are given in the captions to the Figures. Drawings were originally made using imperial measurements but, for all appropriate figures, a metric scale is also included. Measurements in the text are expressed in metric units, with their imperial equivalents given in brackets. The profiles of linear earthworks and Bokerley Dyke itself, which have been taken in the field by the Royal Commission, are distinguished by 'R' and a following number, in topographical sequence for each monument.

The air photographs either reproduced in this volume or quoted as supporting evidence have been taken from a range of sources, indicated on p 6. All photographs, both ground and air, are fully referenced within the text; those given an NMR or RAF reference number are held in the National Monuments Record at the Royal Commission on the Historical Monuments of England, Fortress House, 23 Savile Row, London W1X 2JQ, where they may normally be consulted by the public. All plates reproduced are Crown copyright unless otherwise indicated. North is always to the top of the air photographs unless stated to the contrary.

The material published in this volume, and the conclusions derived from its study, is supported by an extensive programme of survey and recording carried out by the Royal Commission in the counties of Hampshire and Dorset. This information has been produced as a Tabulated Inventory and is available, at a nominal cost, from the Royal Commission at the above address on request.

ACKNOWLEDGEMENTS

The former Secretary to the Royal Commission, Professor P J Fowler, took a lively, encouraging and constructive interest in this volume. Past and present Commissioners who have been especially interested and helpful are Dr P Ashbee, Professor R J C Atkinson, Professor R J Bradley, Professor S S Frere, Professor A L F Rivet, Professor A C Thomas and Professor M Todd. Of the Commission staff involved in the project, particular tribute is paid to the skill and enthusiasm of Mr John Bassham (photography), who sadly died while the work was in progress, and Mr A L Pope who was, most helpfully, a critical supervisor of the drawing programme. Others who made significant contributions were Mr C W Butler (field survey), Messrs J N Hampton, R Palmer and G Soffe (aerial photography and transcription), Mr R Parsons (formerly Chief Photographer), Mr F A Aberg and staff of the National Archaeological Record (National Monuments Record), Miss K Cook (illustrations), Mr R A H Farrar and Mrs V G Swan (Romano-British pottery), Miss V A Smith (word-processing) and Miss K Owen (Managing Editor).

Particular assistance from outside the Royal Commission was given by Professor J K S St Joseph and Dr D R Wilson, who flew special surveys for the Cambridge University Committee for Aerial Photography, and by Mr J R Boyden, who co-operated closely in volunteering to make particular and profitable searches from the air. Dr J G Evans carried out excavations of two major linears to seek answers to specific questions by the recovery of molluscan evidence. Another excavation to resolve particular points was conducted by Mr R T Schadla-Hall, who was also very helpful in other ways. The former Archaeology Division of the Ordnance Survey, and especially Mr C F Wardale, who later joined the staff of the Royal Commission, provided OS Antiquity Models and helped in a number of ways. Dr A J Clark and the Geophysical Section, Ancient Monuments Laboratory (English Heritage), put in considerable effort investigating problems benefiting from sophisticated geophysical survey.

Mr M T Green has made freely available his knowledge of the Gussage area in east Dorset and has allowed the Royal Commission to make use of his air photographs. Mr A Light readily allowed access to the results of the extensive fieldwalking and excavation by the Avon Valley Archaeological Society. Mr P Catherall and a number of workers provided most useful information when a pipeline was being cut right across the area. Mr and Mrs D Jarvis provided invaluable assistance in the matter of the West Park Roman villa, Rockbourne, and Mr I P Horsey, tragically killed in 1988, carried out excavations of importance at the villa.

Thanks are also due to all who gave permission for and facilitated access to archaeological sites, but especially to Mr R S McLeod at Rockbourne and Mr R W Shepherd at Damerham, Mr C C Bonsey, Chief Recreation Officer, Hampshire County Council, and his staff, the officers of the former regional office at Salisbury of the Forestry Commission, and Mr P Toynton, Nature Conservancy Council warden. The Curator, Mr P R Saunders, and staff of the Salisbury and South Wiltshire Museum were most helpful in providing access to selected finds and records. Other acknowledgements for specific assistance are made where appropriate in the text.

H C Bowen
B N Eagles

ABBREVIATIONS

BGC	British Gas Corporation
CUCAP	Cambridge University Collection of Aerial Photography
DoE	Department of the Environment
MBA	Middle Bronze Age
MoW	Ministry of Works
NGR	National Grid Reference
NMR	National Monuments Record
OAP	Oblique air photograph
OD	Ordnance datum
OS	Ordnance Survey
OS AM	Ordnance Survey Antiquity Model
RCHME	Royal Commission on the Historical Monuments of England
VAP	Vertical air photograph

BACKGROUND AND THE LEGACY OF GENERAL PITT-RIVERS

The area in central southern England with which this volume is concerned falls within southern Wessex, the West Saxon kingdom whose historic core lay in Berkshire, Hampshire and Wiltshire. Until 1830, the region lay within the limits of the Outer Bounds of Cranborne Chase. As defined in its legal sense, the Chase extended over more than 700,000 acres (West 1816, iv), stretching from the River Stour in the west to the River Avon in the east and incorporating parts of Wiltshire, in the north, Dorset and Hampshire. The highest part of the region, on the edge of the chalk uplands, some 279 metres above OD at Win Green, lies towards Tisbury in Wiltshire. The Inner Chase, of about 43,000 acres (West 1816, iv), fell either side of the modern county boundary between Wiltshire and Dorset. The archaeological monuments in those parts of the Chase which fall within Wiltshire are not described in the present volume but will be included in another work in preparation by the Royal Commission on south Wiltshire. This book concentrates upon the archaeological sites which lie on the chalk plateau between Chettle in Dorset and, to the east, beyond Bokerley Dyke, Breamore, in Hampshire. To the south of the chalk, extensive areas of generally lower-lying Tertiary clays and gravels fringe the coastal plain (Figs 1, *loose* and 2).

The definition of Cranborne Chase

The legal status of the Outer Chase appears to have originated in the early 13th century and lasted until disfranchisement in 1830 (Pitt-Rivers 1887, xii). The origins of the Inner Chase appear to lie much earlier, in the late Anglo-Saxon period (Poole 1976, 21). The Chase laws provided for the protection of the vegetation or 'vert' as feed for the deer:

> Much of the woodland and commons is capable of tillage, and could be spared for that purpose, were not the conversion forbidden.

> As the sole right to these animals [the fallow deer] is vested in the proprietor of the chace, or in such persons as he appoints, the injury to the cultivated lands may in part be conceived. The deer are in general excluded from them by high and expensive hedges; but as these consist chiefly of dead wood, requiring frequent renewal, and are subject to occasional damage, the depredations on the lands are very

considerable. The woodlands or copses are fenced during three years after each cutting, only by high hedges, in general, as ditches are forbidden by the custom of the chace; and at the end of that time are opened to the deer, by the keepers making gaps called 'leaps and creeps'. The lands subject to damage from the deer are supposed to amount nearly to 32,000 acres; viz. about 7,000 of woodlands, 10,000 of sheep-downs and commons, and 15,000 of cultivated lands.

> (West 1816, v)

The rights of the hunting forest were stoutly defended and they contributed in general to the survival of a variety of ancient earthworks, which elsewhere would have been eroded by more intensive agriculture. In the Inner Chase, where the chalk is overlaid in many places by spreads of clay-with-flints, medieval and later villages are few and there is much woodland today. Here, the conserved earthworks of ancient sites are particularly evident, among them those of the Bronze Age enclosure at South Lodge and the Romano-British villages of Rotherley and Woodcutts – all of them in Wiltshire, bar Woodcutts, and in the neighbourhood of Rushmore Lodge, the family seat of Lieutenant-General Pitt-Rivers. The Inner Chase continued southwards into Dorset, as far as Sixpenny Handley and Farnham, and the present study includes a map of the archaeological sites in that area (Fig 1), many of them having been identified from the air as crop and soil marks in arable since the fifth and final volume of the RCHME Inventory of Dorset was published in 1975. Arable land in the Chase was greatly increased after 1830 but much of it was converted to pasture during the agricultural depression later in the 19th century (Pitt-Rivers 1887, xii). In Bowerchalke, in Wiltshire, West Chase (built c1840), Middle (c1840) and East Chase (c1860) farms were established in Cobley Walk, the easternmost part of the Inner Chase. The former extent of woodland in the area is recorded on a map produced by Thomas Aldwell in 1618 (Pitt-Rivers 1890, Plate 1).

The archaeology of Cranborne Chase

Cranborne Chase is justly famous to archaeologists not only for the quantity of its surviving earthworks but also because some of them are of outstanding importance, most notably, in Dorset, the Neolithic complex and Iron Age hill-fort on Hambledon Hill, the Dorset Cursus (Gussage St Michael (9)), Knowlton Circles (Woodlands (19)–(22)), the barrow cemetery on Oakley Down (Wimborne St Giles (94)–(124)) and Bokerley Dyke itself. The Neolithic sites on Hambledon Hill have been the subject of intensive study (Mercer 1980), particularly through excavation and an extensive programme of fieldwalking; they lie in the south-western part of the Outer Chase, in Dorset, beyond the western limit of Fig 1 and are not discussed in this volume. The Neolithic Cursus extends for 9.5 km north-eastwards from Thickthorn Down, in the parish of Gussage St Michael, to a point just short of Bokerley (Bradley 1986). Its modest earthen banks were in places slighted and overlaid by 'Celtic' fields (see Area Plan 2, loose). At Knowlton, air photographs have revealed the sites of a further seventeen round barrows in the cemetery which clusters around the henges (see Fig 40, page 79). On Oakley Down, some of the barrows, including Wor Barrow long barrow (Sixpenny Handley (29)), excavated by Pitt-Rivers, are shown on Area Plan 3 (loose), which also includes the Angle Ditch (Sixpenny Handley (27)), excavated by General Pitt-Rivers. An important excavation of an Iron Age settlement, at Gussage All Saints (20), was carried out by Dr G J Wainwright (Wainwright 1979); the site is considered below (page 49), in the discussion of settlement types on either side of Bokerley Dyke. Bokerley Dyke, now seen to have been associated with lesser banks and ditches along a 'Bokerley Line' which had a long and complex history, survives today to mark part of the county boundary between Dorset and Hampshire (Bowen 1978).

The archaeology of Cranborne Chase has been richly published, most notably by Colt Hoare, Pitt-Rivers, Heywood Sumner, Crawford and Keiller and more recently reviewed by Professor Hawkes (1947). Sir Richard Colt Hoare's researches early in the 19th century strayed into the area, in pursuit of the Roman road from Old Sarum to Badbury Rings, and his plan in *Ancient Wiltshire* of the earthworks on Gussage Cow Down (Gussage St Michael (7)) remains a valuable record and is reproduced here (Plate 1). His folio volumes also include accounts of archaeological monuments in the parishes of Damerham, Martin and Whitsbury, all now in Hampshire but until 1895 in Wiltshire (Colt Hoare 1810, Station VII, Salisbury).

Between 1887 and 1898 Pitt-Rivers privately printed and distributed four sumptuous volumes in which he recorded the results of his *Excavations in Cranborne Chase*. In volumes I (1887) and II (1888) he presented his discoveries at sites in Wiltshire and Dorset, including the Romano-British villages at Rotherley and Woodcutts, the Iron Age hill-fort of Winkelbury Camp (cf page 5 below) and Bronze Age barrows and an Anglo-Saxon cemetery on Winkelbury Hill, Berwick St John. Volume III (1892) contains an account of his excavations at Bokerley Dyke and Wansdyke. The fourth and final volume (1898) describes Wor Barrow, two Bronze Age enclosures, one at South Lodge, Tollard Royal, and another on Martin Down, in Hampshire (Martin (56), page 107 below), and a further

enclosure at Sixpenny Handley (18), now known to be of medieval date. A fifth book (1890) was devoted to King John's House, also at Tollard Royal.

Heywood Sumner published *Ancient Earthworks of Cranborne Chase* in 1913. In his Preface, he states that his survey, made between 1911 and 1913, was consciously undertaken in response to 'the precepts of the Committee on Ancient Earthworks appointed by the Congress of Archaeological Societies – namely, that Plans and Schedules of our Ancient Earthworks should be made throughout England'. For most sites, he was able to make use of plans published on the 6-inch and 25-inch scale OS maps. The earthworks he recorded in those parts of the Chase which lie in Dorset have been previously inventorised by the Royal Commission (RCHM 1970b, 1972, 1975). However, some of them, notably the complex site on Gussage Cow Down and the linear earthworks on Tarrant Launceston and Thickthorn Downs, are reconsidered in this volume in the context of all the linears now known in the region. On the Hampshire side of Bokerley Dyke, Heywood Sumner's interest in the 'Grim's Ditch' complex of linears led to his excavation of sections across some of them; his observations on their varying profiles were the essential starting-point in establishing the definitions presented below. Other major Hampshire sites to which he gave individual treatment are the hill-fort at Whitsbury and the enclosure on Damerham Knoll (Rockbourne (46)) and the large polygonal enclosures of Soldier's Ring (Damerham (19)) and on Rockbourne Down (Rockbourne (54)). Each of these sites can be found on one of the seven Area Plans included in the present volume and set in the context of the surrounding ancient landscape.

Heywood Sumner had noted the relationship of some sites, such as Soldier's Ring, to 'Celtic' fields. Pitt-Rivers too had recorded lynchets at South Lodge Camp: 'There are not wanting indications that they ['the people of the Bronze Age'] may also have cultivated the soil in fields from the prevalence of lines of terrace near them, but on this subject I had rather withhold my judgment, as no sound argument can be based on proximity in this matter' (Pitt-Rivers 1898, Address of 1897, 19). One of Pitt-Rivers' assistants, H S Toms, who had been present throughout the excavations at South Lodge, returned to Cranborne Chase from Sussex in 1911 and 1912 in order to study these fields, and in 1923 and 1924 he was there again to make measured plans of parts of the systems both at South Lodge and adjacent to the Angle Ditch (Toms 1925). Toms was able to demonstrate that the fields lay under South Lodge Camp and therefore dated from the Bronze Age or earlier. His work produced a lively correspondence with O G S Crawford who, the previous year, had published a pioneering account of 'Celtic' fields, which he suggested were introduced into Britain in the Iron Age (Crawford 1924). Crawford's paper was illustrated by field systems on Figheldean Down (on Salisbury Plain) and in central Hampshire, which had been plotted from air photographs.

In 1928 Crawford and Alexander Keiller published *Wessex from the Air*, at a time when large tracts of the sheep downs remained unploughed. Their volume includes plates and

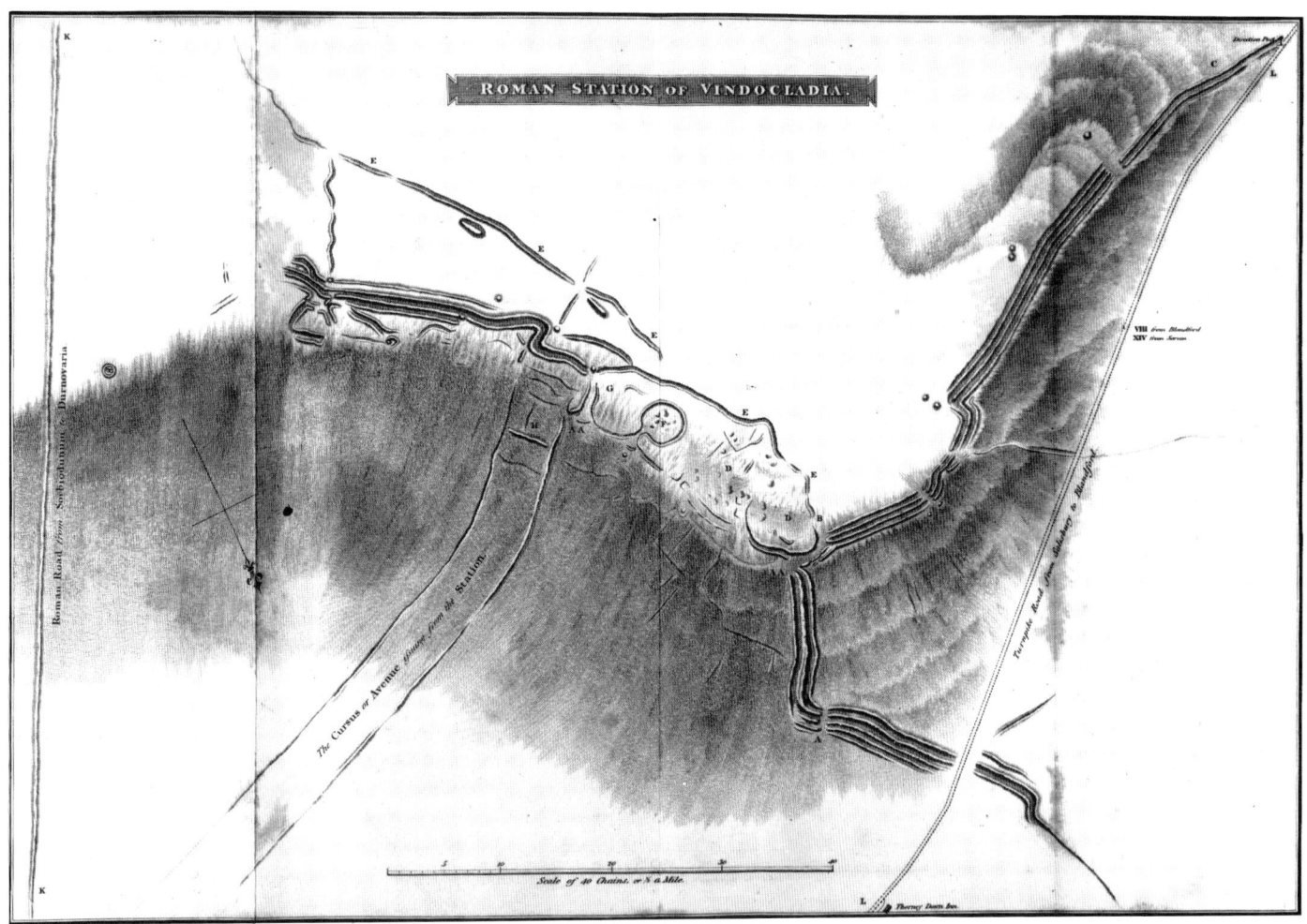

ROMAN STATION OF VINDOCLADIA.

PLATE 1   An illustration of the Roman station of *Vindocladia* taken from Colt Hoare 1821, Roman Aera (Iter 1, between pages 30 and 31). North is to the bottom of the plan.

The plan demonstrates massive destruction before 1821 as well as confirming the former existence of some features now only faintly detectable. Thus, for instance, the Cursus was thought to start here; 'banjo' enclosure **a** is marked only by part of its entrance; there are five parallel banks still at **A**, bottom right, where there was a way through them; two mounds, one being Iron Age barrow Sixpenny Handley (30), flank a gap in four banks centrally to the bow, centre right (cf, Area Plan 2). (NMR BB83/2379)

accompanying transcriptions of a variety of archaeological sites in Cranborne Chase: Badbury Rings, Gussage Cow Down, Handley Hill, Oakley Down, Soldier's Ring and Bokerley Dyke. Their plate of Soldier's Ring is reproduced on page 56 (Plate 23). Crawford's surviving unpublished air photographs have also been consulted in the preparation of this volume.

The work of General Pitt-Rivers

This book would not have been written had General Pitt-Rivers not lived and devoted a considerable part of his work as an archaeologist to an investigation of Bokerley Dyke and its subsequent publication. He applied his innovative genius and the disciplines of technical soldiering to the difficult business of archaeological excavation. His work in some ways has never

been equalled and his prompt and lavish publications will always remain an inspiration.

Augustus Henry Lane Fox (1827–1900), who later assumed the surname Pitt-Rivers (Thompson 1977; Bradley 1983), was commissioned into the Grenadier Guards in 1845. By 1851 he was based at Woolwich, where he was involved in testing the rifle. He soon became interested in the history of firearms and he began to collect them. In a lecture he gave in 1858 he placed emphasis on the 'main chain of improvement' of the musket. The slow and selective modification, or typological development, he had discerned in weapons he was later to extend as a principle to all artifacts, in particular to antiquities and ethnographic material, the collection of which he continued throughout his life. In volume IV of *Excavations in Cranborne Chase* (1898) he included a long discussion on the origin and distribution of chevron-decorated pottery.

Between 1867 and 1869 Fox delivered three lectures on primitive warfare to the Royal United Service Institution, and in these papers the influence of Darwin's *Origin of Species* (first published in 1859) on Fox's approach to ethnological and archaeological material is evident. Fox maintained that the change and development of artifacts through time could only be understood if objects were ordered in a typological series, in the same way that biologists classified plants and animals.

In 1874 Fox placed his own collection on public view at the Bethnal Green branch of the South Kensington Museum. He published a catalogue of part of it, which provides the first information about its precise contents. The display afforded the occasion for a lecture on the 'Principles of Classification'. The exhibition broke new ground in that the objects were set out in a typological rather than a geographical arrangement. The sequences of artifacts, through the selection of one type or form or another, were intended to demonstrate 'either actually or hypothetically, the origin, development, and continuity of the material arts' (Pitt-Rivers and Gray 1905, xiii). Later, the collection, having been offered to, but turned down by, the Government, was presented to the University of Oxford, where it was housed in a specially built annexe to the University Museum. The University established a lectureship in Anthropology, the first in Britain, in connection with the acquisition, and awarded Fox the honour of a Doctorate of Civil Law.

After 1868, Fox became increasingly interested in physical anthropology, greatly influenced by the work of Thomas Huxley, the zoologist, on racial differences and distribution. He was concerned to learn how far the spread of artifacts depended on the diffusion of the races. He also became interested in recording the physical characteristics of living communities. When in command of the 2nd Battalion of the Royal Surrey Militia in Guildford in 1873, he measured and classified the racial characteristics of his men. Later, he conducted a similar exercise with estate workers in Cranborne Chase. He invented his own craniometer in order to obtain precise measurements of the skull (Pitt-Rivers 1898, 118).

In 1867 Fox was in Yorkshire where he undertook fieldwork and visited Canon Greenwell's excavations. Later that year he began the first of his own excavations, at Cissbury in Sussex. His motive was not to investigate structures but only to obtain flint artifacts which could be placed in a typological series in order to demonstrate their development.

Fox later described himself as a pupil of Greenwell (1820–1918), who excavated more than three hundred prehistoric burial sites; his collection remains of fundamental importance to scholars today (Kinnes and Longworth 1985, 10–14). From 1875 Fox excavated with friends, most notably George Rolleston, at several hill-forts in Sussex. He returned to Cissbury and now distinguished the flint mines from the later defences through their stratigraphical relationship on the site. Sections were recorded for the first time and a model section made for display at Bethnal Green. He also excavated Caesar's Camp, Folkestone, which he showed to have been a Norman castle. In 1879, sectioning of Danes Dyke, Flamborough Head,

in the East Riding of Yorkshire, failed to produce dating evidence. This salutary experience might well have discouraged Fox later from excavating at Bokerley Dyke had it not been for the chance discovery there of Roman coins in the rampart (page 38 below). Professional recognition of his work, both as a distinguished ethnologist and as an archaeologist, had resulted in his having been elected a Fellow of the Royal Society in 1876 (he had been a Fellow of the Society of Antiquaries of London since 1864).

In 1880 Fox, through the deaths of intermediate heirs, very unexpectedly inherited an estate of 29,000 acres, of which just under 3,000 lay in Wiltshire, on Cranborne Chase. By the terms of the will of his great uncle, the second Lord Rivers, Fox was required to take the surname of Pitt-Rivers. In volume I of *Excavations in Cranborne Chase* he states clearly his delight at his inheritance and the archaeological opportunities which now opened up before him: 'I had an ample harvest before me, and with the particular tastes that I had cultivated, it almost seemed to me as if some unseen hand had trained me up to be the possessor of such a property, which, up to within a short time of my inheriting it, I had but little reason to expect' (1887, xiii). Pitt-Rivers set about the excavation of round barrows at Barrow Pleck and the Romano-British villages at Rotherley and Woodcutts. In a part of Roman Britain where there were no Roman towns and few villas, he wished to investigate 'the condition and physical peculiarities of the Romanised Britons ... a race about whom less is known to anthropologists than of those which preceded and followed it'. He had 'no doubt that the chief interest of this investigation will be found to consist in the discovery of the remarkably small race of people that were buried in its pits and ditches' (1887, xiv).

Pitt-Rivers' own military background inevitably drew him to consider the problems of the date and historical context of the massive defences of Wansdyke and Bokerley Dyke. He considered that they showed evidence of 'some great war, in which the whole of the south-western portion of the country was arrayed against the rest of Britain' (1892, xii). He was also interested in investigating Bokerley Dyke in another context, because 'the district at the present time forms the frontier of a changed ethnological area, and that as we go westward, a short dark-haired and dark complexioned people begin to show themselves in this neighbourhood for the first time' (1887, xvi). The opportunity to study the racial composition of the ancient population of Cranborne Chase therefore provided him with a focus for his general interest in ancient ethnology. Pitt-Rivers was concerned to determine as precisely as possible the height and head form of each of the skeletons he had excavated and to compare any differences in the groups from the Romano-British settlements at Rotherley, Woodcutts and Woodyates (the settlement at Bokerley Junction (Pentridge (15)), page 21 below) and the Anglo-Saxon cemetery at Winkelbury.

Pitt-Rivers' *Excavations in Bokerly ... 1888–1891* provides the rich ground on which all subsequent consideration is based. He himself saw clearly, however, that his actual methods and results would be improved upon in later years: 'Notwithstanding the care that I have taken to omit nothing, I am aware that my investigations fall short of what they ought to be, and probably will be, in the future' (Address to the Archaeological Institute (1897) in Pitt-Rivers 1898, 28). His belief in evolution involved a passionate conviction in the development to higher and better states in virtually all matters. In the case of Bokerley Dyke he allowed implicitly and explicitly for new information and explanations. Thus, his dating evidence was allowed to relate only to the spots where he examined it while he gave only a *terminus ante quem non* for the visible rampart (which cannot be refuted) (Pitt-Rivers 1892, xiii). He believed (correctly) that a major settlement would be found just south west of Bokerley Junction and he acknowledged that the date of the rampart south of the Epaulement area remained uncertain.

It was not until 1947 that a major step forward was taken in the evaluation of Pitt-Rivers' works. In that year Professor C F C Hawkes did an invaluable service by reconsidering all the General's excavations in Cranborne Chase, bringing them before a much wider public than ever before and suggesting how they might fit into the rapidly growing framework of concepts for Romano-British history, stimulated particularly by R G Collingwood (Hawkes 1947). New evidence since then has made it inevitable that Hawkes' brilliant analysis in its turn be reconsidered, the quite unsuspected reduction of the Rear Dyke to an apparently limited and isolated creation being the most fundamental (cf, page 20). Thus it is necessary to begin by looking again at Pitt-Rivers' own positions.

Pitt-Rivers operated self-consciously in the van of what, to him, was science. He was rigidly systematic and thought out all problems from first principles. His publications look astonishingly modern, even a century later, not least because they set standards of display which are still an inspiration. To some extent, however, they can mislead, as a few select points indicate:

1. His method of excavation was, by modern standards, coarse and relied greatly on pick and shovel. All the actual excavation was done by labourers and, although there was always a young supervisor present, the General himself said, even in his early years and with reference to sites near his home, that he would sometimes visit only three times a day (Pitt-Rivers 1887, xviii). Re-examination at South Lodge has emphasised that he frequently failed to observe post-holes and small pits (Barrett and Bradley 1978).

2. He recognised 'seams' (layers) in section; his recording, however, was not by layers but by depth from the surface.

3. His sections (where not 'ideal', ie, composite, as in the distorted section of Martin Down 'camp', Martin (56), or across linear Martin (72)) give the stratigraphy where drawn, but the finds from the entire trench are usually 'projected' on to this and do not necessarily relate to the layers drawn.

4. He did not draw disturbances even where, as in the region of his Section 1 across Bokerley Dyke, he says that the rampart had been dug into for 'top dressing'. (The Dyke was also in places heavily rabbited, as early air photographs show.)

5. He operated almost in an archaeological vacuum and had limited parallels on which to draw, although he had a very wide experience of fieldwork in the British Isles, notably with Canon Greenwell, and elsewhere. He had excavated at several hill-forts but he still did not recognise much in the way of artifacts or earthworks that today would be called Iron Age. He saw little sign of the Iron Age in Cranborne Chase, even after digging Winkelbury (Pitt-Rivers 1898, 18), and he thought the little hill-fort on Penbury Knoll (Pentridge (18)) might have been a Saxon *burh* if not Norman.

His observation and consideration of surface features were generally weak. For instance, he did not ponder the implications of a Bronze Age ditch (Martin (72)) ending, as he thought, on Bokerley Dyke, and his plans of the Bokerley Dyke area do not even show the linear Martin (78), which abuts the Dyke, though it had been drawn by Colt Hoare in his Salisbury Station map (Colt Hoare 1810, map of Station VII, opposite page 223). He made no comment on the scarp line shown in Fig 13 in the present volume (page 28), which is based on Pitt-Rivers' own plan (Pitt-Rivers 1892, Plate CLXIX), parallel to the Dyke just east of the Epaulement, though it is part of a linear (Martin (70)) actually facing Bokerley Dyke.

6. He made little attempt to investigate relationships based on stratigraphical sequence, although well aware, conversely, of the dangers of equating proximity with contemporaneity. Thus, for example, he observed ancient fields but never considered how they related to features possibly built on them, such as was the South Lodge enclosure (cf, above, page 2).

More surprisingly, he did not consider the physical evidence for sequence where two ditches intersected. In this instance he was misled by his own logic. He thought, from digging dry wells and so on, that his settlements belonged to a 'pluvial age' and that, therefore, the ditches on such sites were 'drains' (eg, Pitt-Rivers 1898, Address of 1897, 26). Assuming this, he believed that at any intersection the deeper ditch must be later because it would tap, and so render ineffective, the shallower (cf, page 24 below for comment on the Boundary Drain in his settlement (Pentridge (15)) at Bokerley Junction).

The richness and variety of the archaeology of Cranborne Chase has long attracted the attention of archaeologists, whose fieldwork, excavations and publications have provided much basic information about many of the sites, several of them of major importance, in the area. The study and re-examination of this earlier material forms an essential part of any new analysis of the ancient landscape, and the Royal Commission's investigation which follows, properly and inevitably, includes some re-interpretation of previous work.

THE NATURE OF THE EVIDENCE

This volume was originally conceived as the first in a series of Royal Commission publications on Hampshire in which overall archaeological patterns, so profusely displayed on the chalk, would be especially examined. It extended investigation of a geologically homogeneous block of land from the Dorset boundary up to an obvious topographical break on the east, the Hampshire Avon.

Detailed investigation of Bokerley Dyke involves re-examination of the whole so-called 'Grim's Ditch' and therefore, as anticipated in the fifth Royal Commission inventory on Dorset (1975, 56), was only possible on a two-county basis. The need to examine the origins of this work was emphasised by the Royal Commission's study of *Long Barrows in Hampshire and the Isle of Wight* (1979), in which it became clear that a Neolithic cultural zone extending from the River Stour in Dorset to the River Avon in Hampshire had been cut by the Bokerley Line (Fig 2). Equally, a need to reconsider the final development along this Line, the Dyke that is seen today, emerged with new discoveries made since the last major examination, by Professor Philip Rahtz, in 1961.

The project therefore expanded into a statement and review of the different strands that make up the Bokerley Line and of the archaeological monuments on either side of it, to provide a record on which an appreciation — and further work — could be based. It had already been noted (Bowen 1978) that the use of very long ditches for land allotment in what is now Hampshire seemed to end on the Bokerley Line. It was therefore decided to investigate further potential differences, looking both at pattern and at monument type, examining all discernible ditches over a wide area of Dorset west of Bokerley (already studied by the Royal Commission in its inventory volumes on Dorset (RCHM 1970b – 1975)) as well as in a lesser area of Hampshire east of it.

Sources of evidence

The investigation around Bokerley and in the Hampshire parishes has depended primarily on analytical field survey, aerial photography (some of it done to resolve particular issues), the manuscript drawings by the OS known as 'Antiquity Models' and the reconsideration of published work in the light of new knowledge. Some small excavations carried out by other parties during the RCHME investigation have been of mutual benefit. Work on Dorset sites has been confined largely to aerial photography, with select field visits especially where independent work has been most active, as in the Gussage/Farnham area (*see* Acknowledgements, page xii).

Fieldwork

Analytical field survey, with which aerial photographic studies must be bracketed, involves the identification of surface features and their plotting, at an appropriate scale, to show shape, relationships and setting. It is frequently possible to determine sequence.

One limitation on fieldwork should perhaps be given special mention: the extremely wide incidence of former ploughing on downland, often assumed to be free of such earlier disturbance. Frequently the evidence lies, not in the positive existence of visible vestiges like ridge-and-furrow (of a sort Sumner once excavated and thought to be natural; *see* Rockbourne (53) and (54), page 71) but, negatively, in the fact that 'Celtic' fields or linear features have been degraded or levelled, mostly by post-Roman ploughing. The point to be emphasised is that much of this downland, having reverted to grass, has lost both all surface traces of its earthworks and (in most years) the possibility of revelations that occur in ploughland as soil and crop marks. However, the marks in grass above the ditches of one major settlement, Damerham (18), were surveyed on the ground, this being the only circumstance when crop marks can be reasonably and freely walked over.

Air photographs

The chalk country to which the area covered in this volume has been deliberately confined is especially apt to yield clear air photographic marks of levelled archaeological features, although chance plays a big part in what is recorded. All available air photographs have been used, including those of Cambridge University (the CUCAP), the RAF, commercial firms — such as BKS for the 1971 census year sorties — private fliers (especially Mr John Boyden who flew some special

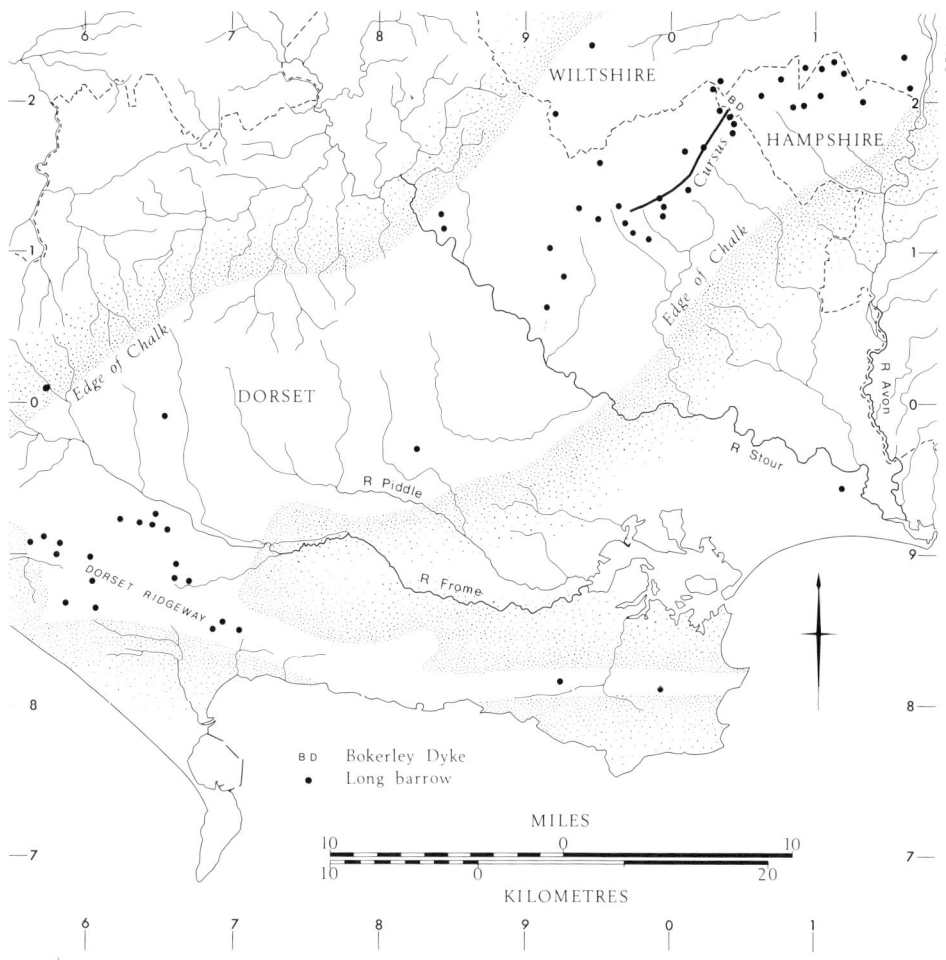

FIG 2 The Dorset Cursus and long barrows in Hampshire, Dorset and south Wiltshire (1:500,000)

sorties) and the RCHME itself. All these photographs can be found in the NMR, arranged by NGR kilometre squares.

Confusion or uncertainty about the validity of ancient soil marks is usually due to uneven spreads of clay-with-flints, sometimes difficult to distinguish from what Bersu at Little Woodbury would have called 'working hollows' (cf, Plate 21). The shallower of such natural spreads are sometimes 'filtered out' under crop conditions when only the deeper soil anomalies register. Innumerable tracks, sometimes heavily used for short indeterminate periods, can add to the difficulties. Generally speaking, a number of different air photographs have been used in this volume to build up a site picture. Different aspects are seen, or corrected, on different flights. Establishment of the certain absence of gaps in a ditch line, for instance, requires a number of air photographs, preferably taken on different occasions, but the presence of a gap can be satisfactorily established by one good picture (cf, especially Plates 18, 29 and 33). The absence of a ditched side to an 'enclosure', even where repeated on some air photographs, has on one occasion been so unlikely as to need testing by geophysical means (Rockbourne (55), page 71).

The only chance of finding air photographic marks in 'old' pasture, much of it apparently untouched but once heavily ploughed, is in the later stages of a drought. When this occurred in 1959, the RCHME asked a co-ordinating Whitehall air photographic committee to direct one or two RAF training flights on certain lines, and in 1976, the next drought year, Royal Commission and other fliers over this area, especially Mr John Boyden, produced notable results.

In the context of air photography, archaeological knowledge overall is certainly very incomplete: there is a whole range of archaeological marks which cannot be seen on any but very close air photographs, taken in the best of conditions. These include all minor features without elements cut into the underlying chalk and post-holes and the smaller pits and ditches narrower than, say, 1 metre. This helps to explain why no houses have been certainly identified on air photographs in this volume and, more importantly, why the former presence of open settlements is often barely hinted at, even where ditched enclosures representing one phase of such settlement activity draw attention to the area (cf, further discussion on page 84). It is possible that many settlements, in which there was never a ditched phase, remain totally undetected, though occasionally unconformity in field pattern, fragments of track, etc, are suggestive and warrant closer attention by fieldwalking and so on. Some sites, even well ditched and in situations expected to produce good contrast, will so far have failed to register on air photographs. Martin (64), disclosed after surface stripping, is an example of this.

There remain numerous problems in the interpretation of air photographs. If ditches intersect, for instance, there is mostly no indication of allowance for a bank or banks which, in most cases, would have been thrown up alongside a ditch. Logically, such intersections should represent the destruction of one of the banks; it is a point that needs looking for in excavation. (Cf, discussion, in Pentridge (15), about the Boundary Drain and ditches approaching or intersecting it.) A different assumption, which is hardly open to doubt, is that complete ring ditches can only display themselves fully if cut into the bedrock so that, for instance, the coincidence of a ring ditch Whitsbury (13) and the flattened bank of linear Whitsbury (22) can only be explained by the ring ditch being there first, and the bank later covering it and any − probable − mound within it.

Broad dark bands around 8 metres across can now reasonably be considered as hollow-ways of possible Roman date (Fasham 1979, 51); such an assumption would have been doubted recently because the density of traffic required seemed more likely to be due to medieval and later droving. The earlier identification is now demonstrated by the Royal Commission air photographs of the important settlement at Wimborne St Giles (36) and the roads indubitably coming from it (Area Plan 3).

Geophysical aids

A fluxgate gradiometer was used in all but one instance in attempts to detect whether or not a ditch continued beyond its apparent termination. Behind Bokerley Dyke a search for any continuation of the linears Martin (73), (78) and (80) produced no trace; taken alone, this fact cannot be regarded as conclusive evidence since the Geophysical Section of the Ancient Monuments Laboratory (English Heritage) reported only the slightest reaction above the flattened ditch of Pentridge (17), against which the Martin linears would certainly have ended. Dr A J Clark of the Section, using a larger gradiometer, worked on the line of Martin (80) C, east of Damerham Ridge, where the relatively slight ditch was picked up in an area dappled with clay-with-flints, but very mixed surface soils defeated all attempts at detection in the area north of Whitsbury hill-fort. A most useful negative result was obtained on the 'enclosure' Rockbourne (55), where Dr Clark's pulse induction meter confirmed both the presence and absence of the ditch as indicated on air photographs.

The present study

The aim of the present study is to show, through fieldwork, that Bokerley Dyke served as an ancient frontier in a different,

cultural, context. A sharp contrast will be identified between the system of land division marked by 'spinal' linears, some of which extend for many kilometres, on the east side of Bokerley, and any system west of it, where linears are short and many of them are multiple (Fig 1). This volume also includes a discussion of the occurrence of various settlement types, and other archaeological features, on either side of the Dyke. Other studies have demonstrated a cultural divide in the area of Bokerley Dyke; for example, the complementary distribution of Deverel−Rimbury fine wares (Globular Urns, types I and II (Calkin 1962)), a pattern mirrored in the more localised distributions of the contemporary everyday wares (Ellison 1980).

As will be shown in this study, marked differences in the nature of the linear boundaries on either side of Bokerley Dyke have become apparent through a combination of intensive fieldwork, the examination of air photographs and the results of some, generally very limited, excavations carried out at widespread intervals during the last century. These various sources of information are here brought together, and this has allowed the analysis and definition of many widely differing types of 'linears', and the recognition of their greatly varying dates. It has become equally apparent that the many linear strands along the Bokerley Line itself also have a long and complex history. The development of the Bokerley Line can therefore be understood only through the analysis of the linear boundaries and the ancient landscape to either side of it. This study is an initial attempt to disentangle some of the complexities of these relationships; it also offers a critical reassessment of the most important of the linears, Bokerley Dyke itself.

Note on the preservation of monuments

This volume, as has been emphasised, is different in character from other Royal Commission publications by reason of its emphasis on a single but complex problem involving areas already covered by the Royal Commission in its Dorset inventory volumes. The latter, in accordance with the Commission's Royal Warrant, contained Reports which specified those monuments thought most worthy of preservation.

For the discoveries of recent years, recorded in the present volume, no such systematic extraction has been made; instead, a short note has been forwarded to English Heritage, the statutory advisory body concerned, for consideration, in particular, in its scheduling enhancement or Monuments Protection Programme. The substance of that note is as follows:

1. Bokerley Dyke is still a largely enigmatic work and should be preserved intact. If, at some time, part of it is subjected to an inexorable threat, it is hoped that further archaeological investigation will be conducted with due consideration to the outstanding questions implicit in the list on page 41.

2. Equally, all monuments close to Bokerley Dyke are important, notably Wimborne St Giles (36) and Pentridge (15), and any proposed development whatsoever within, say, 400 metres of it should be made known well in advance so that steps

might be taken to carry out further investigation, in particular at the terminals, the Epaulement, and on Blagdon Hill.

3. Particular consideration should be given to those monuments which, though not quite levelled, are being steadily reduced by ploughing, especially the long mound within Martin (66) and the rare ring-and-tongue barrow, Rockbourne (23).

4. Most of the newly discovered monuments near Bokerley Dyke, however, are known only as crop or soil marks and are generally unrecognisable at ground level, among them several large settlement complexes probably embracing long periods of development, eg, Martin (58). It is highly desirable that no part of these should be allowed to disappear, whether by quarrying, building development or other cause, without excavation. The Area Plans in this book have been selected to focus on those areas where intricate patterns of the Bronze Age, Iron Age and Romano-British landscape, which are still little understood, are particularly well preserved or may still be recognised through aerial photography.

PART I
LINEAR WORKS

Description

Terminology

It is proposed, throughout this study, to use the adjective *linear* in a substantive sense for brevity. Linear features (Fig 3, *loose*) may, for instance, be primarily boundaries or primarily roads. They may consist of single ditch (or hollow) and bank *or* two banks flanking a medial ditch (difficult to establish unless there are earthwork indications) *or* multiple parallel arrangements of bank and ditch *or*, occasionally, ditch *or* bank alone (though the presence of a ditch is normally taken to indicate the former presence of the latter).

Recognition

This section defines linears of the prehistoric or Roman periods. A multiplicity of lines in the landscape are marked in different ways; some are partly fossilised in 'footpaths' and hedges. Confusion of origins and functions and the 'channelling effect' of any linear boundary creates difficulty in deciding which lines can be excised as not demonstrably Romano-British or earlier. It is made the more awkward when there are clear air photographic marks across present field boundaries and where there is the possibility of a butt junction with a definite element of the Wessex linear ditch system. Such an example occurs in the north-east corner of Martin parish and the immediately adjacent sliver of Stratford Toney, Wiltshire (*see* Fig 52). In this latter parish, air photographs show a pronounced dark band with white edging extending north east from 08902235 to meet an angle in 'Grim's Ditch' Martin (69) at 09362283. This approach feature lies athwart field boundaries seen on an air photograph (CUCAP, VAP RC8 W 37). Reference to earlier 6-inch OS maps, however, reveals that the linear mark follows the course of a former field boundary, set diagonally to the present arrangements, to within 200 metres of Martin (69). The same air photograph shows, in the intervening space, a faint dark line flanked by two thin white bands, similar to those which mark Martin (69). The alignment of the old diagonal hedge is continued south west from 08602209 by a footpath and thence a lane to East Martin. The linear feature is omitted from the archaeological presentation because it can be explained as

a road line of historic date. Its exact conjunction with the sharp angle in linear Martin (69), however, is of a sort that might be expected to indicate a link with another feature, while the way in which its comparable marks elide with those of Martin (69) remain a challenge to interpretation that might be helped by excavation. Inferences are not always clear. Excavation of Pentridge (17) on Blagdon Hill (page 14) shows such a shallow ditch as to be comparable with Damerham (22), considered as a road and certainly leading to settlement Damerham (18).

Among the pitfalls of definition and recognition are the problems set by certain double ditches. It is particularly important for this investigation to distinguish between roads and multiple linears. The ditches may be set at different widths apart. A country road needs at least 5 metres of usable space between the flanking features and 8 metres would be more likely (cf, RCHM 1976, page xlv, for a discussion of repeating widths in the Cotswolds). The safest assurance that double ditches represent roads is that they are at least so spaced, allowing for external banks, are individually small (under, say, 2 metres across) and correspond in size with each other (cf, leading to Woodcutts, Sixpenny Handley (19), RCHM 1975). Certain roads may be much less tidily marked by sporadic single or asymmetric ditches, with or without the broad, long dark bands that can now be safely taken to mark hollow-ways (Wimborne St Giles (36), Damerham (18), Rockbourne (54), etc).

Parish boundaries can provide problems of identity when ancient linears are certainly embodied in some stretches of parish (eg, Charlton Marshall (Fig 4; Plate 2)), and county, boundary but may remain unrecognised, suspected or not, in others (eg, Long Crichel (Area Plan 2)). The way in which present boundaries sometimes relate to barrows makes it the more difficult; for example, barrow Whitsbury (3) is incorporated at an angle in the parish boundary with Rockbourne. The boundary bank dividing the Shaftesbury and Pitt-Rivers estates also hinges on a cluster of three barrows on Handley Hill, incidentally seen in Plate 38, one of which prominently displays its obvious use as a marker when viewed from downhill on the west (Wimborne St Giles (88)).

Linears can rarely, if ever, be dated purely by the pattern they make. The local pattern on Hambledon Hill (centred at ST 850120, Fig 3), for instance, is now known to be Neolithic but could not alone be safely used as a criterion for the date for similar arrangements. The 9.5 km length of the Cursus makes

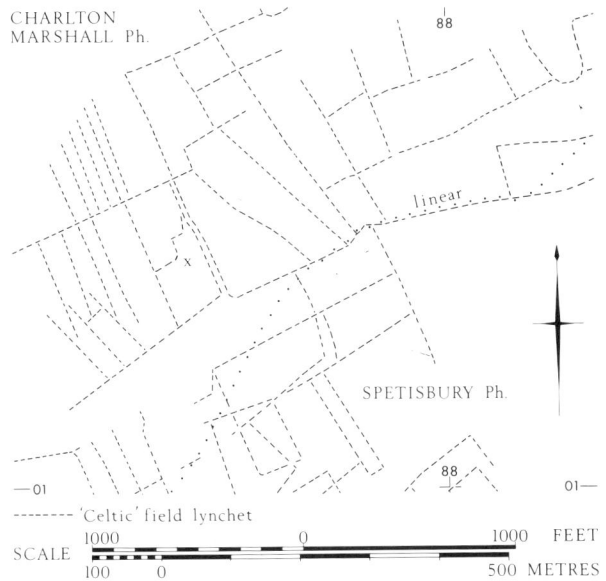

CHARLTON MARSHALL Ph.

linear

SPETISBURY Ph.

CHARLTON MARSHALL Ph.

x

88

88

—01

01—

01—

------- 'Celtic' field lynchet

SCALE

1000   0   1000 FEET

100   0   500 METRES

FIG 4 Charlton Marshall, Dorset: plan of unditched linear and 'Celtic' fields (see Plate 2) (1:10,560)

it even dangerous to assume that great length puts Neolithic dates beyond belief.

Character and features

A coarse distinction may be made between very long linears, plausibly related to the dividing up of large tracts of country, and local arrangements restricted to discrete blocks. 'Spinal' linears lie, by the arbitrary definition adopted here, between two distant points, 5 km or more apart, which may or may not be intervisible. Their course between these points may be irregular, involving a variety of deviation, like Martin (69), inviting the suggestion that they became very long features as a result of the accretion of lesser stretches, or, alternatively, were affected *en route* by natural obstructions, such as heavy timber, or by adjacent human activity. On the other hand, they may be generally regular and follow a direct line, such as Martin (80) between Tidpit Common by Martin (63) and a pair of barrows, Whitsbury (9) and (10), on the ridge north of Whitsbury. Such a straight course as that mentioned probably reflects the early importance of Knoll Down, by Damerham (20), and the surveying skill available, since Martin (80) diverges here at a point not visible from the Whitsbury ridge. The original line to the west is presumably that taken by Martin (80) B, which roughly continues the overall axis towards Bokerley; its bifurcation west of settlement Martin (63) (cf, Plate 51) recalls the possibly cognate splaying of two strands of different dates at Bokerley Junction. It might be suggested that there is an optimum maximum size in spinal linears, as represented by Martin (80) A on Knoll Down or by Whitsbury (22) on Gallows Hill. Local deviations may be due to poorly directed gang lines necessitating sharp correction, or they may describe broad sweeps, as at the east end of Martin (69), or briefly 'undulate', as

in Whitsbury (24) or in Martin (69), at its west end where it approaches the Shire Rack, the quite separate county boundary bank which also undulates (Plate 48). There are patchy spreads of clay-with-flints and it is possible that in these areas large forest trees were being avoided.

'Local' linears are ditched arrangements of considerably lesser length (for example, Martin (82)–(85) on Area Plan 5), occurring in plausibly self-contained blocks.

'Multiple' linears are structurally different. They are seen in the area under study only in Dorset, around Gussage Hill to Crichel (Area Plan 2), related patchily to a particular specialised management policy over 9 or 10 sq km (say 3 square miles) but still regarded here as 'local'. Local dispositions of ditches are, then, variable and doubtless reflect different purposes conceived at different times in varying ways but with elements of continuity visible in, for instance, the reuse or refurbishing of particular lines. The spread of ditched boundaries in the area of Badbury (Area Plan 1), the only other large local block in this area of Dorset, has no physical link with the hill-fort (Shapwick (34)), for example, but, while excavation has pointed to Bronze Age origins, there is apparent Iron Age fortification (Shapwick (35)) on a line of that earlier date. The great importance of the area in, and perhaps after, the Roman period allows a correspondingly late date for some of the ditches in the complex.

Linears may be arranged in such a way as to suggest particular usages to do with local containment or penning. For instance, there is the looped end to Martin (84), which contains settlement Martin (67) (Area Plan 5), or the two sharply pointed features, Gussage All Saints (a 68) and (a 69), crossed by the Roman road, which plausibly represent a contemporary arrangement for herding towards the apices (Area Plan 2).

Relationships with barrows

The relationship with barrows is of two kinds: skirting round or beside them, which could mean no more than the use of the barrows as reference points along a boundary (as, perhaps, at Blagdon Hill (Fig 23)), and an apparent incorporation of barrows in or on the line of a bank, as in the differently arranged Martin (24), Whitsbury (22) or the ring ditch in multiple linear, Long Crichel (7) on Thickthorn Down (see Area Plan 2). The Romans were so careless of barrows that they could build over or mutilate them (eg, the Roman road over Witchampton (a 26) and disc barrows on Oakley Down (Area Plan 3)), but the respect shown for almost all barrows in prehistoric times in this area makes wilful harm unlikely. Martin (24), an elongated barrow, is very deliberately incorporated (as Colt Hoare described) within the line of Martin (80). This example suggests indeed that some barrows, at least, may have demarcated an actual frontier before the construction of the linears, and plausibly have had a function in the staking out of territorial bounds. There are not enough of them to represent the leaders of a population of a size manifest in the sort of control and power shown by the widespread linears and fields. There is no simple answer, nor any that can ever be proved, and because it

North ➤

PLATE 2 A linear with no visible ditch and 'Celtic' fields on Charlton Down, Charlton Marshall, Dorset. An oblique air photograph looking east from **P** ('Holly Brake' on 6-inch OS map), grid square reference ST 875015.

The linear, recognisable by the continuous and partly curving run, probably extended for more than one mile (2 kilometres). It is completely integrated with 'Celtic' fields. Unconformities show different groups and phases in the fields: left of **a** one lot of fields overlies another. The dark line at **b** is the ploughed-out parish boundary emerging from the linear which it partly followed. Adjacent to **P** is a 'parcel' of close-set parallel lynchets **p** and at **x** an arrangement of curving lines, probably to do with settlement, on the far side of which is a probably ditched line marking a subsidiary boundary springing from the linear. (NMR OAP ST 8701/4; © John R Boyden)

will never be possible to be sure of the time that elapsed before the conjunction with barrows (unless they are on top of linears, nowhere so far provable), it is not a safe pointer to date.

Relationships with 'Celtic' fields

Linears frequently cross 'Celtic' fields diagonally (cf, Plate 28 (Knoll Down)), though may, less often, be integrated (Plate 2, Charlton Marshall). The strict inferences to be drawn are: the fields traversed were almost certainly put out of use at the time, since triangular fields are particularly awkward, but not impossible, to plough; whatever happened, their arable use must have been seen as less important than the function performed by the new linear; the management of a block of fields must also have been disrupted by the restraint on physical access, and the block itself probably ceased to be an entity. Subsequent ploughing might be determined by inspection of any plough-effect, negative or positive lynchet formation, against the linear.

Consequences for dating are difficult to assess. Lynchets cut by linear ditches will, by their size, give a very rough indication of the length of time that the fields had been in cultivation. Pottery found in lynchets immediately adjacent to such ditches would almost certainly relate to manuring before the linear construction. Conversely, however, pottery found sparsely scattered in linear ditches, unless demonstrably from some other source, will most likely relate to the same former manuring of the ground in which the ditches were cut and so, while the sherds may indicate the date of the fields concerned (no more, because pottery will not necessarily go out with manure), the date of the linears must generally be sought in some other relationship. Martin (72), for instance, was dug out over a length of 300 feet (90 metres) by Pitt-Rivers in a manner never since repeated. The pottery found sparsely in the lower silting of the ditch was Middle Bronze Age. It is known that the ditch had been cut across 'Celtic' fields and that the finds almost certainly, therefore, belong to the fields. It leaves linear (72) itself undated, though of the Middle Bronze Age or later. (The lack of Iron Age pottery by itself just suggests that the ditch was cut in a preceding period.) Martin (69), too, is usually assigned to the Bronze Age because Martin (72) joins it and so they are of the same or earlier date. It is also now seen that Martin (72) abutted the newly discovered linear Martin (73), which must therefore be of the same or later date. This was almost certainly continued east by Martin (74) which, when excavated, produced Middle Bronze Age pottery identical with that from Martin (72). There were no signs of 'Celtic' fields at this latter point but there was a pronounced 'S' curve in the line, probably marking the former existence of some particular natural or human obstacle other than fields. There were no later finds. It is the more likely, therefore, that Martin (72) and Martin (73/4) really are of Bronze Age date. This being so, the termination of Martin (73) against Bokerley Dyke, if actual and not just apparent (that is, if it did not continue beyond to meet Pentridge (17)), would imply the former existence of a linear, of at least the same date on that line, in a function later to be taken over by the Dyke. Martin (80) A, by contrast, whose bank covered late Iron Age material in J G Evans' excavation on Knoll Down, is probably of that date; (80) B may belong to an earlier period since it was certainly superseded, while Martin (80) C, continuing the earlier line, may simply have been abandoned. Datable associations are ambivalent. The many ditches cut across already well-developed 'Celtic' field lynchets (both by (80) A and (80) B on Knoll Down, Area Plan 5) could obviously suggest either very early 'Celtic' fields or late ditches (Evans and Vaughan 1985).

Relationships with hill-forts

The relationship of spinal linears to hill-forts is of particular consequence, not least to dating, and the obvious questions are whether the linears were sighted on the hill-forts themselves or on barrows, for instance, or just distant high points encircled by the hill-forts, or whether they were physically linked to some element of the hill-fort, making them contemporary in origin. The apparent position of Whitsbury (17) hill-fort in relation to the spinal linear Whitsbury (22) and the lesser linears Whitsbury (24) and Whitsbury (26), as shown in Area Plan 7, made it particularly important to investigate these relationships (page 77). In this example, the balance of judgement just suggests that the hill-fort corresponds, perhaps coincidentally, with one node but is not connected specifically to the spinal Martin (80). It is further worth noting that the other spinal linear, Whitsbury (22), which Martin (80) might be found to abut, extends 5 km north east, ignoring the site of Clearbury (the next, but much smaller, hill-fort), as Colt Hoare observed (Colt Hoare 1810, 231). In Dorset, the linears around Badbury hill-fort do not connect with it (Area Plan 1). The evidence from elsewhere increasingly indicates that spinal linears were mostly not directly associated with hill-forts. In Hampshire, for instance, the recent RCHME survey of 'Woolbury fields' (so-called by Crawford and Keiller (1928, 154)) has indicated that the linears there were making for points on the hill not necessarily connected with Woolbury hill-fort; the sole linear

east from Danebury is of a local type and late; Quarley as a hill-fort is clearly not connected with the spinal arrangements (Hawkes 1940). In Berkshire, recently published plans show spinal linears ignoring hill-forts (Ford 1981–2). The evidence overall thus points to a widespread division of the landscape by the spinal linears independently of, and possibly before, the establishment of hill-forts. In this, as in other matters connected with the linears, a very great deal could be learnt by relatively small excavations aimed at answering specific questions.

Relationships with enclosures

Enclosures in the study area are very occasionally tacked on to linears (eg, Long Crichel (32) or Farnham (a 15)) and there are possible examples of terminal position (cf, Fig 46a). Settlement Martin (61) may have been remotely terminal to linear Martin (78) through Martin (79), its just possible former continuation (see Fig 6, loose).

There are, however, two settlements, Martin (63) and Damerham (20), tucked in beside the spinal linear Martin (80) and, in both cases, their presence is probably the reason for a local alteration of its line.

'Ligatures', local ditches possibly related to tracks, linking two or more enclosures in sometime contemporary relationship, are well seen in the local plan of Tarrant Hinton (18) and Pimperne (18) (see Fig 47).

'Grim's Ditch'

The following account, as well as the inventory, of elements in the traditionally named 'Grim's Ditch' (Pentridge (17) in Dorset; Martin (69) and (80) and Whitsbury (22) in Hampshire), draws variously on previously published work, especially that of Colt Hoare (1810), Heywood Sumner (1913), Mrs C M Piggott (1944) and Dr J G Evans (Evans and Vaughan 1985), and on the OS Antiquity Models (LIN 76, now held in the Royal Commission's public archive, the NMR).

'Grim's Ditch' is a folk name that is inherently confusing because of its widespread and imprecise use. The attribution to the mythical figure 'Grim' implies an unknown origin for the feature in question, but in the area under study (as in others) it has been used to dub a number of ditches upon which it confers a quite unreal homogeneity. The term is Saxon and is equatable with 'Woden' which, by a process of Christian association, explains why (according to Heywood Sumner (1913, 62)) 'Devil's Ditch' was the countryman's name.

Sumner himself calls 'Grim's Ditch' 'a continuous earthwork . . . across the eastern portion of Cranborne Chase. The length of its course is about fourteen miles' (Sumner 1913, 57). This is misleading and needs correction more in harmony with Sumner's actual awareness of the general nature of these linear ditches.

Sumner's 14 miles (23 km) of ditch comprise, taken clockwise from the north west, what in this volume are called Martin (69), Whitsbury (22), those parts of Martin (80) then known, and

Pentridge (17). The diversity of these elements can be briefly stated, firstly in plan (Fig 1; cf, Fig 3). Martin (69), which is some 14.5 km long, its west termination undiscovered, includes very erratic stretches with its ditch generally on the south side ('facing' both Bokerley Dyke and the linears trailing west from its north-west end and Martin (80)). At its east end, it abuts Whitsbury (22), which is at right angles to it, and continues indefinitely northwards in fairly straight stretches. Martin (80), which is most conspicuously different from Martin (69) in that its course is largely set in direct lines, hingeing on Knoll Down (by Damerham (20)), is roughly parallel to it and almost certainly did connect at one time with Whitsbury (22), forming thus the south side of a great 'enclosure' (whether it was ever conceived as such or not) whose fourth side was incompletely filled by Pentridge (17). A weak case could therefore be made for the whole being a stock enclosure with the ditch conventionally facing inwards (cf, Pitt-Rivers' very tentative proposal (1892, 291–3) that Martin (69) and the linear west from Pentridge (16) A to West Woodyates might form a 'funnel' through which deer could be driven). These ditches may have been to do with stock control but it is known that they had origins at varying dates, experienced different stages, and certainly manifested diverse physical forms. The shallow ditch of Pentridge (17), for instance, on Blagdon Hill, is shown by excavation to be by itself quite unsuited for the containment of animals and there is no positive evidence for any palisade or hedge on the bank. Conversely, the sections of Martin (80) on Knoll Down (Evans and Vaughan 1985) or Damerham Ridge (Sumner's G–H; see Fig 60 on page 114) seem absurdly massive for such a purpose. It remains a fact, however, that containment of stock requires different types of bounds for different types of animal. This applies to ditch size and form as well as to type of fence; sheep, for instance, especially of the Soay sort, would require a dense as well as high 'hedge' (necessarily laid, therefore, if 'live'), or a ditch with bank so arranged that it could not be jumped. This raises another problem. If the ditch were the critical element then it would only be effective on one side of the linear (as, for example, in deer pales, where a steep ditch on the inside with a bank rising sheer beyond made escape extremely difficult but in certain places allowed access from the outside to the top of the bank, from which jumping in over the ditch presented no difficulty). And, of course, it would have had to have been kept scoured to the effective profile – so, if scouring did take place, it suggests the importance of maintaining a particular profile. The great variations in size and form on continuous runs are indeed very difficult to rationalise. Martin (80) B (see Fig 61) was so much smaller than Martin (80) A, and the extra work involved in the latter's construction so very much greater, that there must have been a good reason for the change – but why only for half the distance postulated for Martin (80) as a whole? The dating of all these features is uncertain (cf, page 12) and, as with the inextricably involved strands of the Bokerley Line, it has to be asked again whether or when all the pieces functioned as a whole.

It is most unlikely that confident answers can ever be given to all the obvious questions but one fact must surely be assumed, that the Bokerley Line includes a strand as early as any on the eastward side of it – since it is the 'stopper' for the whole widespread ditch system of which 'Grim's Ditch' is but a part. And so this strand must be prehistoric in origin. Whether it is encapsulated in the winding Bokerley Dyke (as its use as an apparent termination by Martin (73), (78) and (80) suggests), or is marked by Pentridge (17), must remain unresolved without excavation since there still remains the remote possibility that Bokerley Dyke really did cut through Martin (73), (78) and (80).

PART II

THE BOKERLEY LINE

The name *Bokerley Dyke* or *Bokerley Ditch* appears first in the medieval period (*Bockedic*, 1280). The earliest, 10th-century, reference is merely to 'dich'. It becomes 'Blakedounes dich' in the 13th century and this localises the name in what Pitt-Rivers would call the right centre to right flank, on Blagdon Hill at the south of Martin parish. The name 'Bokerley' appears to be descriptive and to relate quite specifically to deer (?'buck' and 'wood, clearing') and so plausibly to the 'chase' and the 13th or early 14th-century Blagden deer park, which at that time was bounded at the north east by Bokerley Dyke (Mills 1980, 235−6). It is of note − and consistent with the fact that linear earthworks are variously regarded and used at different times − that Bokerley Dyke was embodied within the deer park when an eastward bulge was constructed in the 15th century (RCHM 1975, 15: Cranborne (32)).

The various strands which together make up the full length of the 'Bokerley Line' are shown, and labelled, on Figs 6 and 7 *loose* (each at 1:10,560 scale). Fig 6 shows the position of all the other, larger scale, plans included in the volume, the sections and profiles outside the area of those plans (on which the remainder are placed) and the location of photographs in the volume's Plates. Fig 7 indicates the variety of land use, both along Bokerley Dyke itself and the areas to either side of it.

Definition and terminology

The remains of Bokerley Dyke are much more complex than Pitt-Rivers could possibly have appreciated − as aerial photography, some further excavation and intensive fieldwork over wide areas have now shown. Further analysis of Pitt-Rivers' own methods and assumptions (cf, pages 3-5) strengthens the need for some cautious reassessment.

A whole pattern of lesser ditches ends on or near the Bokerley Dyke line or moves towards it from the east and north east. According to present knowledge, these linear works do not extend west of Bokerley. Pentridge (17) follows straight lines just west of it. Bokerley Dyke (Pentridge (16)), by its proportions indicating defence or intimidation, faces east or north, as does Pentridge (16) A, and as did, probably, the Rear Dyke.

The terms that have been used to describe different parts of the Dyke and how they, and others, will be used in this present

account are shown on Fig 5 and in a concordance table (pages 16-17). Pitt-Rivers' usages show a belief in the military nature of the Dyke (though he was never quite sure, cf, Pitt-Rivers 1892, Appendix A) and that it therefore blocked a gap between two blocks of 'primaeval' forest, the product of a 'pluvial age' (Pitt-Rivers 1892, 9). The latter idea caused him to include relatively slight earthworks extending the line 1.6 km further west than any dyke of plausibly defensive proportions. Since he had excavated substantial ditches totally levelled by his day (the Rear Dyke the best example here, though this was detectable on the ground by Mr Aubrey Parke in 1942), it was reasonable to believe that slight remains − or none, if between likely upstanding sections − might still once have been a defensive line.

The Dyke as defined and accepted here is an earthwork bank and ditch of considerably larger dimensions than those which constitute the normal run of Wessex boundary ditches (cf, the discussion on 'Linears' on page 10). The 'model' ultimately required was, it may be thought, something like the Fore Dyke in Sector C (cf, Pitt-Rivers 1892, Plate CLXIV, Section 2; Figs 8 and 9 in this volume: plan and profiles), inhibiting and impressive enough, but the course of development along a topographically non-defensive line gave rise to larger sections of undeniably defensive proportions in Sector A, south of the Epaulement. The whole line was probably refurbished at some late stage, making a feature over 5.2 km long whose final unitary nature was confused by the incorporation or nearby survival of many diverse strands, some certainly prehistoric, some slight, some only postulated because of the placing of other features, probably embodied in or destroyed by the later Dyke, and others running roughly parallel. Some are so disjointed that it is not clear how they might have originally joined up. For this reason the RCHME nomenclature deals in sectors using, wherever possible, the terms which the earlier writers have applied to the works. All these strands (Fig 6, *loose*) lay along and form the Bokerley Line.

Topography

The topography of Bokerley Dyke can be described summarily and is seen best on Fig 7 (*loose*). The Fore Dyke ends at the west by a shallow valley and Pentridge (16) A lies on the slight shoulder

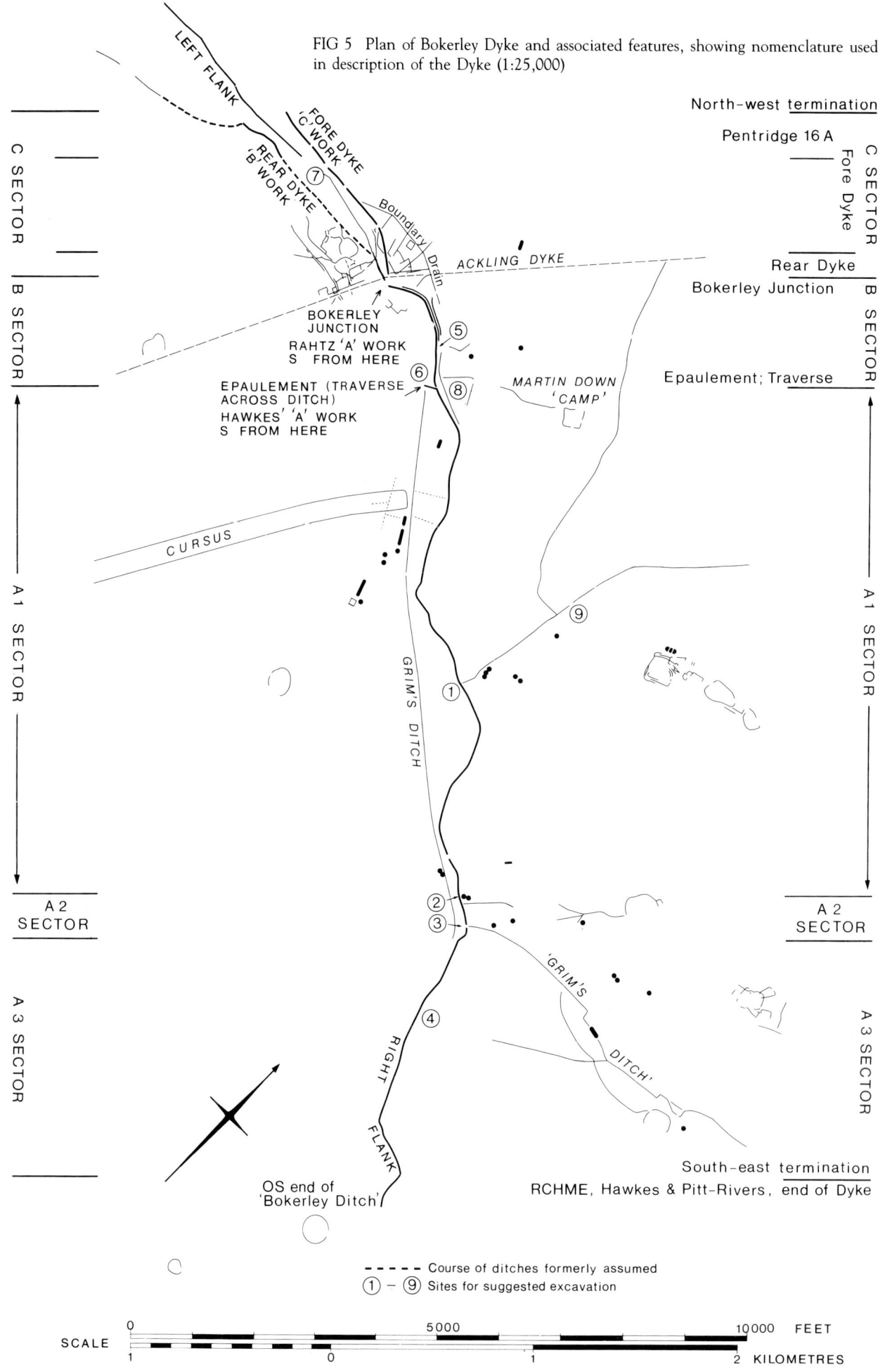

FIG 5   Plan of Bokerley Dyke and associated features, showing nomenclature used in description of the Dyke (1:25,000)

North-west termination

Pentridge 16 A

C SECTOR
Fore Dyke

Rear Dyke

Bokerley Junction

Epaulement; Traverse

A1 SECTOR

A 2 SECTOR

A 3 SECTOR

South-east termination
RCHME, Hawkes & Pitt-Rivers, end of Dyke

LEFT FLANK

FORE DYKE 'C' WORK

REAR DYKE 'B' WORK

Boundary Drain

ACKLING DYKE

BOKERLEY JUNCTION
RAHTZ 'A' WORK
S FROM HERE

EPAULEMENT (TRAVERSE ACROSS DITCH)
HAWKES' 'A' WORK
S FROM HERE

MARTIN DOWN 'CAMP'

CURSUS

GRIM'S DITCH

'GRIM'S DITCH'

RIGHT FLANK

OS end of 'Bokerley Ditch'

- - - -   Course of ditches formerly assumed
① – ⑨   Sites for suggested excavation

SCALE

0   5000   10000   FEET

1   0   1   2   KILOMETRES

Bokerley Dyke: components, terminology and concordance of definitions related to the work of Pitt-Rivers (Fig 5)

Original terminology used in Pitt-Rivers 1892	Components and location of elements of Bokerley Dyke as defined by Pitt-Rivers	Approx length miles/metres(m) according to Pitt-Rivers	Later terminology			Length in miles/metres(m) according to RCHME	Comment (RCHME)
			Hawkes 1947	Rahtz 1961	RCHME 1990		
Left Flank	single dyke: 01241990– 03331996 Denbose Wood to A354		*	*	not accepted as concept	—	*military definitions not used after Pitt-Rivers though defensive explanation maintained
Fore Dyke	Fore Dyke	1⅕ 1900m	Fore Dyke = **C** work	as used by Hawkes	Fore Dyke ends on W at 02342004	½+ 900m	nothing big W of this; uncertain whether former parish boundary bank immediately W of 02342004 was on line of earlier ditch
Rear Dyke	variety: 01501962 NW of West Woodyates Manor to A354 on line S of Fore Dyke	1+ 1640m	Rear Dyke = **B** work west of A354	**B** work entire apart from Traverse	not accepted as concept; 'Rear Dyke' restricted to short, unfinished work roughly from A354 to 03021988	130m	built over earlier slight ditch which might have linked to Pentridge (16) A but follows different line from former concept
					Pentridge (16) A is discrete dyke, undated, W from 02471999	250m	
Left Centre	variety: from A354 to 04361892 by Bowling Green Lane (Sillen Lane)	1 1600m	* **B** work E of A354 to Epaulement plus; **A** + **B** to Bokerley Gap plus further part of **A** work	*	not accepted as concept		*see entry for Left Flank. Pitt-Rivers recognised a difference in date E from Epaulement (1892, 95)
Epaulement	03771968 to SW	75m	as Pitt-Rivers: termination of **A** work	as Pitt-Rivers: flanks entrance through **A** work?	as Pitt-Rivers		? discrete dyke or element, unfinished?
Traverse	03771969 crosses Epaulement Ditch	20m	as Pitt-Rivers: start of **B** work	as Pitt-Rivers: entrance through **A** work blocked in **B** phase	as Pitt-Rivers: part of final phase		
Right Centre	variety: from Sillen Lane to Blagdon hill top 05631801	1 1600m	**A** work	as Pitt-Rivers	**A** 1 to junction M (68) plus part of **A** 2 to SE side Blagdon Hill		
Right Flank	from Blagdon hill top SE to termination on knoll 06251698	⅘ 1100m	part of **A** work	as Pitt-Rivers	**A** 3		OS had a slight ditch extending further 200m

above the same bottom. This is away from the clay-with-flints that so happily supports much of 'Cranborne Forest'. The ground rises gently east to a low local ridge crossed by the Fore Dyke. The probable Iron Age settlement Pentridge (15) A is on the south shoulder of the ridge top. The ground rises at only 2° from the Rear Dyke to the Fore Dyke; a military position would have been nearer to that of the Boundary Drain, commanding the re-entrant gulley east of it.

Between the Junction and the Epaulement, in Sector B (Fig 5), is the south-west continuation of the gulley already mentioned. In this, the Dyke is at its most unmilitary, its size similar to that on Pitt-Rivers' Section 2 (Fig 9 and Plates 3 (looking into the valley from the north) and 4 (a close up of the ditch seen in the distance on Plate 3)). Where it meets the Epaulement, the Dyke is much lower than that which continues south east (Plate 5). The course continues to be markedly ill-sited for defence. Just south of Sillen Lane it is sunk in a valley as again it is, south of the meeting with Martin (73), where Pitt-Rivers' suggestion that it came forward to embrace a spring is wholly unconvincing. The position on the top of Blagdon Hill, capped by gravel and favouring trees is commanding but, thereafter, even though it follows a ridge top it fails to take advantage of this, as the bank frequently sits on the rear edge with 'dead' ground close in front of it. Its termination is already 800 metres within the tree-favouring gravel zone.

Before going on to the more detailed description against the background of particular larger scale plans, and of sections and profiles, some brief notes may be made of the evidence for a long history of damage.

Treatment and alteration (Fig 7)

Any consideration of the interpretation of the Dyke must allow for alterations and modifications, levelling and even total destruction. This has occurred at different times and for different reasons. It is reasonable to assume also that narrow ditches emerging from bigger ones which superseded them (as in the case of the Rear Dyke) imply the likely total destruction of the slighter feature, whether or not a bank, or part of it, might be, or have been, preserved within a later bank. In the case of the Rear Dyke all traces of bank(s) have been removed. The further significance of this is discussed below (page 20) but it must be allowed that other banks and ditches were totally removed in antiquity, while in quite recent times remarkably large parts of major works have been carried away, as from Bokerley Gap and much of the Fore Dyke. Also, at the 'Shoulder Angle', quarrying into the Bokerley rampart for 'top dressing' (marl for arable fields) — whereby, it may be noted, archaeological material, too, may have been far removed from

PLATE 3   Bokerley Dyke, Sector B, crossing the valley bottom. A distant view looking south; the figure is standing on an inconspicuous bank where profile R 4 was drawn (Fig 12) (cf, Plate 4). (NMR BB80/481)

PLATE 4 Bokerley Dyke, Sector B, at the position of profile R 4 (Fig 12) (*see* Plate 3), looking south. (NMR BB80/491)

PLATE 5 Bokerley Dyke from the north east, looking towards the high dyke at the left. The beginning of Sector A 1, with the Epaulement hidden behind it (cf, Plate 9), the dip at Pitt-Rivers' 'Traverse' and, right of it, the low line of the Dyke in Sector B can all be seen. (NMR BB80/487)

its source — has removed substantial parts of its back and summit in the 70 metres east from Pitt-Rivers' Section 1. Small, shallow quarry pits also occur in a rough line beyond the counterscarp of the single visible 'main' ditch.

There are suggestions of extensive levelling of a bank outside the double ditch along the whole length of Sector A1. In places the top of the rampart is up to 6 metres wide and flat, as in the section opposite the junction with Martin (73) and south east of it for some 300 metres, probably due to a digging away rather than non completion. (The present county boundary bank sits on it.) Certainly, partial quarrying, rabbiting and tree growth have damaged long stretches. 'Original' passages through are not easy to detect. (Whether the A354 road goes through one such is discussed below (on page 27), with Pitt-Rivers' Section 1.) That at the west end of the Bokerley Gap must be as old as the old road going through it, significantly an extension of Earth Pits Lane. The same applies to that taking Sillen Lane while, as at the Junction, there is a 'stagger' in opposing ends of the banks which suggests that at some time there was a break (if not just a very sharp but inexplicable twist) in the line. The hollow-ways of Sillen Lane confuse the issue. On the top of Blagdon Hill there is again a stagger but quarrying and the construction of the park pale have once more obscured original conjunctions or a possible gap.

Widespread cultivation has, on the Dorset side, probably come up to the Dyke along almost the entire length of the Fore Dyke in Sector C and in Sector B, except, possibly, just north west of the Epaulement. In Sector A 1, 'Celtic' fields have themselves been almost obliterated. Some of this may have been by ridge-and-furrow of medieval type (cf, Plate 10). Modern cultivation has again almost flattened 'Celtic' fields to the north in this section. Much of the thin pottery scatter reported by Pitt-Rivers under the rampart in the Bokerley Gap area suggests that, here at least, the Line lay over 'Celtic' fields.

A description of Bokerley Dyke sector by sector

Sector C

Bokerley Dyke, defined as a substantial, continuous earthwork, is in this area represented only by the Fore Dyke (Fig 8). The so-called 'Rear Dyke' (Figs 8 and 9) was totally flattened by the time of Pitt-Rivers' excavation, is different in nature, its large ditch no more than 130 metres long, almost certainly unfinished and not, as such, continuous with the major earthwork south of the road. Its nature is different in critical

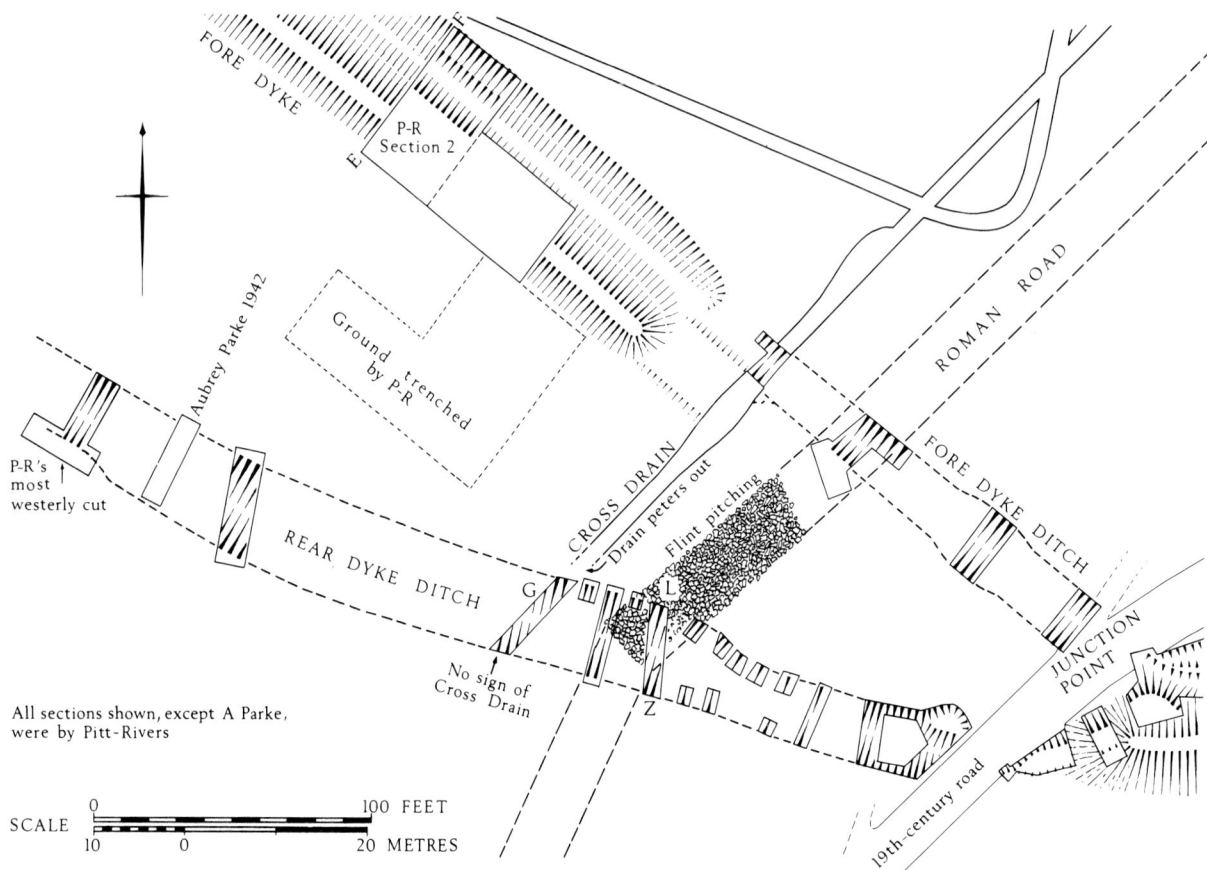

FIG 8   Sector C of Bokerley Dyke: plan of the Fore and Rear Dykes (enlarged detail from Fig 10) (1:800)

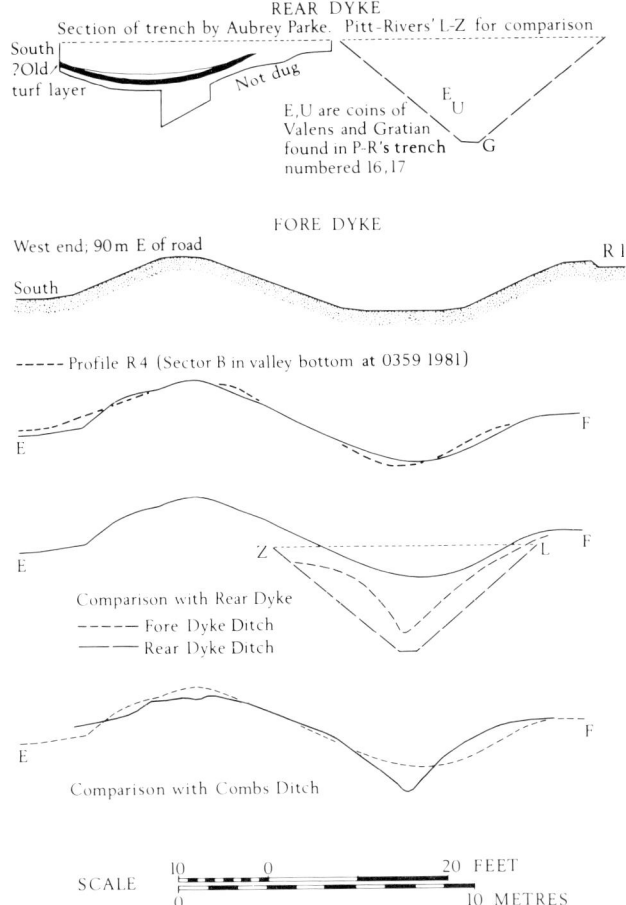

FIG 9 Bokerley Dyke: profiles and sections of the Fore and Rear Dykes. E−F represents Pitt-Rivers' Section 2 and is included for comparison (1:250)

ways from that formerly supposed. It is a massive defensive work where Pitt-Rivers found and described it, being 'a large ditch, some 30 feet [9 metres] wide and 12 feet [3.6 metres] deep, with a regular escarp and counterscarp' (Pitt-Rivers 1892, 69; cf, Fig 9 in this volume, showing his section L−Z). Pitt-Rivers himself had shown, however, on the same plan that the ditch was decreasing in size to the east and air photographs (Plate 6) now show unambiguously that at the west, 20 metres beyond where Pitt-Rivers dug his most westerly section (where the ditch was only just over 20 feet (6 metres) wide), the ditch tapers irregularly until it is seen only as a continuous narrow line perhaps 1.5 metres across. This almost certainly represents a linear, on part of which an unfinished stretch of fortification, the Rear Dyke, some 100 metres long, had been imposed.

Professor Rahtz, in his excavation of 1958 at Bokerley Junction, had already, before the new air photographs were available, questioned 'the continuity and contemporaneity of the Rear Dyke with the "link" E. of the road, and thence with the outer member of the double ditch [as seen in Pitt-Rivers' Section 1] ... on the grounds of its disparate depths and its irrational course' (1961, 76). The Rear Dyke is thus not to be regarded as part of any 'B' work (cf, Rahtz 1961, Fig 7, with Figs 5 and 6 in this volume).

It is not known whether the narrow ditch, Pentridge (16) B, continuing west from the Rear Dyke and which surely antedated it, was part of an antecedent linear, totally destroyed south of the A354, as seems most likely, or associated with one of the 'strands' external to Bokerley, discussed further below, or with a lost part of the line of Pentridge (17), for instance. To the west it probably links with Pentridge (16) C. It is just conceivable that at Bokerley Junction there was a divergence of spinal linears, one destroyed by the Fore Dyke, of the sort that occurs between Tidpit Down and Bokerley (Martin (80) A and B), but it seems very likely that, from some early date, perhaps before the time of construction of the Fore Dyke, there was an 'entrance' here, presumably replacing that which at one time took the Roman road through or across an early linear or even the Rear Dyke itself. The sharp bend in the Roman road over the actual ditch of the Rear Dyke surely relates to the previous existence of a ditch on the same line. Pitt-Rivers' excavation of the Rear Dyke revealed a bigger ditch, where widest, than the ditch of the Fore Dyke.

The Fore Dyke is a work of apparently uniform size with bank and ditch congruent. Its bank is rather smaller than that south east of the Junction (Fig 9). It is put forward here as a different type of work from the short Rear Dyke.

The area of the settlement Pentridge (15), in Sectors C, B and A 1, is the only one in which Bokerley is related to a demonstrable settlement and also the one about which there is most information (Figs 10, loose (1:2,500 plan), 8 (1:800 plan of part of Fig 10, giving greater detail of the Rear and Fore Dykes) and 9 (comparative sections and profiles), and Plates 6 and 7).

The sources used for Fig 10 are the plans and sections published by Pitt-Rivers (1892, passim) and by Rahtz (1961), air photographs by John Boyden, Cambridge University, the RAF, BKS and by the Royal Commission, as well as new field survey by Royal Commission staff. Note has also been taken of an excavation carried out in the difficult wartime conditions of 1942−3 by Mr Aubrey Parke. The new information requires some revision of the theories propounded by Hawkes in 1947 and modified by Rahtz.

The elements in Fig 10 are: settlement Pentridge (15), much more extensive over space and time than appreciated in RCHM (1975), and, in the present volume, allotted letters for the 'new' parts ('A' incorporating Iron Age elements); Bokerley Dyke, Pentridge (16), also allotted letters for elements that require separate reference in Sector C; Fore and Rear Dykes, the latter, as explained above (page 20), quite different from former concepts; the earthworks south of the A354, and the Roman road, Ackling Dyke. Discussion of this area begins with a short description of the new information about Pentridge (15).

Iron Age and Roman settlement, with possible post-Roman elements, is spread in varying and uncertain density over some 12 hectares (30 acres) (Plates 6 and 7). The 2.8 hectares (7 acres) of settlement hitherto recognised lie north east from the Rear Dyke. Pitt-Rivers 'trenched over' about ⅛ of the total area beyond the Fore Dyke and dug out most of the ditches ('drains') but only sections of the Boundary Drain (1892, 45−6). Most of the pottery and nails found close to the Rear Dyke persuaded

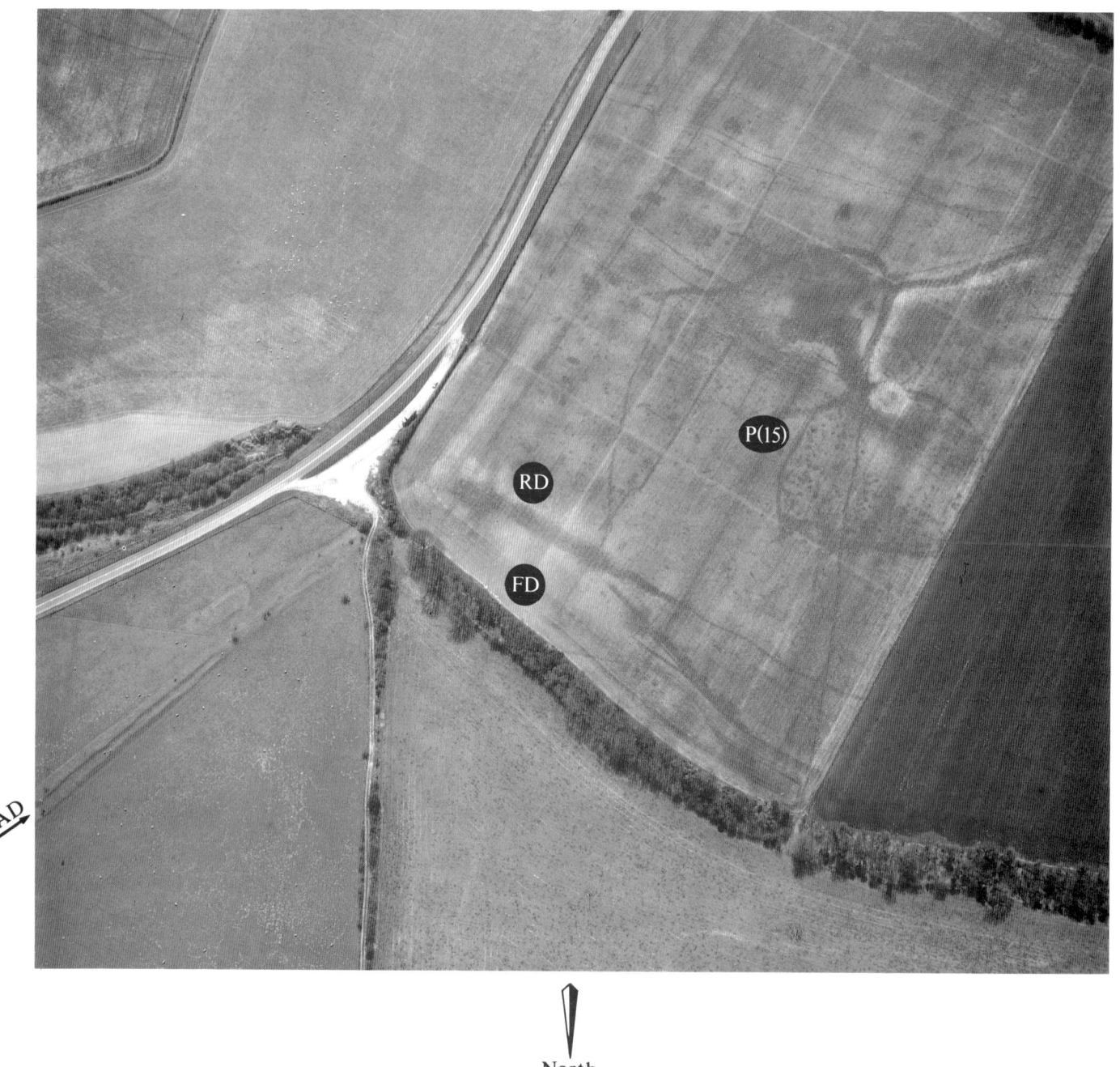

North

PLATE 6   Bokerley Junction, Pentridge, Dorset, and Martin, Hampshire. A near-vertical air photograph, with north to the bottom, with the Rear (**RD**) and Fore Dykes (**FD**), the settlement Pentridge (**15**), part only being visible, and the Roman road 'Ackling Dyke' (**AD**) (cf, Figs 8 (1:800 plan) and 10 (1:2,500 plan), and Plate 7). (NMR OAP SU 0319/14/283)

Pitt-Rivers that 'the ditches to the north and east must in all probability have been the boundary drains of fields'. Both he and Hawkes, in his reassessment of the site, thought that a major site lay to the south, nearer Woodyates (Pitt-Rivers 1892, 18; Hawkes 1947, 68). This probably correct proposition must be tempered by an appreciation of the substantial finds and evidence for settlement activity found on the outer side of

Bokerley Dyke by Pitt-Rivers and by Rahtz (eg, Pitt-Rivers 1892, 13; Rahtz 1961, 74), discussed further below.

Quite unexpected increments, displayed on recent air photographs (eg, Plate 6), to the settlement area are (15) A and B. The enclosure (15) A is associated with spreads of storage pits of almost certain Iron Age date. It is on the shoulder of the modest hill west of Bokerley Junction on which, over 40 years

PLATE 7 Bokerley Junction, Martin, Hampshire. An oblique air photograph looking south west across the area of settlement Pentridge (15), excavated by Pitt-Rivers. The Rear Dyke **RD** is just detectable beyond the wooded line of the Fore Dyke **FD**. The marginal annotation **AD** shows the Roman road, Ackling Dyke, **BD** the Boundary Drain, **WD** the West Drain and **FDE** the Fore Drain East, both now seen to continue north out of the settlement area, and **ED** the East Drain, curving away from the Roman road. The Cross Drain displays a thin ditch line beside the thick. (NMR SU 0320/5/2)

ago, circular platforms were built for a wartime radio location centre (cf, Fig 7), making any further investigation in that area very difficult. An oval of almost 0.7 of a hectare (1¾ acres) opens through a broad ditched funnel to an arcuate area also containing pits. The arrangement is bigger and less regular than would be usual for a 'banjo' but suggests some affinity. A long ditch, part of a pattern which — if contemporary — divided much of the settlement area north of the A354, is possibly continuous from the Fore Dyke and extends further south, bisecting the enclosure. A chalk pit, shown on late 19th-century maps, cuts it at the southern part, where it meets a small ditched compound possibly attached to (15) B. Downhill of

(15) A, and probably later than it, (15) B consists of two broad ditches not necessarily part of a single feature, the more westerly probably with its north bank partly overlying the ditch of (15) A. A large depression up to a metre deep, as seen on the ground today, lies within an intensely black spread on air photographs in the area of B on Fig 10. Pits that could be Iron Age extend in less density over a hectare (2½ acres) or two outside A, but few can be seen within B.

(15) C consists of rectangular ditched arrangements, mostly without pits, along the north side of the Roman road. Just north of C on Fig 10, extending from west to east, are ditches suggesting a track leading to the Roman road. A broader 'way'

east of the road, flanked by a much re-cut acute angle of a probable enclosure, and another, 70 metres north, of two parallel ditches, intersecting (15) B, are contemporary. There are dark patches, some rectangular, 6 to 9 metres long, perhaps deriving from structures, at least three adjacent to the Roman road (Plate 6) and one in (15) B.

East of the present road, test excavation within an area of about 0.8 of a hectare (2 acres) immediately south east of Bokerley Junction was carried out in 1958 by Professor Rahtz, who found scattered indications of settlement, possibly near its edge, including an oven, small pits and ditches, Roman coins and pottery. Subsequent air photographs by John Boyden suggest small, linked subrectangular features, which are undated, just east of the 1958 excavations and on slightly higher ground.

North of Bokerley Dyke the 'drains' do not necessarily depict a contemporary pattern (cf, page 5). There seems little doubt that the Roman road is later than the Boundary Drain, and it was only thought by Pitt-Rivers to be the latest feature on his site because it was the deepest, a character which only tends to mark it out as different, plausibly prehistoric, and so unrelated to the settlement he was excavating. (The skew setting of the 'square', an apparent cemetery enclosure of the 4th century AD, strongly suggests this, and also indicates either that the former bank which once accompanied the 'drain' lay on the far side from the settlement, making the ditch 'face' it, or that it had been flattened and was of no account.) Its total length is unknown. Its likely junction with the Fore Dyke to the west could hint at the former presence of a linear followed by the Fore Dyke. To the south east, 250 metres away, it extends into a broken area where it is possible that Pitt-Rivers missed evidence for continuation (as he did in the case of the Fore Drain which, together with the West Drain, continued north for at least 200 metres). The East Drain, east of the Roman road, raises another possibility. If related to the Cross Drain as a side ditch to the road, it is curious that it should diverge south from it, unless to form a sort of triangular 'open space' associated with the settlement arrangements. It may have some bearing on the interpretation of the Shoulder Angle earthworks or of the outer ditch found in Pitt-Rivers' Section 1.

Sector B

The visible dyke east and south from Junction to Epaulement is probably largely of one final construction, apparently — according to surface inspection — with a single ditch that may have been deepened on the same line though notably 'undefensive' in appearance. Plate 3 shows a distant view across the combe bottom, Plate 4 a close-up of the same view and Plates 5 and 8 illustrate the view at the Epaulement, showing 'strong' work to the south and much lesser work to the north.

Pitt-Rivers' surface profile at his Section 1 (Fig 11; Pitt-Rivers 1892, Plate CLXIII) shows a ditch depression 3 metres wider

PLATE 8 Martin Down closely north east of Bokerley Dyke in Sector B, looking north on former rifle range. The 500-yard firing point bank is marked by the near ranging rod. The photograph illustrates the impenetrable growth on an area shown totally bare in 1959. (NMR BB80/517)

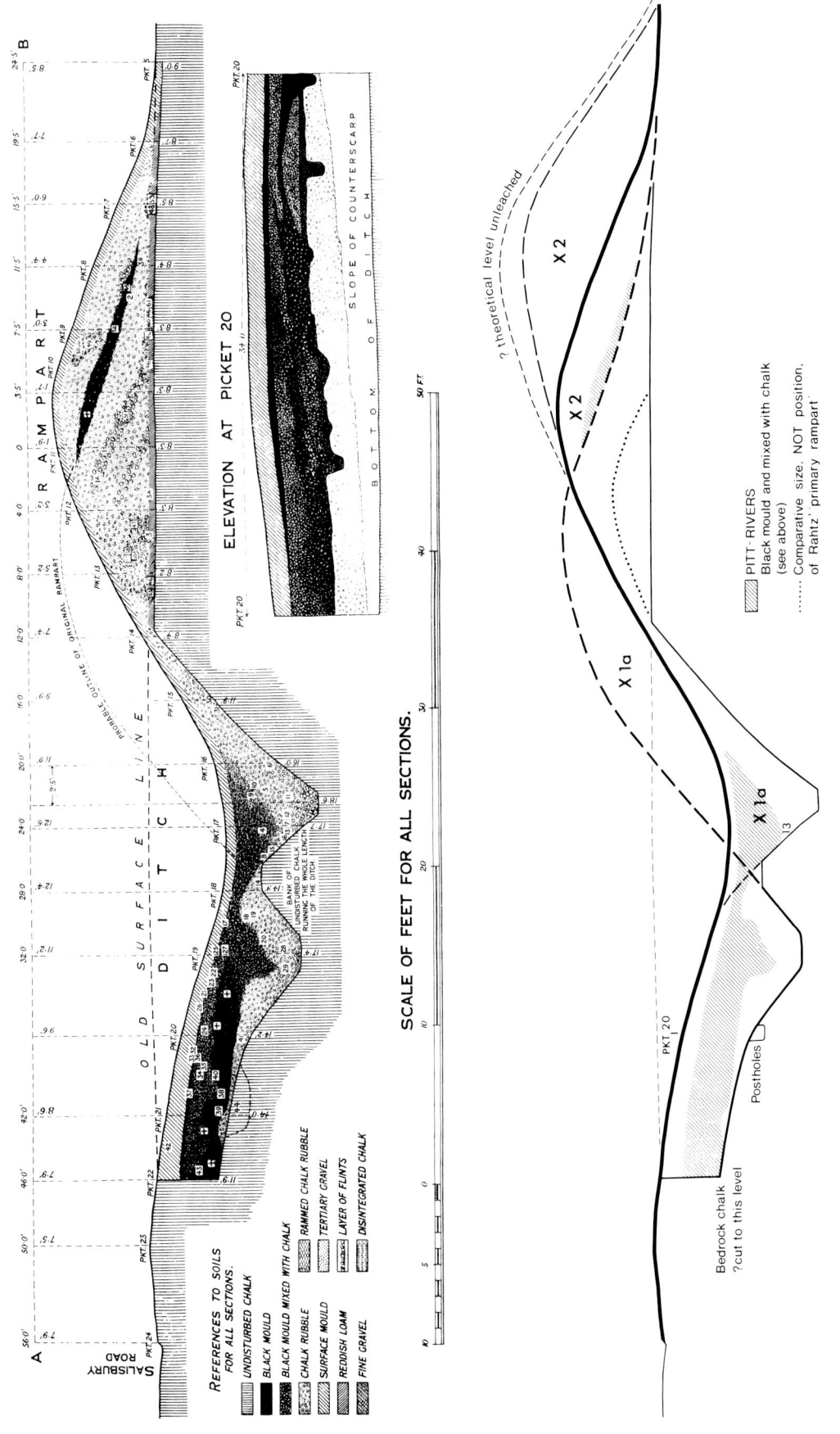

FIG 11 Sector B of Bokerley Dyke: Pitt-Rivers' Section 1 and its analysis (1:125)

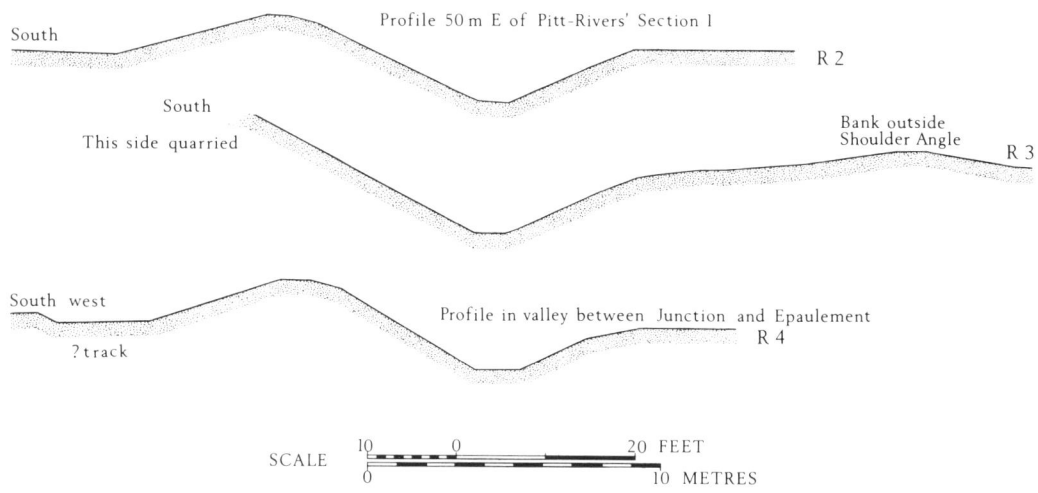

South   Profile 50 m E of Pitt-Rivers' Section 1

R 2

South

This side quarried

Bank outside
Shoulder Angle

R 3

South west

?track

Profile in valley between Junction and Epaulement

R 4

SCALE

10   0   20 FEET

0

10 METRES

FIG 12   Sector B of Bokerley Dyke: profiles R 2, R 3 and R 4 (1:250)

than that seen in other surface profiles for most of the length in Sector B (Fig 12). Comparison with his Section 2 across the Fore Dyke shows that a ditch of similar size to the 'inner' ditch at Section 1 has been dug here through some other feature(s), exemplified by the black humus undifferentiated in the 'old surface line' (Pitt-Rivers 1892, Plate CLXIV), the nature of which is less than certain. There is no surface sign of any 'outer' ditch in the valley bottom profile (Fig 12: profile R 4), though it is less possible to be dogmatic in the area around the Shoulder Angle.

Running closely along the outside of the extant Bokerley ditch south of the A354 outside the Shoulder Angle, is a bank now traceable for at least 250 metres (not just a feature at the angular turn of the Dyke). Outside this again is another possible ditch and bank, 'possible' not because they lack size but because they could be largely formed by the hollowing effect of former heavy animal traffic climbing out of the little valley below, south east of the Dyke.

Certainly, the surface manifestations south of the Epaulement at Pitt-Rivers' Sections 9 and 10 and in Sector A 1 as a whole, where two ditch lines are clearly visible (see Plate 11), are quite different from those north west of the Epaulement. Pitt-Rivers himself saw no trace of a second ditch continuing into what is here termed Sector B but, with uncharacteristic lack of logic, averred that he would have found it had he dug further north west!

It should therefore be assumed, unless further excavation reveals an earlier major ditch, that there is only one continuous substantial work (the obvious extant one), extending north west from the Epaulement, and therefore it is necessary to consider more closely the 'outer ditch' at Section 1 and Pitt-Rivers' explanation for it, which depended largely on the assumption that it was the same as seen in Sections 9 and 10. It is this which allowed the hypothesis, further developed by Professor Hawkes, of two successive dykes of similar size extending west from the

Epaulement, one shifted bodily south for 3 metres to cut back a hypothetical decayed face in the earlier dyke.

The theory put forward by Pitt-Rivers is difficult to believe, even on grounds of volumetric comparison (Fig 11: annotated Section PR 1), but this sort of analysis cannot be safely taken as a proof — since the identity and size of earlier, encapsulated, features within the rampart are on every count uncertain and there are incalculable factors, in this settlement area, of adjacent upstanding earthworks possibly being used as a quarry for the new bank.

The tip lines in the rampart do not have to be truncated as Pitt-Rivers suggests but the face may have been sharpened by scarping as it probably was south of the Epaulement. Dating from Pitt-Rivers' section is unsafe because, as already noted, the objects projected do not necessarily belong to the drawn layers and may, in any case, have been displaced by the quarrying that drew Pitt-Rivers to this spot. The ditch is not likely to have been so disturbed and can be related in terms of type of layer to the bank section. The 'black mould' in the rampart is indistinguishable from that almost spanning the outer ditch, and it seems very likely that a continuation of that layer was the source (not a static turf growth).

The actual nature of the 'outer ditch' is difficult to understand in its complexity. The outer slope is 1.2 metres lower at the 'counterscarp lip' than the old ground surface under the rampart and is of too slack a section to be explained by crumbling. It is best understood as quarried away before, but not long before, the digging of what are surely post-holes into the chalk since, otherwise, these post-holes would have been up to 1.5 metres deep (see Fig 11: section along Pitt-Rivers' Picket 20). It seems that Pitt-Rivers did not recognise the curious scoops that Rahtz identified as F 21 and F 22 in his section adjacent to Pitt-Rivers' R, but something like them would plausibly explain the depressed level of the 'counterscarp'. Pitt-Rivers was surely wrong in his assumption that the 'outer ditch' cut through settlement, 'pits or dwellings, which were on the ground before the Dyke was made' (Pitt-Rivers 1892, 73), and it is probable that settlement activity over the 'outer ditch' left the thick black layer which may be the equivalent of that in Rahtz' layer G. This latter produced copious finds, including late 4th-century AD coins and a small bronze figurine of a nude female. Clearly there was occupation over a substantial period; a bronze arrow head (Pitt-Rivers' find 13; see Fig 11) in his inner ditch is Early Iron Age at latest (according to Mr Brendan O'Connor, in a private communication). Whether there was an 'entrance', more or less on the line of the A354 is problematic. It is still uncertain, but likely, that a continuous small bank and ditch reached at least this point from the south east in a relatively early period. Rahtz very cautiously thought his 'primary rampart' should be at least before AD 300 (his own work had exposed only Iron Age or early Roman sherds in the covered ground surface but he was still trying to synthesise his observations with those presentations and interpretations which had been previously put forward and generally accepted (Rahtz 1961, 76)). There is an obvious stagger in the disposition of the ditches east and west of the present road and the banks could only originally have continued without a violent twist if the bank of the Rear Dyke had been on the north side of its ditch.

Therefore, though there are difficulties, it seems most likely that this 'outer' ditch had been virtually destroyed, though made use of, possibly for industrial purposes (accounting for the blackness and possibly the money), and that the entirely new rampart was built as seen today after the settlement east of it had ceased to exist, or count.

Sector A 1

(For the Epaulement and its immediate area, see Figs 13 and 14 and Plates 5 and 9. Fig 13 (plan) is based on Plates CLXIX and CLXX in Pitt-Rivers 1892. Profile R 5 in Fig 14 — across the Epaulement — is included to correct the distortion in Pitt-Rivers' staggered section B−C−D.)

The **Epaulement** itself is a massive work with rampart volume rather bigger than ditch, suggesting that it might encapsulate an earlier bank. It extends from a shoulder down a medium slope to the valley bottom and thence 35 metres out into the valley (now arable), ending in a tongue of ditch only three-quarters of the previous width. It has to be noted that if Pitt-Rivers' explanation of the two ditches south from here is not correct, then there is no need to postulate a major work continuous with it when the Epaulement was built to this size. The line of the

PLATE 9 Bokerley Dyke: the Epaulement swinging west from the end of Sector A 1 towards the valley bottom. The fence, roughly on the county boundary, dips over Pitt-Rivers' 'Traverse'. (NMR BB80/482)

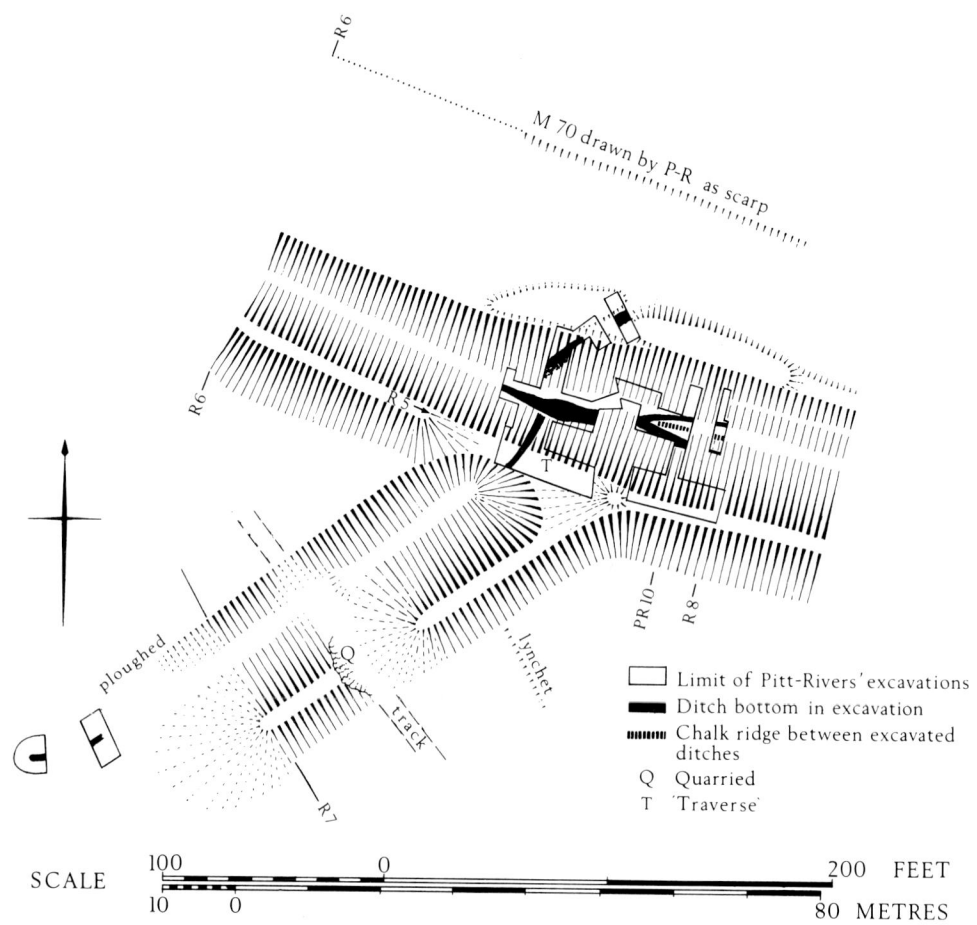

FIG 13   Sectors B and A 1 of Bokerley Dyke: plan of the Epaulement (1:1,250)

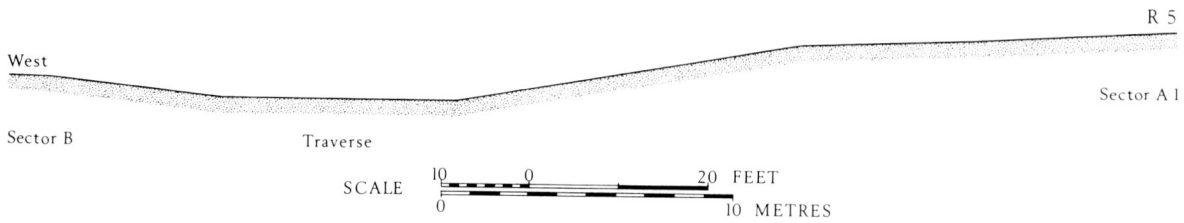

FIG 14   Sectors B and A 1 of Bokerley Dyke: profile R 5 (1:250)

Epaulement ditch, as he shows it, is not swinging to meet the 'outer' ditch, although there is almost certainly a connection since the outer ditch is apparently absent north of this point. It is therefore just possible to envisage the Epaulement in one phase as an independent inhibiting work facing north west.

The small finds in this area may be regarded as indicating some degree of settlement activity. There are irregularities in the ground immediately to the east, of unknown significance. At some stage the rampart was built up in Sector A 2 to proportions which match those of the Epaulement.

The scarp shown parallel with Bokerley Dyke to the north

east is part of Martin (70), its flattened ditch almost certainly lying along the south-west side, 'facing' Bokerley.

In the area opposite the Epaulement an outer ditch begins within the Bokerley Dyke ditch, and this continues, with variable profile (and partly quarried away for a short stretch, cf, Fig 7), to just south of the link with linear Martin (78) (Figs 15, 16, 17 and 18; Plates 10 and 11). Outside this, in places, a bank runs alongside it.

The tapering of the Epaulement, and its change of direction in the valley bottom to the west, invites questions. One such is whether the developed Epaulement was following an earlier

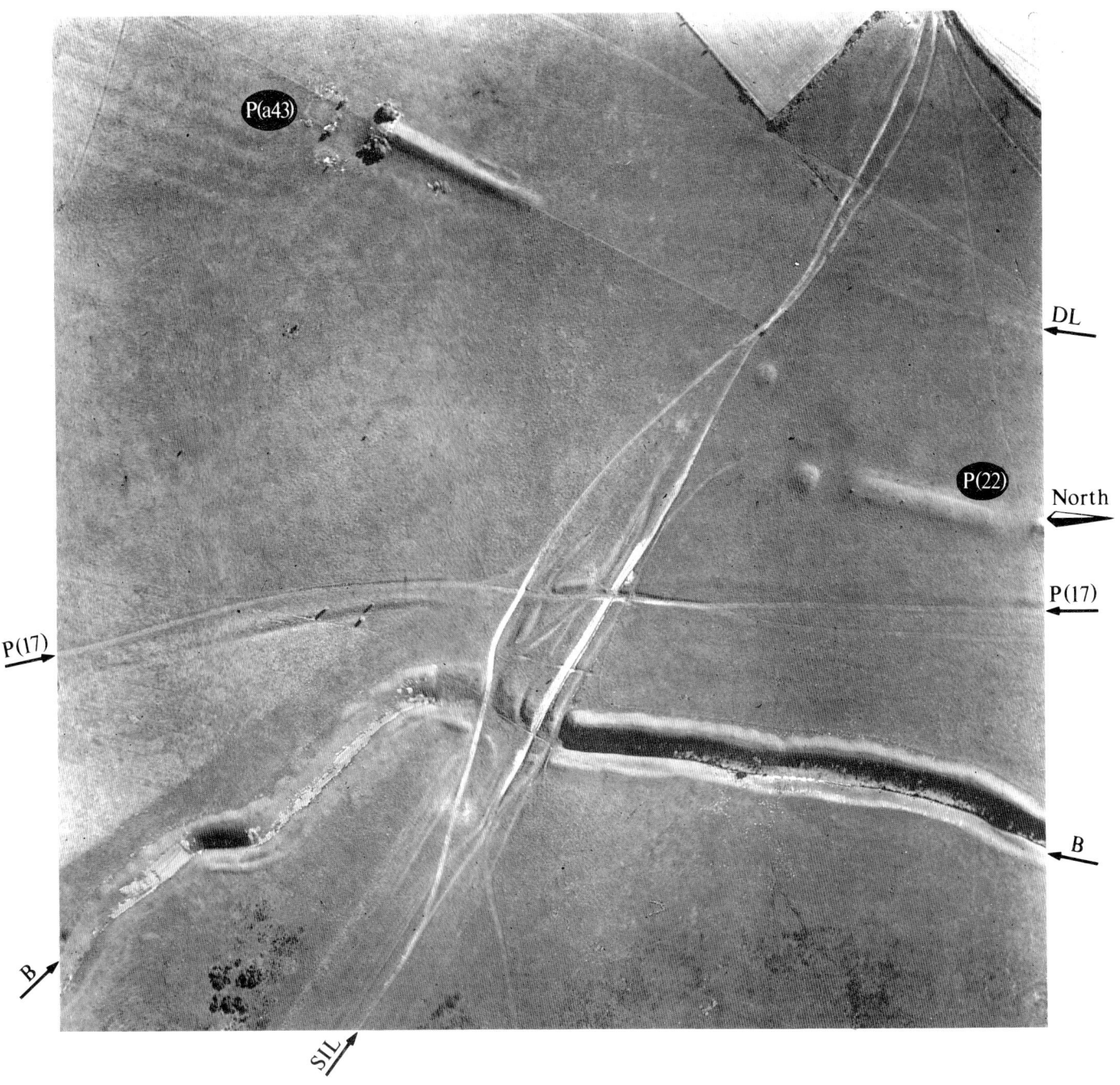

PLATE 10 Bokerley Dyke: Sector A 1 which illustrates the Dyke, barrows and cultivation remains of different periods in the area of Sillen Lane (SIL). A near-vertical air photograph, with west to the top, taken by O G S Crawford on 14 July 1924 (part of Plate XLIII in Crawford and Keiller 1928). Compare Figs 6 and 7 and Fig 19 (detail of Sillen Lane area) in this volume and p 32 for consideration of possible early passage through the Bokerley Line at this point.

The apparent long mound between the tracks of Sillen Lane could be an elongated barrow (cf, Martin (24)) incorporated in the line of Pentridge (17), which appears here to swerve to one side of it, but was more likely a fragment of the linear itself.

The double ditches along Bokerley Dyke are flanked by an external bank which might have followed a slightly different line at the Sillen Lane intersection; whether there was an original or very early passage through Bokerley Dyke, there is no sign of an original break in Pentridge (17), which changes direction on either side of the Sillen Lane tracks.

The parallel lines (DL) are almost certainly a double-lynchet track associated with the probably 'Celtic' field scarps making a right-angled turn by the round barrow just south of long barrow Pentridge (22) and ending against Pentridge (17). Ridge-and-furrow of medieval form is clear to the top left of the picture, with traces of 'Celtic' fields on the near side. There are signs of some quarrying of the earthworks. Scrub grows in the ditch of the small square enclosure Pentridge (a 43) but not generally over the barrow ditches. The prolific spreads of white on Bokerley Dyke (B) are almost certainly due to rabbits. (NMR OAP SU 0419/4)

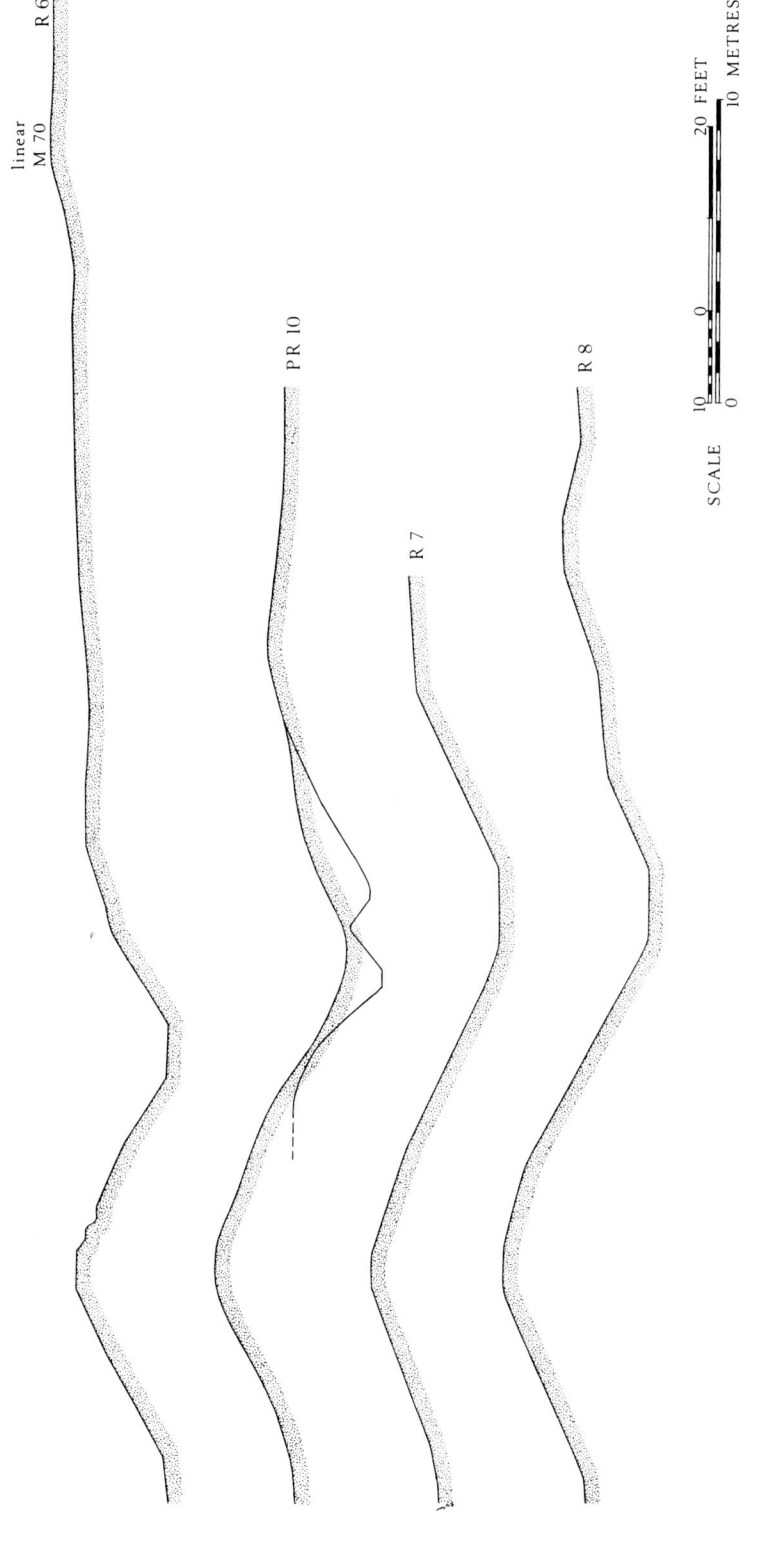

FIG 15 Bokerley Dyke: profiles R 6, PR 10 (with section), R 7 and R 8 (1:250)

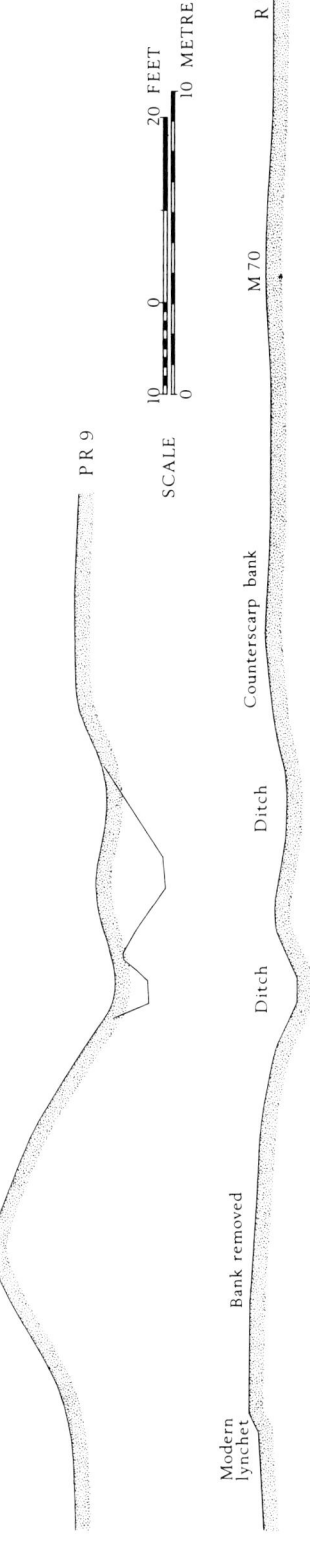

FIG 16 Sector A 1 of Bokerley Dyke: profiles PR 9 (with section) and R 9 (1:250)

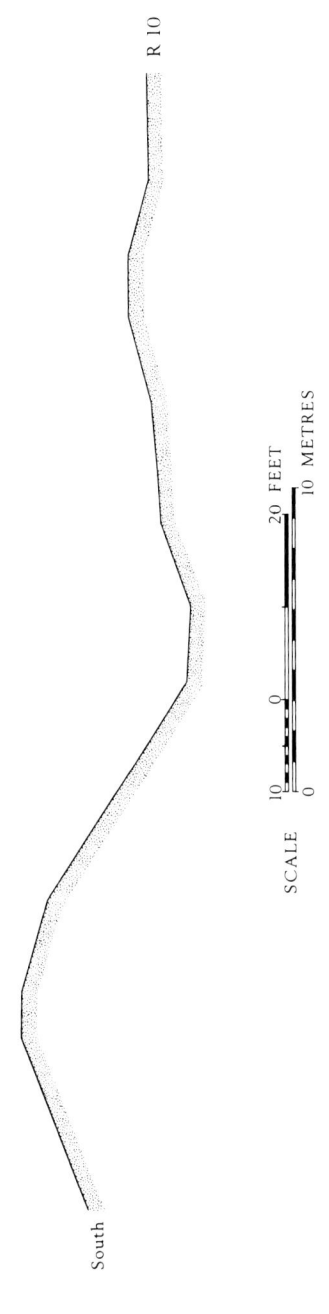

FIG 17 Sector A 1 of Bokerley Dyke: profile R 10 (1:250)

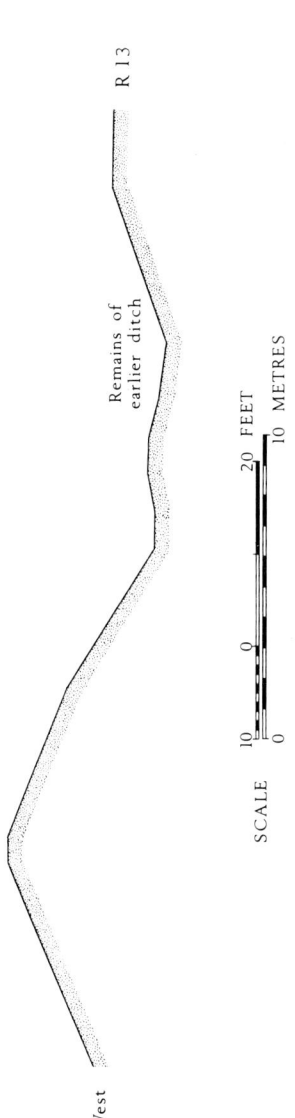

FIG 18 Sector A 1 of Bokerley Dyke, north west of Blagdon Hill: profile R 13 (1:250)

PLATE 11 Bokerley Dyke in the southern part: Sector A 1 looking north, showing double ditch. (NMR BB80/490)

linear. Pitt-Rivers did not detect any but he was looking for a ditch of massive proportions, and lesser ones were not always recognised by his team (eg, the northward continuation of the 'Fore Drain East' in Pentridge (15) now seen on air photographs). Traces of a possible slight linear climbing the side of the valley have been seen on air photographs taken in years so far apart as to discount ephemeral farming effects (V 58 RAF 3250, 0125 and 6 (9 Oct 1959); Carto-graphical Services sortie 530, 1342 (7 Nov 1975)), but there is no confirmatory sign on the ground.

At **Sillen Lane** (Fig 19), the ground, which is here dimpled by a slight re-entrant from the east, falls to the true valley bottom 100 metres further south. Fig 19 is a 'measured sketch plan' to show the pronounced bend in the Bokerley Line where Sillen Lane and parallel abandoned hollow-ways cut through the Dyke. It is the only point at which there are multiple breaks. The rampart to the north is some 7 metres above a sharp 'V'

ditch, whose profile suggests recutting. Its end, abutting a hollow-way, is clearly rounded. The continuation of the rampart across the gaps is only 3 metres high. The 'counterscarp bank' seems to deviate slightly from its line. (For a note on the possible antiquity of Sillen Lane see linear Martin (73), page 109.) The ditch of Pentridge (17) can be seen across Sillen Lane, some 70 metres up the slope west of this point.

At the point where Bokerley and linear Martin (73) meet (Figs 20 (plan) and 21 (profiles)), the 'outer ditch' to Bokerley takes the form of a slightly dished 'berm' or 'ledge' with what appears to be local scooping along it. The 'counterscarp', which rises some 1.5 metres above this ledge, gives the impression of truncating the linear ditch. There is little trace of a bank beside the 'counterscarp' in this area, ie, from the combe north of Martin (73) to the combe south of it, though the quarrying just north of the southern combe has apparently removed the 'outer ditch' entirely. Bokerley rampart itself is of curious form close

32

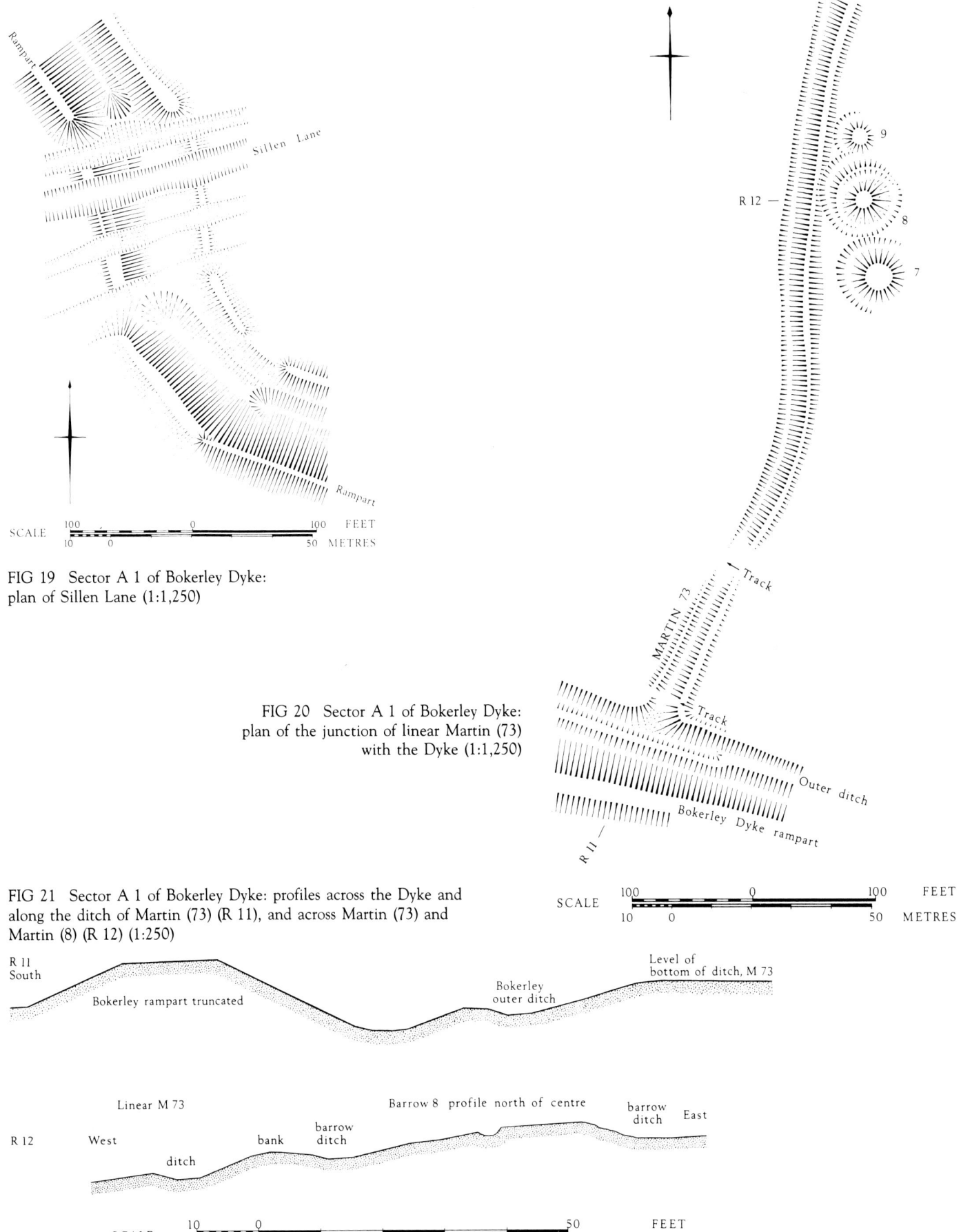

SCALE 100   0   100   FEET
10   0   50   METRES

FIG 19   Sector A 1 of Bokerley Dyke:
plan of Sillen Lane (1:1,250)

FIG 20   Sector A 1 of Bokerley Dyke:
plan of the junction of linear Martin (73)
with the Dyke (1:1,250)

SCALE 100   0   100   FEET
10   0   50   METRES

FIG 21   Sector A 1 of Bokerley Dyke: profiles across the Dyke and
along the ditch of Martin (73) (R 11), and across Martin (73) and
Martin (8) (R 12) (1:250)

R 11
South

Bokerley rampart truncated

Bokerley
outer ditch

Level of
bottom of ditch, M 73

Linear M 73   Barrow 8 profile north of centre   barrow   East
                                       ditch

R 12   West   bank   barrow
                              ditch
              ditch

SCALE 10   0   50   FEET
10   0   10   METRES

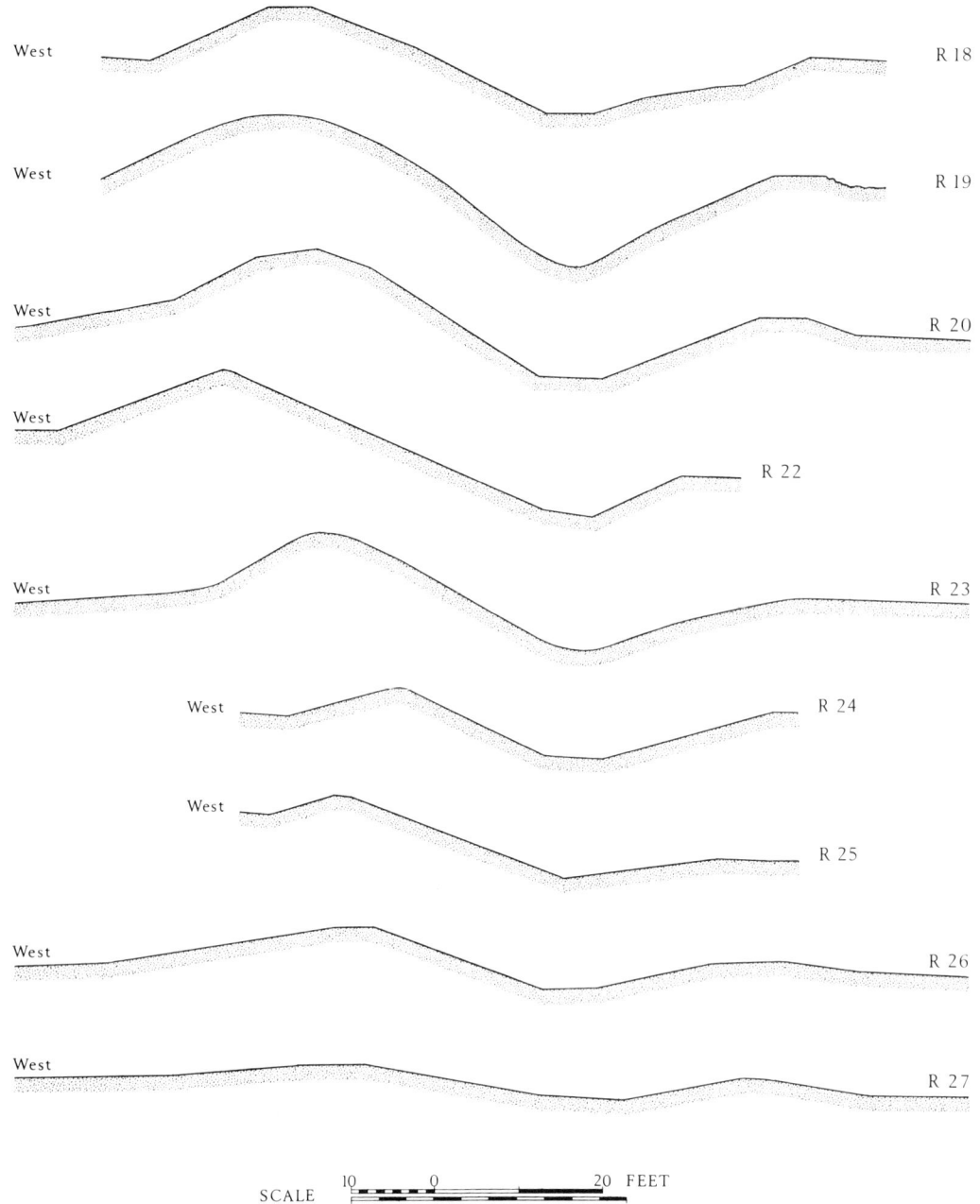

West   R 18

West   R 19

West   R 20

West   R 22

West   R 23

West   R 24

West   R 25

West   R 26

West   R 27

SCALE   10   0   20 FEET
         0   10 METRES

FIG 22 Bokerley Dyke: profiles (1:250)

to Martin (73) with a flat top either original (? unfinished) or cut down (? quarried away) at some time prior to the construction on it of a small bank to mark the county boundary.

The cluster of three barrows, Martin (7)–(9), set tight against Martin (73), can be seen prominently on the skyline from the combe bottom to the north. The proximity to the linear, strikingly similar to that of barrows to Pentridge (17) and Martin (78) (*see* below, Blagdon Hill (Fig 23)), is such that there is no possibility of the bank being associated with a ditch on the south (as it would appear to be north of Sillen Lane). Surface inspection suggests that the ditch of barrow (8) has actually cut the tail of the linear bank (Fig 21), though it would be unsafe to accept this as evidence for a sequential relationship.

Sectors A 2 and A 3

Sector A 2 merits a separate designation because here the rampart achieves its greatest height and the ditch is of proportions only emulated in the Rear Dyke. It may be supposed, therefore, that this was raised to such a markedly defensive size for some local reason, and so it becomes another 'strand' (Fig 22: eg, profiles R 22 and 23).

Sector A 3 has a single ditch for its whole length, but its form changes: at first the bank dominates but, for the second half, a counterscarp bank becomes prominent until, in places, there is a wide medial ditch between banks of almost equal size (Fig 22: profiles R 24–27).

PLATE 12   Bokerley Dyke in Sector A 2, looking south east, approaching its most massive size on top of Blagdon Hill. The figure is in the ditch of Martin (78). A single ditch only is visible where the ranging rods are positioned. (NMR BB80/1118)

South from the termination on the knoll there is no substantial bank.

From the Cranborne 'road' gap to the summit of Blagdon Hill (Figs 22, 23 and 24: 1:2,500 plan and profiles)

The ground here falls to the north from Blagdon Top by Martin (78) (Plate 12). Bokerley Dyke south of the junction with Martin (78) consists of a single bank and massive ditch narrower in span than that to the north but of larger dimensions, being the highest and most clearly 'defensive' part surviving of the whole Dyke (profiles R 18 and R 19/20 in Fig 22 make the comparison). The difference in size and the complex strands in Bokerley are reflected in profile R 18. The 'ledge' immediately outside the deep Bokerley ditch is certainly another, earlier, ditch. This is somehow related to Martin (78), which is plausibly prehistoric, but it has to be observed that Martin (78) which stands at a higher level than the 'ledge' (as was Martin (73)) crosses the line of any Bokerley 'counterscarp' bank. Such a feature is present in a marked form south of the conjunction,

but almost non-existent immediately north and then, north of the Cranborne 'road' gap, is particularly prominent (as seen on Plate 13). It seems probable that a single deep ('inner') ditch which extends along the length of the line by Martin (78) is the latest element in the Dyke's construction.

The present gaps containing the Cranborne 'road' and that opposite Martin (80) could at some stage have marked original ways through the Dyke and thus reflect, in some sense, the importance that might be attached to such routes and their blocking. The 'stagger' opposite Martin (80) A might, alternatively, be related to a former integration with that linear. Pentridge (17) seems to be continuous, blocking any line from these gaps. What the relationship of this linear was to Bokerley Dyke, or to any earlier, encapsulated linear, remains problematic, but is discussed further below.

The relationship between the barrow pairs Martin (26) and (27) and Pentridge (33) and (34) and the linears is unresolved, and perhaps unresolvable because of former excavation and disturbance, particularly of Pentridge (33) (cf, profile R 15 (Fig 24) with Plate 14). Their placing must be a deliberate choice and if, for instance, such barrow pairs have a territorial

35

PLATE 13   Bokerley Dyke in Sector A 2, pierced by the Cranborne 'road' and looking south east. The figure is beside the outer bank of Bokerley Dyke, here at its biggest for a short length. The stepped aspect of the double ditch is apparent on the right, and beyond the Dyke is linear Pentridge (17) (cf, Plate 14). (NMR BB80/494)

significance, this could even be a factor in explaining the close proximity of the two linears. There can be no 'defensive' advantage in the situation of Bokerley Dyke over Pentridge (17), and, were this a real consideration influencing the choice of ground, the opposite would clearly be the case since Pentridge (17) is uphill from Bokerley Dyke and clearly seen to be better placed where, for instance, the Cranborne road intersects both dykes.

Despite its remarkable straight alignments, Pentridge (17) is not a completely uniform structure, as is shown by a change of size (between profiles R 16 and R 17 in Fig 24) and by the remarkable difference between Dr J G Evans' exposure of an extremely shallow ditch at his BP II and the much deeper one where intersected by the BGC pipeline (BS M 71) (both Fig 24). At no point, however, is there a counterscarp bank and in this, as in the flat-bottomed ditch profile, it differs from the nearby Martin (80) (profile R 21, cf, 'V' sections in Martin (80) excavations on page 114 (Figs 60 and 61)), formerly thought to be its continuation. The absence of a link is something that still requires final confirmation by excavation, but it seems demonstrated by the just detectable continuation south of an extremely degraded bank, reasonably regarded as part of Pentridge (17), extending beyond the parish boundary in a wooded and scrubby area which has suffered a variety of disturbance. There is, moreover, no sign of Martin (80) west of Bokerley as has sometimes been suggested. Its line is indeed roughly continued west by the pale of Blagden Park (Cranborne

(32)), itself surmounted by a parish boundary bank, but these structures sink into the ditch of Pentridge (17) as they cross and so are much later than it.

Pentridge (17) was excavated where shown on Fig 23 to decide, initially, whether there were any environmental pointers to the former existence of a hedge or the like on the bank (page 14) (Evans and Vaughan 1985).

Since it is in this area that Pentridge (17) is best preserved, more general comments can be appropriately added here to those in RCHM 1975.

Pentridge (17), unhelpfully known as part of 'Grim's Ditch' (cf, page 13), is the most distinct separate strand of the Bokerley Line. Its course (Fig 6) is clear from near the Epaulement, which it is seen approaching as a very slight line hollow in arable, descending the small valley side and converging on the hedge there. To the south east it proceeds in remarkably straight stretches, making slight angular bends roughly opposite the two 'bulges' in Bokerley Dyke and turning subtly between those points as if to achieve clearance of the bulges. Nowhere can its course be regarded as tactically determined. It was recorded by the OS before ploughing had levelled most of it, except in parts of Blagdon Plantation and on Blagdon Hill (Fig 23). Its bank has been long since flattened up to just short of the Cranborne parish boundary, the bank of which, as noted above, crosses the course of the ditch. South of this, in scrubby woodland, are the broken traces of a very low bank, about 5 metres across, and with faint traces of a ditch plausibly part of Pentridge (17), which changes direction roughly opposite the point where Martin (80), with which Pentridge (17) was formerly thought continuous, comes up to Bokerley.

PLATE 14 The Bokerley Line: linear Pentridge (17) in Sector A 2, looking south east to Blagdon Hill from the Cranborne 'road' gap. The tail of barrow (34), with a white marker on it, is apparently over the bank of (17), but the barrow has been disturbed by digging. Barrows Martin (26) and (27) are to the top left of the photograph, in front of the black trees, with linear Martin (78) meeting Bokerley right of the white track. (NMR BB80/1114)

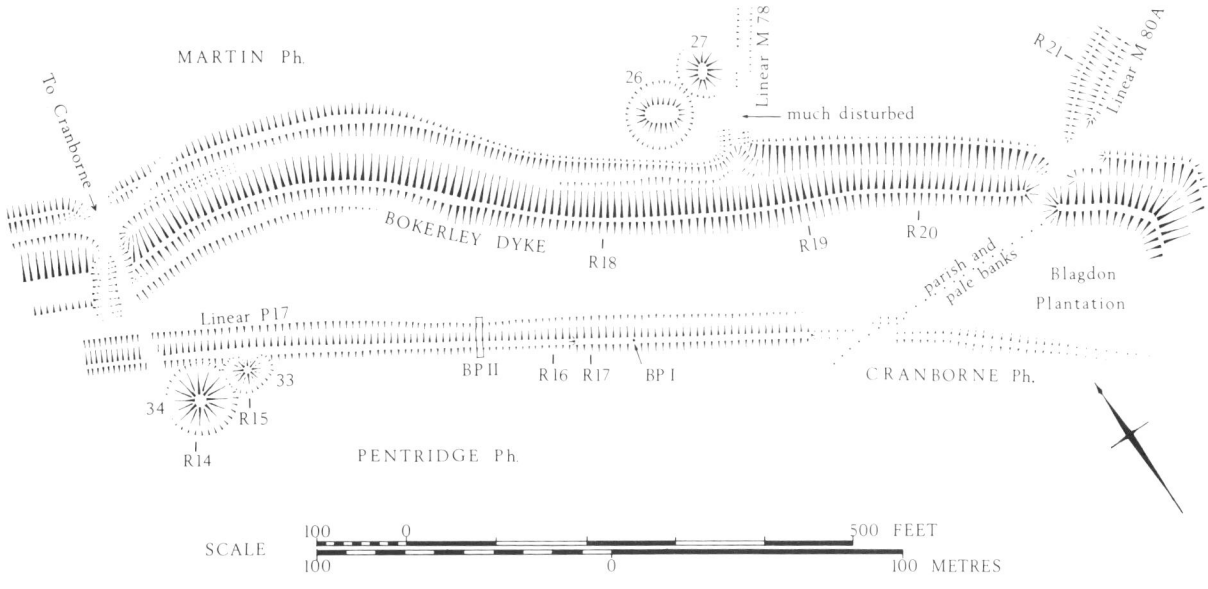

FIG 23 Sectors A 1 and A 2 of Bokerley Dyke: plan of features on Blagdon Hill (1:2,500)

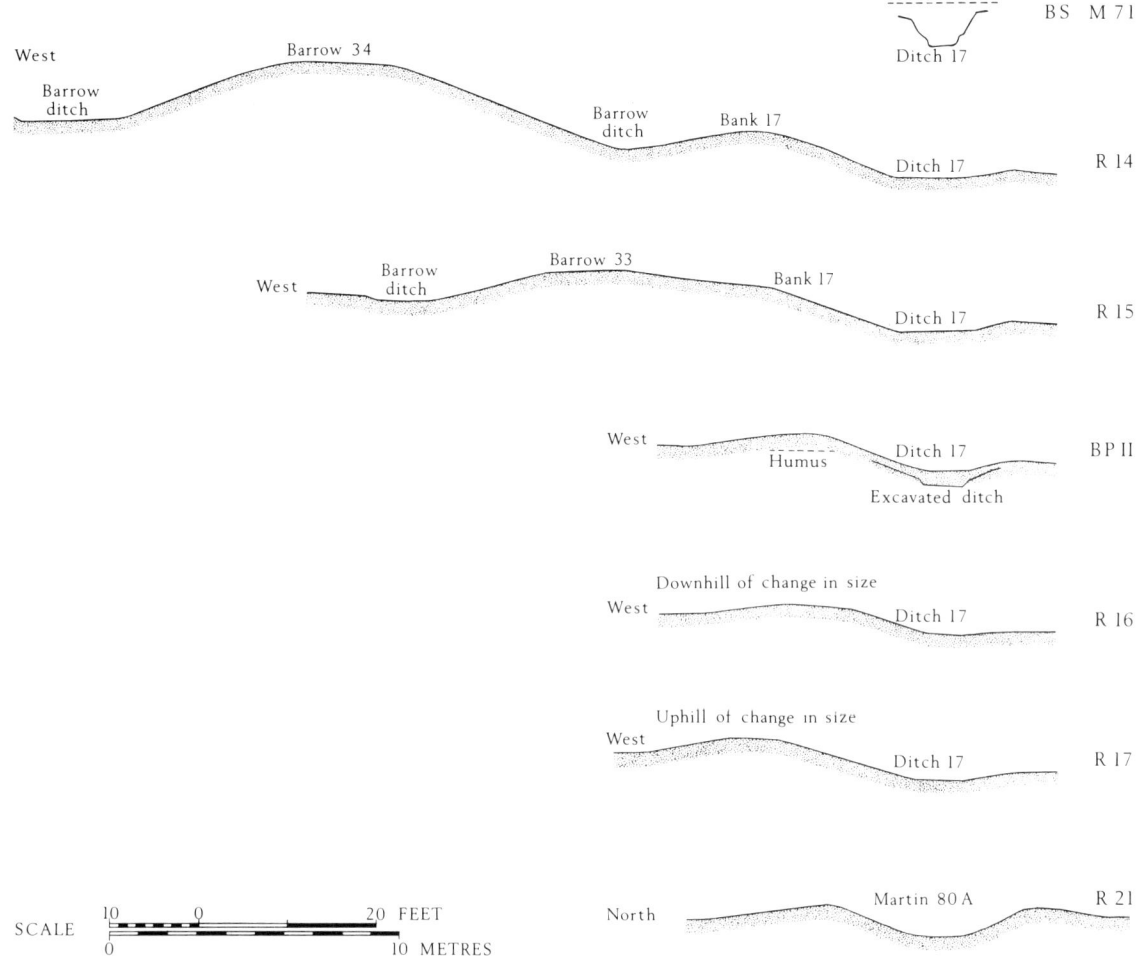

FIG 24   Sectors A 1 and A 2 of Bokerley Dyke, Blagdon Hill: profiles R 14, R 15, BP II, R 16 and R 17 across linear Pentridge (17). Comparison with section BS M 71 and profile of Martin (80) A (R 21) included (1:250)

In mean size, where well preserved, though not in form, Pentridge (17) is comparable with the bigger linears like Martin (80) A (Fig 24). It is only possible to guess at the original north and south terminations and other relationships. It either ended at the Epaulement, or somehow intersected it, and it may have been continuous with linear Pentridge (16) B which, emerging west from the Rear Dyke in a straight run followed by an angular bend, suggestively recalls the unusual character of Pentridge (17) as a whole. To the south the bank, presumably prolonging Pentridge (17) although relatively short, displays a similar quality of straight runs and angular turns, and is last recognised 'pointing' at the virtually straight run of Bokerley in Sector A 3.

The date of the work is unknown: there were no finds in the excavations and no datable relationship has been proved, though logic might infer that some ancestor of Bokerley Dyke with its western bulges already existed.

The chronology of Bokerley Dyke

It has been said that 'the most difficult of all problems in the military archaeology of the Late Roman and post-Roman centuries: [is] that of the "dykes"' (Alcock 1971, 349). Dykes are particularly difficult to date unless involved with other, datable, features. Pitt-Rivers saw this clearly, and it was only when, in 1888, his bandmaster discovered the farmer digging away Bokerley rampart just east of the Junction with the modern and Roman roads, thus exposing coins and artifacts indicative of settlement, that he knew he could settle once and for all whether or not it was 'Belgic' (Pitt-Rivers' Section 1 (see also Figs 10 and 11)). He went on later to excavate Wansdyke as well and was able to say, with admirably careful wording, that both dykes 'at the places where I excavated them, are Roman or post-Roman' (Pitt-Rivers 1892, xiii). Martin (80) and other prehistoric linears probably end against the present Bokerley Dyke, as all tests short of excavation have so far indicated, and it must be supposed that it incorporates a work or works of comparable or earlier age (pages 12, 21).

Consideration of the date of the Rear Dyke is affected to some extent by Pitt-Rivers' presentation of his excavation which can be criticised for mistakes, omissions and unwittingly misleading techniques. His section L–Z (see Fig 9) almost certainly shows, for instance, a couple of coins (E and U, the latter of Valens

(AD 364—78)) under the actual Roman road, whereas, as Hawkes notes (1947, 73), they were found in section G in Plate CLXVI, not drawn but where the ditch was described to be 12 feet (3.66 metres) deep. Hawkes shows that coin number 16 (Carausius (AD 287—93)) was there at a depth of 5 feet 6 inches (1.68 metres) and number 17, the Valens, at 6 feet 3 inches (1.91 metres). Pitt-Rivers' plan also misleadingly suggests the Cross Drain flanking the Roman road crossed (and so could have been dug into the fill of) the Rear Dyke on the line of this section. The section was certainly cut in pursuit of any continuation of his Cross Drain but he unambiguously stated that the drain 'was found to die out on the surface' (Pitt-Rivers 1892, 69) before it reached the line of what was subsequently to be recognised as the Rear Dyke and which, at the time, he thought might have been a 'soaker' for the Cross Drain. (The Cross Drain itself is conventionally thought of as a 'road ditch' but there is no certain ditch to balance it on the other side of Ackling Dyke, and there is no certainty of any immediate continuation to the south west.) The lack of displayed finds in the fill actually under the Roman road will be returned to since it could be taken as a reason for considering a pre-Roman date for the big ditch.

The incidence of both Samian and Roman coins as late as Gratian (AD 367—83) throughout the fill (Pitt-Rivers 1892, 91) strongly suggests that it largely derived from a scatter on the surface mixed up with later material and that filling did not commence until the late Roman period or later. Attention can now be drawn to the difficult, but most useful, wartime (1942) excavation carried out by Mr Aubrey Parke (Fig 8). Mr Parke shows a 'layer of turf' (not mentioned anywhere by Pitt-Rivers, though he recognised such features elsewhere) which 'sharply divided' 'two main fillings'. This turf line (layer 4) was nine inches (0.23 of a metre) of 'grey ashy substance. Turf allowed to grow . . . ' and was overlaid by a thin stratum of 'puddled chalk' (layer 3) (typescript account of excavation (copy deposited in the NMR), p 1). Below was layer 5, which was only examined within the confines of a pit dug hurriedly below the level that Mr Parke had been able to achieve across his whole trench.

'Most of the Samian fragments [all undecorated] came from the lower filling of the ditch and most of the New Forest sherds were found in the top main filling' (typescript p 4). Some New Forest sherds were found in layer 5: 'There was a certain amount of very hard grey ware which had no grit but appears to have been bound by grass. It tended to be undecorated, but showed signs of having been turned on the wheel' (typescript p 3).

All of this pottery, and the other finds, have been lost after leaving Mr Parke. What is clear is that both Samian and late Roman wares occur throughout as in Pitt-Rivers' description. Any real, as opposed to apparent, predominance of 'early' finds in the lower levels could be explained by the ditch being dug through an area not much occupied in the later period. There is conclusive evidence, not least on air photographs, that settlement in this area shifted in different periods. The final, overwhelming mass of 'late' material in the upper levels would be due to the effects of violent destruction, the product of clearing burnt and broken dwellings — an abundance of nails

was found — from further south west and throwing them into the ditch. Material from the bank may well have been used largely to level off the ground over the ruins rather than thrown into the ditch.

Pitt-Rivers' Section L—Z is singularly uninformative about the relationship of the Rear Dyke to the Roman road. He does not describe this section in any detail. No finds are recorded in the ditch under the road (page 38). The inference to be drawn from the level line of metalling is that there is a carefully packed fill here, possibly dug from elsewhere and put in after the old heterogeneous fill, unstable and likely to sink differentially, had been entirely removed. His convention shows a remarkably homogeneous 'light mould'. He noted: 'The Roman Road must have existed before the [Fore] Dyke was made, and must have been cut through to form the ditch of the Dyke, and the earth thrown up over the road to form the rampart . . . [section 5 along the Roman road *under* the Fore Dyke]. At this time, the Rear Dyke had been filled in, and the flint pitching of the Roman Road had been laid over the top of the *filling*' (1892, 70), and so 'the Roman Road must have continued in use after this Rear Ditch had been filled in' (1892, 69).

Whether the road originally went across a natural chalk causeway in an early linear cannot, of course, be known, but its width would be greater than might be expected of a 'passage' through a relatively small linear.

The undoubted survival of this boundary line throughout the Roman period and across a settlement, as well as the careful, engineered foundation of the road across the ditch, either at the very end of the Roman period or at a later date, are matters of considerable interest.

The purpose of the Dyke

It seems reasonable to suppose that the variety of slight works shown as strands were not 'defensive'. The 'Bokerley Line' evidently had some sort of cultural significance in prehistory determined by features not primarily military. While, then, dykes and parts of dyke on this line have, in places, a defensive potential, the course as a whole is decidedly unmilitary. (For an example of an almost certainly defended, as opposed to defensible, work in what appears to be a most inappropriate military siting, however, cf, Shapwick (35) in Area Plan 1.)

Pitt-Rivers always wanted to associate Bokerley Dyke with the Roman road but the evidence does not sustain this. The Rear Dyke as hitherto envisaged does not exist; however, there is, instead, a pair of short, discrete, massive works; that is, the Rear Dyke as now defined, and Pentridge (16) A, each plausibly blocking a road approaching from the north east and east north east. This suggests that Pentridge 16 (A) and Pitt-Rivers' Rear Dyke are indeed contemporary but separate attempts, not necessarily linked to the Dyke south of the A354, to establish control points on roads from the north east. Although Hawkes postulated a Roman estate in Cranborne Chase west of Sector A, there is no positive evidence for it. But the Epaulement, over

500 metres south west of the Roman road, does mark a significant and definite end to a major stretch of the Bokerley Dyke, and this remains unexplained.

Combs Ditch

Some brief comment must be made on Combs Ditch (RCHM 1970b, Winterborne Whitechurch (19)). This is about 10 km south west of Bokerley Dyke and runs roughly parallel to it for a distance of at least 1.75 km (Fig 3). There was a confused suggestion in the 19th century that it was somehow continuous with Bokerley as part of a 'Belgic' defence. Pitt-Rivers himself thought it 'not beyond the pale of possibility' that, if Combs Ditch had been a fragment of a first line of boundary, then Bokerley might have been a fragment of a second line (1892, 2). What it shares with Bokerley is a complex development on an old boundary line, and a final phase late or post-Roman in date of a size bigger than known in any linear of the Wessex linear ditch system (Bowen 1978, 122). Fig 9 shows it to be not very much less than Bokerley Dyke in Sector B where it crosses a narrow valley bottom. Here Bokerley is at its smallest but in a form that represents its final phase (cf, profile PR 2 (profile E−F) in Fig 9).

The full extent of Combs Ditch is not yet certain. In its ascertainable form, however, the main obvious difference from the final Bokerley arrangements is that it did not cross the Roman road.

Conclusion

> . . . no theory relating to past events can ever be final. Not only has the last word not yet been spoken, it never can be spoken.
> AC Renfrew on 'Models in Prehistory', *Antiquity* **XLII** (1968), 134

The discussion above has altered the bases for former assumptions. Only one published excavation, by Rahtz, can be relied on in detail and there is still much that requires confirmation, some of it achievable by small excavations (a list is suggested below). The following are 'stage hypotheses'; that is, they are proposals still based on very scanty and unsatisfactory information.

1. The Bokerley Line was stabilised as a political frontier, indicated by differences in land allotment patterns, sometime in the Bronze or earliest Iron Age. A Neolithic zone of control was thereby bisected.

2. Linears marking the limits of a particular type of land allotment were built on the Bokerley Line in unknown sequence and detail. One of these, Pentridge (16) B, was extended into and across the area occupied by settlement Pentridge (15).

3. The Roman road very likely passed through what was, or had become, an entrance in this linear (Pentridge (16) B), though any entrance would surely have required substantial widening.

4. The main Iron Age element of the settlement, Pentridge

(15) A, was uphill of the Roman road. Virtually all the pits probably associated with this were to one side, that is, south of the linear (16) B.

5. Ditches, probably prehistoric, to the north included Pitt-Rivers' 'Boundary Drain', here regarded as one of the Bokerley Line 'strands'.

6. In the Roman period settlement expanded. Subsidiary roads from the north and south probably led into a new roadside establishment marked by ditched rectangular enclosures. In the 4th century AD there was also substantial occupation just south east of Bokerley Junction on the 'outside' of Bokerley Dyke.

7. A massively deep ditch, the Rear Dyke, was dug in a discrete length, apparently unfinished, for 100 metres along part of the line of the old linear Pentridge (16) B across, and west of, the Roman road, blocking it. Not long afterwards the ditch was filled in sufficiently to take a rebuilt road. It can be suggested that the settlement had already been withdrawn behind this line and the Dyke was intended to deter hostile movement into what is today the county of Dorset. It failed; the Dyke was slighted, perhaps by the people against whom it had been thrown up. Another discrete length of dyke (Pentridge (16) A), if not Iron Age (like Great Ditch Banks), might be seen as intended to obstruct access from the 'Ox Drove' direction. This was not flattened. Some particular significance may therefore be seen in the apparent destruction of the Rear Dyke.

It might be suggested that the Epaulement was thrown up as another discrete work when the inhabitants of Pentridge (15) were evicted. But this also would be an emergency measure since that work, too, appears to have been unfinished. There is insufficient evidence to place the Sector A Dyke but it is conceivable that heightening to defensive proportions on Blagdon Top was also carried out at this time to block approaches from due east, the area of Charford that is, from the direction perhaps first seen as a Saxon threat. The Fore Dyke line is different in character from the Rear Dyke, both by reason of its lesser size and by its continuous extent, as has plausibly been said, between impenetrable scrub developed after total abandonment of much 'downland' settlement and therefore, possibly, post-Roman. It at least looks like a frontier − impossible to ignore but, equally, not truly defensive. The way through seems to have been south of the Roman road, at Bokerley Junction.

8. The date of all this, even if validated, is uncertain. There is nothing at Rockbourne Villa (Fig 25, *loose*) to suggest any form of disturbance in the latest phase of Roman Britain (RCHM 1983). Grass-tempered ware found by Parke in the fill of the Rear Dyke is, for this area uncharacteristically, in a hard fabric and may conceivably support a post-Roman date but its precise provenance is unknown. It should be noted that there is no grass-tempered ware amongst the finds from the excavations of 1888−90 now held in the Pitt-Rivers' Collection at Salisbury Museum (information from M C B Bowden). Much of the material found in excavation, except in the 'outer' ditch at Pitt-Rivers' Section 1, may be from abandoned settlement.

9. Where the battle of *Mons Badonicus* may have fitted in (if at all) is quite uncertain, for although Badbury is often advanced as a possible site, the battle is unlocated (*see*, for example, Thomas 1981, 245–51; Alcock 1987, 229–30). A severe military defeat for the Saxons, of the sort indicated by Gildas around AD 500 (*De excidio et conquestu Britanniae c* 26), would accord well with the political impasse that probably led to the final creation of 'Bokerley Dyke'. The Saxons were present in the Salisbury area by *c*AD 500 (Evison 1965, 82) and there are ?6th-century Saxon finds from around Oakley Down (Wimborne St Giles (120); Pitt-Rivers 1898, Plate 258, 15).

Perhaps then, and on the basis of inevitably slight evidence, Bokerley Dyke in its final form can be conceived as a single frontier work of post-Roman date, placed where it was very largely because it followed a major boundary line established in prehistory but plausibly ending against areas of thick scrub which, at the north end, would have regenerated in former arable. Combs Ditch (RCHM 1970b, 313, Winterborne Whitechurch (19)), 10 km south west of it, seems a similar, if smaller, work (Fig 9). The former concept of two long works, the Rear Dyke and Fore Dyke, is no longer tenable. The interpretation of the 'double ditches' which went with this theory is equally insupportable. The nature and, indeed, identity of the earliest boundary works is still open, although the pattern of linears proves, so far as archaeology is capable, that a major system of land allotment terminated here. Massive and widespread destruction, indicated by fragmentary and degraded earthworks, of which the levelling of the only short stretch that can be called 'Rear Dyke' provides a most striking example of virtually total destruction, is masked by the presence of 'old pasture' on areas where archaeological knowledge is negligible. Sector A 1/2 south from the Epaulement presents perhaps the most challenging problem: the Dyke here is considerably more massive than in the B and C sectors; it certainly ended at the Epaulement (which itself could have been a separate entity) and is blatantly separate from the Woodyates settlement. What was it protecting? There is no convincing answer to questions of purpose or of date. There certainly are, however, in this Sector as far south as a meeting with a linear from the east, a clear two ditches (possibly more) on the line itself, considerable traces of a further independent line which extended unbroken across the A 1/B Sector (ie, south *and* north of the Epaulement with its ditch 'facing' Bokerley) and, to the immediate west, Pentridge (17), which can no longer be regarded as overlain by Bokerley on Blagdon Hill but could be complementary to it.

Suggestions for further research on the chronology and function of Bokerley Dyke

It is suggested that limited excavation at the points indicated below (*see* Fig 5 for points 1 to 9) might resolve the following problems.

To check the assumption that prehistoric linears ended at Bokerley Dyke in butt junctions

1–3 Between Bokerley Dyke and Pentridge (17) on continuation of the line of Martin (73), (78) and (80), to establish whether any or all of these three linears extend beyond Bokerley;

4 Along and outside counterscarp of Bokerley Dyke opposite Martin (80) B to establish whether it continued to Bokerley.

5 To establish that there is no second ditch embodied in the apparent single ditch of Bokerley Dyke in Sector B between Bokerley Junction and the Epaulement: trench the counterscarp in the combe bottom at profile R 4 (cf, Plate 4).

To investigate the nature and course of 'strands'

6 To establish whether a slight ditch continued the line of the Epaulement west: trench on the west side of the combe where air photographs suggest the possibility.

7 To establish whether ditch Pentridge (16) B continues west beyond the modern circular platform: strip to bedrock over the area immediately east of the platform in the pasture.

8 Excavate linear Martin (70) opposite the Epaulement to confirm the assumed existence of a south-west-facing ditch and its nature; continue surface stripping to the south east to get the first indications of whether the lumpy surface here is due to ancient or modern activity.

9 Trench Martin (73) just east of the junction with Martin (72) to provide a section for comparison with that across Martin (74) (cf, Plate 50).

Major excavation is needed to look into innumerable unresolved matters such as:

10 The Rear Dyke: a full, true analytical section (for the first time) to establish the nature of backfill/silt at a number of points, including whatever is possibly under the Roman road to throw light on Pitt-Rivers' Section L–Z.

11 The Epaulement: full, true sections (again for the first time), to establish whether it encapsulates an early linear and to determine the relationship with Pentridge (17).

12 Bokerley Gap: the ditches, the 'counterscarp bank' and the discrete bank outside it where the main rampart has been removed, to establish terms of reference for a major section through the main rampart (the nature and relationship of the double ditch and the outside linear Martin (70) being still unresolved).

13 Pentridge settlement (15) C: investigate the dark rectangular marks along the west side of the Roman road.

PART III

AREA PLANS

Introduction

The following areas have been selected for illustration at a minimum of 6 inches to 1 mile (1:10,560). Only one area, Badbury (1), is not also shown on Fig 1, and is included as Area Plan 1 because of its pattern of 'local' ditches around the hill-fort, not before published, which requires comparison with arrangements east of the Bokerley Line. Area Plan 2 illustrates, in particular, a remarkable concentration of multiple linears between Thickthorn Down and Gussage Hill in Dorset. Linear ditches on Oakley Down, also in Dorset, are now seen to have been related to roads which linked several settlements (Area Plan 3). The relationship between linears and another hill-fort, Whitsbury (Hampshire), is considered in Area Plan 7. Area Plans 4, 5 and 6, all relating to Hampshire, show the setting of settlements and enclosures and also illustrate a variety of archaeological features which have been included in the comparison of monuments on either side of Bokerley Dyke, set out in Part IV below (pages 79–99).

The limits of the Area Plans, numbered below, are shown on Fig 3 (loose):

Dorset
1 Badbury Rings and west (page 43)
2 The Gussages and adjacent areas west (loose)
3 Oakley Down (loose)

Hampshire
4 Soldier's Ring and area, Damerham (page 53)
5 Knoll Down and north (page 58)
6 Rockbourne Down (loose)
7 Whitsbury and Breamore (page 74)

The outline plan of the area Pimperne/Tarrant Hinton, Fig 47, too small to warrant particular description in this section, is also shown on Fig 3, at grid reference ST 9211, marked 'TH'.

For air photographic references, see detail given in the Inventory, Part V of this volume (and also in the Tabulated Inventory available on request from the Royal Commission).

Area Plan 1

Badbury Rings and west, Shapwick and Pamphill parishes, Dorset

This plan provides a closer view of most of the second largest block of linears in Dorset. It shows a tightly concentrated web of localised arrangements lacking the multiple linears of Gussage Hill (see Area Plan 2) or the very long runs on the far side of Bokerley (cf, Fig 3). Included, below, is a preliminary consideration, with separate illustrations, of an excavation by Major and Mrs H L Vatcher, across a remarkable earthwork fragment, now levelled, of one of the linears (Shapwick (35)), close to Badbury (Plate 15). There is an apparent lack of physical link by any linear with Badbury itself. It is possible that linears do connect with the curiously bounded settlement (Shapwick (31)), more like a terminal loop to a linear springing from the Roman road line (the road otherwise masking it?) than an 'enclosure', outside Badbury. Linear Shapwick (a 95) may be integral with it and it is very possible that there was a link with (35) to the west. The focal importance of the whole area, apart from the well-known Roman crossroads just north west of the hill-fort, is further emphasised by the density of occupation around the almost certain Roman fort, Shapwick (a 85), and the ultimate, unexplained, but certainly massive defensive proportions of part of the linear (35) already mentioned.

Almost the entire area, apart from Badbury and a sliver of land immediately north west, has been ploughed. Very faint traces of probable 'Celtic' fields are suggested, even in the areas of former open fields. A sizeable block of downland was shown around the hill-fort on the first (early 19th-century) edition of the OS 1-inch map but part of this, the present grassland around and south of Shapwick (31), had been ploughed at some earlier date (Shapwick (30): ridge-and-furrow, partly overlying (31)) and, from air photographic evidence, was probably ploughed again more recently (cf, Crawford and Keiller 1928, Plate IV). Here, too, are fragmentary scarps and banks of different (including ancient) periods as well as deep-cut hollow-ways. The sudden slight drop south in the height of the outer hill-fort bank near the west entrance suggests it was possibly built over 'Celtic' fields. It is, however, in this small piece of downland, with its phases of former ploughing, that the archaeological picture is least clear.

There is enough clay-with-flints on the chalk in the area to make ponds an obvious source of water and in Badbury itself, capped with Reading Beds, there are two, of uncertain but probably quite recent date, shown on the plan, possibly developed from quarry pits.

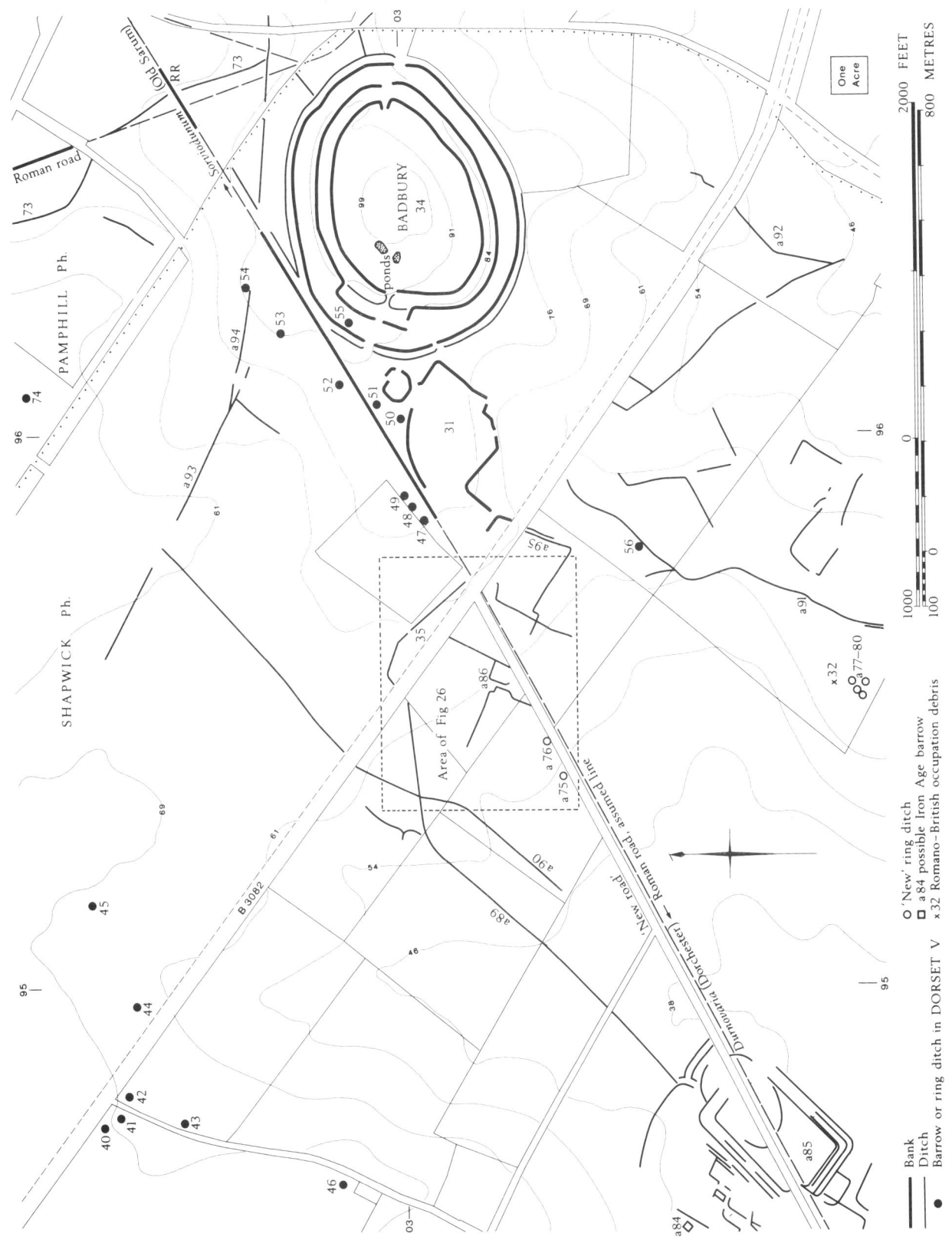

Area Plan 1 Badbury Rings and area to the west, Dorset (1:10,560) (**NB** modern field boundaries are omitted around the Roman fort)

○ 'New' ring ditch
□ a 84 possible Iron Age barrow
x 32 Romano-British occupation debris

——— Bank
——— Ditch
● Barrow or ring ditch in DORSET V

1000   0   2000 FEET

100   0   800 METRES

One Acre

PLATE 15 Shapwick (35) with Badbury hill-fort beyond, to the south east. Photograph taken in 1964, after ploughing and before excavation. (BB89/454)

`New´ Road

North

PLATE 16 Shapwick (a 85): a probable Roman fort. An oblique air photograph looking south (cf, Area Plan 1). The fort's north-east corner is labelled **a**; **b** is Shapwick (a 84), possibly an Iron Age barrow. The Roman road to Dorchester ran on the far side of, and roughly parallel to, the modern ('**New**') **Road** metalled road seen on the photograph. (NMR OAP ST 9402/3)

The probable Roman fort (Shapwick (a 85)) is similar in size to that in Hod hill-fort, Stourpaine (11) (Plate 16). There are curious features, especially the apparent lack of entrances. It seems to overlie a ditched enclosure of likely Iron Age date. A small rectangular enclosure, probably an Iron Age barrow, lies north of this (Shapwick (a 84)). A rectangular layout over 1½ hectares (3 to 4 acres), especially north west and possibly to be seen in the fort interior, represents earlier or contemporary settlement. It is certainly aligned axially with the fort, which the arterial Roman road from *Sorviodunum* (below the Iron Age hill-fort of Old Sarum, Salisbury, Wiltshire) to *Durnovaria* (Dorchester, Dorset) decidedly is not. Early Roman surface finds could belong to either settlement or fort. Excavation has now indicated that the Roman road 'V' (for roads 'V' and 'III', *see* RCHM 1975, xxx) to *Durnovaria* intersecting the fort is a very

early one (probably pre-AD 50) and is perhaps half a century earlier than the constructed road 'III' from Hamworthy on the south coast to ?Bath which intersects it at 'RR' (cf, Johnston 1982). The bank accompanying the ditch, Pamphill (73), was levelled during the construction of the road 'V' (cf, 18 km (11 miles) north east, the almost certain levelling of the Boundary Drain adjacent to Pentridge (15) where this same road cut across it). It is likely, too, that for a short way the Roman road 'III' precisely followed, and obliterated, the line of (73) continuing north north west from grid reference 96530340 as, again, it seems to have done for a longer stretch over linear Martin (69), also north east of Pentridge (15).

The bank and ditch, Shapwick (35) (Plate 15), is almost certainly part of a linear arrangement, as is indicated by the continuation of the main ditch from both ends and the

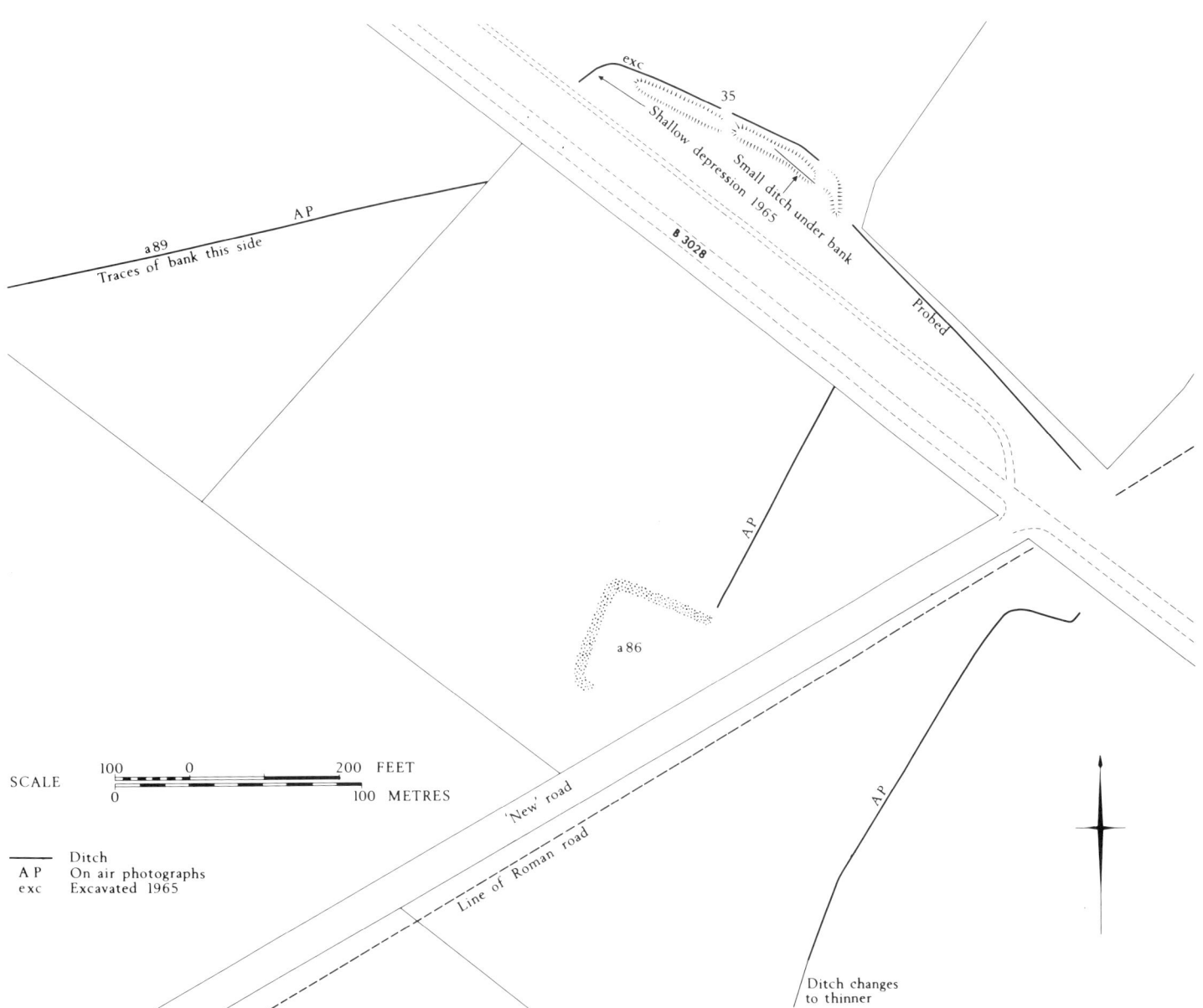

FIG 26 Plan of Shapwick (35) with linears and enclosure (a 86) (1:2,500)

suggestion on the plan that it joined (a 89), south west of it, with a bank on the same side of the ditch (Fig 26). Its history and form at this point have particular importance: it is locally protuberant in plan (perhaps the equivalent of a 'bow' elsewhere; for further discussion of salients in ditch lines, banks over and following ditches and local enlargement, *see* page 10); it appears to be built on a Middle Bronze Age line; there was a probable original entrance where the ditch was interrupted by a narrow causeway; it is ultimately developed in part (perhaps unfinished ?) to hill-fort proportions with a ditch 13 feet (4 metres) deep; a *ballista* bolt found on the tail of the bank (Vatcher 1965) could be connected with events leading to the establishment of the probable Roman fort (a 85).

The excavators' sections, here shown much simplified on a bare version of their plan, together with the plan made by the Royal Commission when the earthwork was in the condition shown in Plate 15 (Fig 27), strongly suggest that the palisade trench could have been clearly visible, at least as a shallow ditch line between low banks, when the apparently Iron Age bank was built along and over it.

(This account is partly based on information kindly supplied by Major H L Vatcher and the Trust for Wessex Archaeology, on behalf of the DoE (now English Heritage).)

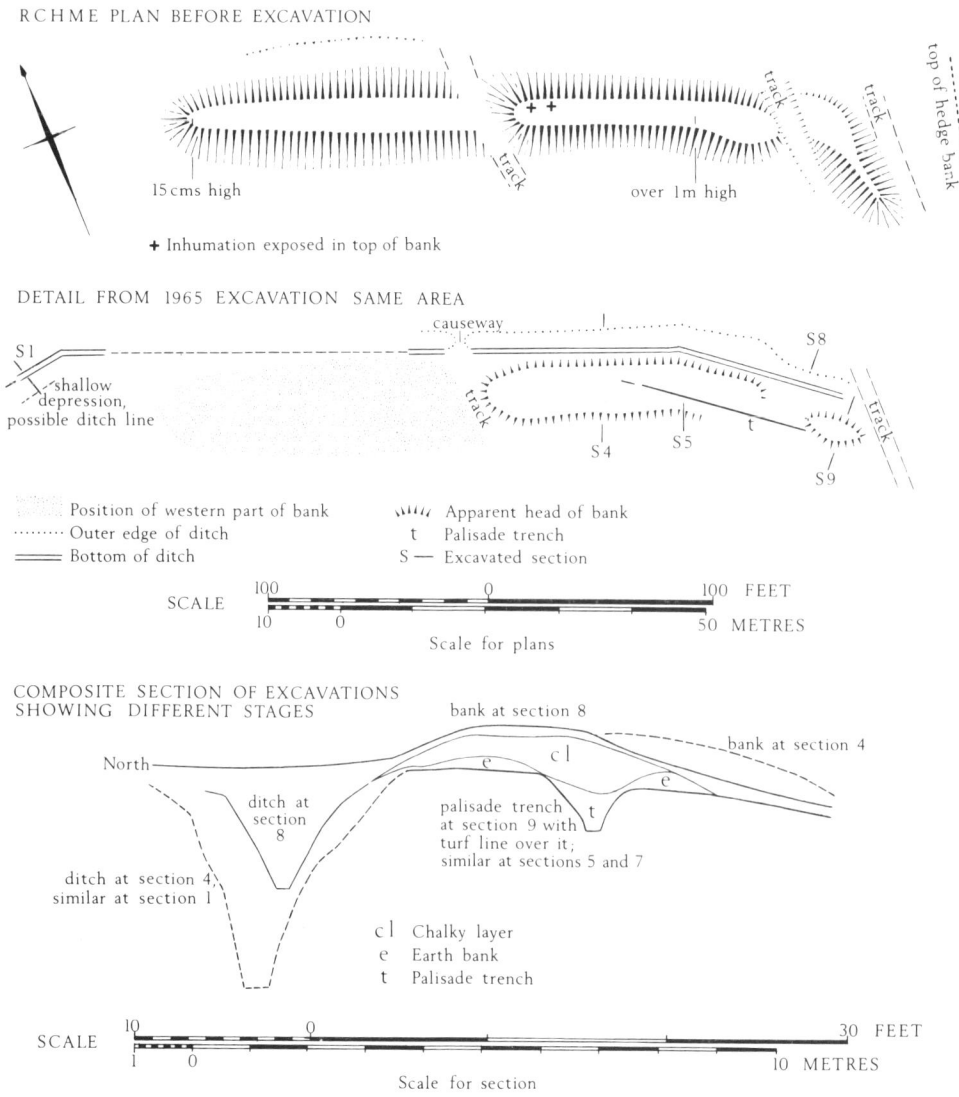

FIG 27 Plans and sections of Shapwick (35) (1:1,000; 1:125)

Area Plan 2

The Gussage parishes, Dorset, and adjacent areas west

This plan covers Gussage Hill (or Cow Down) and Thickthorn Down and parts of the parishes of Gussage St Michael, Gussage All Saints, Sixpenny Handley, Chettle, Farnham, Long Crichel, Tarrant Hinton and Tarrant Launceston. It is a compact area in which, uniquely for Dorset, multiple linears are found. The plan and account that follows include revisions of, and additions to, material published in RCHM 1975 (opp p 24) and in Bowen 1979 (Fig III).

There can be little doubt that the similarities of structure in the linears reflect a common control or, at least, tradition, as may be demonstrated in the closely comparable profiles on Thickthorn Down and Gussage Cow Down (Fig 28, *loose*). The comparative extra breadth of 'inner' banks in those examples is seen also, for instance, at grid reference 992146, north of Gussage Hill.

How far the detail within this pattern of multiple lines now recognisable is a true picture is uncertain. Some runs certainly seem to have been partly of multiple and partly of single form, though to what extent this was the product of addition and change over a period is unknown (cf, Plate 17: Tarrant Hinton (22)). Some arrangements are difficult to categorise, for example, Gussage All Saints (a 68) and (a 69). There are demonstrable small alterations. Just south east of ring ditch Gussage St Michael (a 44), for instance, air photographs show a narrow ditch continuing straight where a larger ditch diverges to make a 'bulge' or 'bow' (Plate 18). Some linears, eg, Long Crichel (a 35), end at enclosures. Others are flanked by enclosures, eg, Farnham (a 15). Degradation of earlier features was taking place in Roman times, if not before, as the imposition of 'Celtic' fields on and over the Cursus sufficiently demonstrates, but much destruction is more recent.

Gussage Cow Down is one of the very rare major sites planned and described at different times over the last 170 years. Part of Colt Hoare's plan, made before 1817, is reproduced in this volume as Plate 1 (page 3). It shows certain elements now destroyed but also, importantly, fails to show considerable features recently brought to view by air photography. The

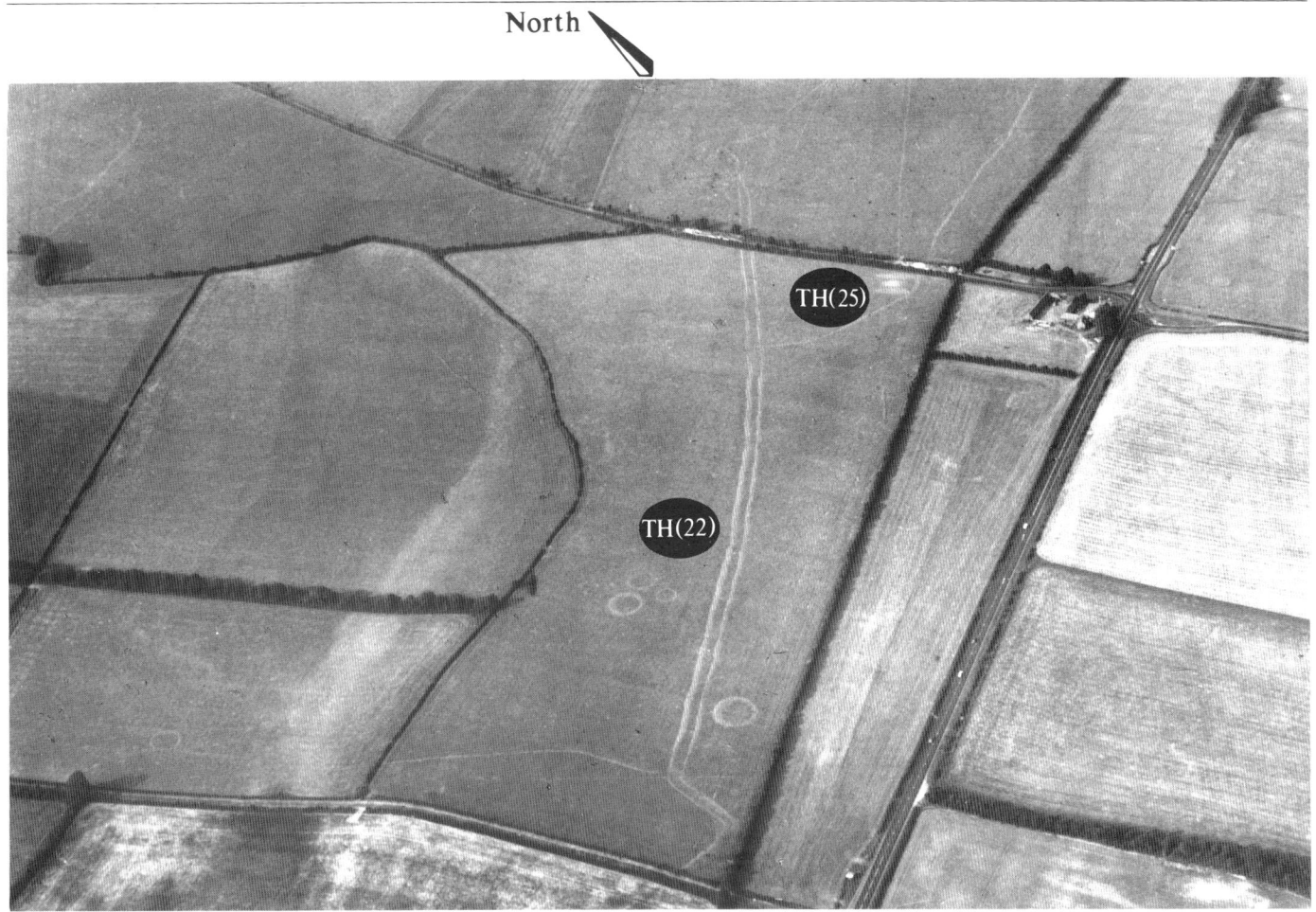

North

PLATE 17   Linear Tarrant Hinton (**22**): an oblique air photograph looking north east. Ditches show as parch marks. Bank arrangements are uncertain but there is possibly one on the north side of each ditch. A single linear ditch butts (22) after skirting long barrow Tarrant Hinton (25) (**TH (25)**) (*see* Area Plan 2). (NMR OAP ST 9613/2)

apparent accuracy of the plan, where verifiable, makes it good evidence and indicates, for instance, that 'banjo' enclosure (7) a, unrecorded by Hoare, though the adjacent (7) b was percipiently described, had almost certainly been flattened, to allow other constructions in Roman times. The remains of these, seen by Charles Warne fifty years later, were too 'irregular and eccentric' to be described in detail, though enclosure (b) was still well preserved (Warne 1872, 25). Allowing for the possibility that not all mounds shown are barrows, it is interesting to see that Iron Age barrow Sixpenny Handley (30) has another mound very close to the west of it, on the opposite side of a gap in the bowed multiple linear. Barrow Gussage St Michael (27), just to the west of these, is also shown paired. There is so far no confirmation of the further pair drawn by Hoare at grid reference 988142. When he returned to the area in 1817, Hoare found that the downland was being broken up, and his description shows that he did not recognise the earlier, ancient, destruction (Colt Hoare 1821, Roman Aera, 33):

> ... on revisiting this spot in the autumn of 1817, did I notice the encroachments of the plough on this memorable, and till lately, well preserved monument of early antiquity. A new farm has been created in the valley, and the lines of the Cursus cut across and levelled; thus interrupting a course which, within the few last years, was perfectly distinguishable from beginning to end.

As further noted below, this refers to Gussage Hill and the area to the east only.

It is known that the area of (7) a and b was part of that put under the plough because, in 1913, Heywood Sumner specifically notes on his plan that it had 'reverted from cultivation' (1913, Plate XLIV). In or about 1924 it was once more under corn, as is seen in an air photograph (Crawford and

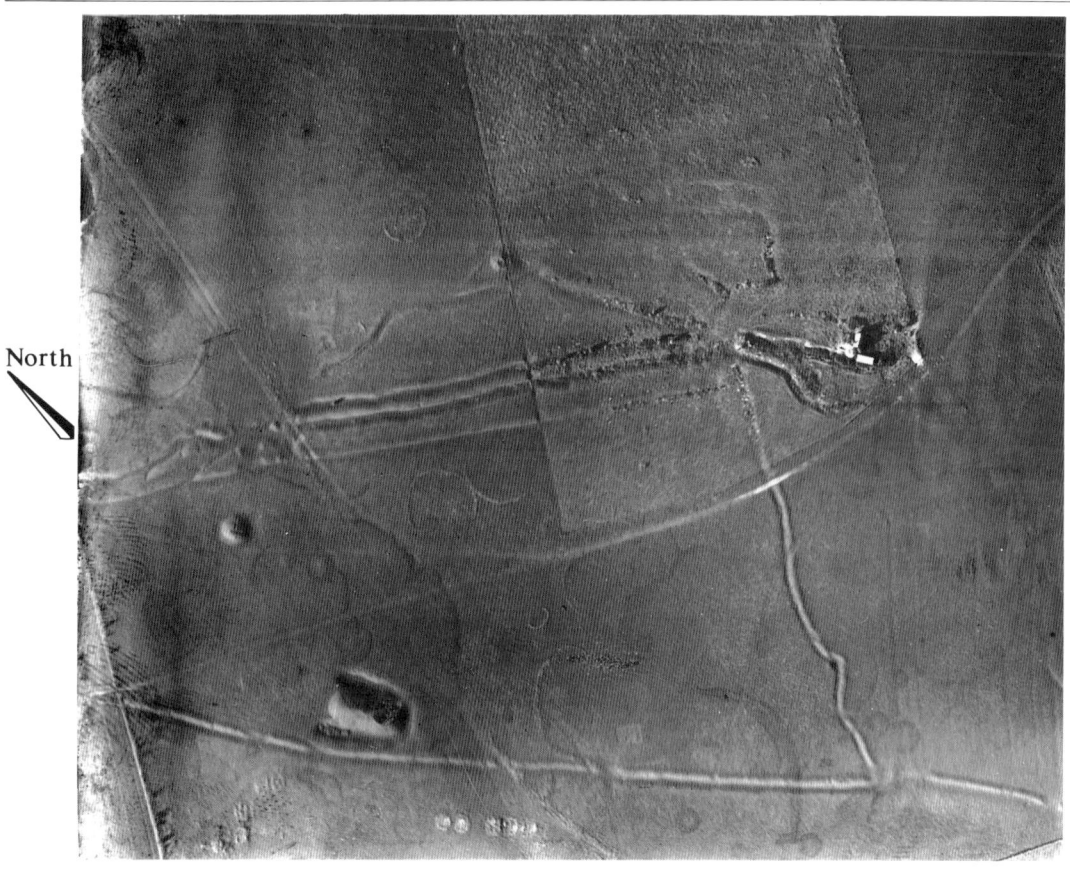

PLATE 18 Gussage Hill, south-east parts: a near-vertical air photograph taken in 1924, with north east to the top. It shows at least two related systems of linears, simple and multiple: to the south west (bottom of photograph) a single linear is interrupted by an apparent original gap (cf, Plate 29) 110 metres south east of a junction with another single linear meeting it from the north east; this latter includes an inverted triangular diversion (cf, Plate 49) with the original line apparently cutting straight across its base. In turn this line is met by, or turns at right angles, to form a straight line extending north west. Almost parallel to this on the east side is a more massive multiple linear notably less regular in its course and apparent construction. Near the point of the junction at the south east is a complex of banks and ditches partly overlaid by farm structures. The pocked, ploughed-over ground south of this is an area of Romano-British and possibly earlier settlement (Crawford collection of air photographs). (NMR VAP ST 9914/1)

Keiller 1928, Plate XVI). Massive destruction is emphasised around grid reference 992147, where now only one bank is clearly seen against five on Hoare's plan. It may be noted that one previous assertion, by Pitt-Rivers, that at 'Gussage Down ... the [Roman] road makes no turn' (1892, 20) is refuted. It actually bends beside Gussage All Saints (a 63).

The largest increments to knowledge of the area since previous publication are the revelation of the Bronze Age enclosure Gussage St Michael (a 49) and the aerial discovery of the two, possibly three, 'banjo' enclosures south of Gussage Hill (grid reference 999132) (Plate 20). Their presumed connection with the multiple linears is based especially on proximity as well as, now, the recently discovered dating provided by Iron Age barrow Sixpenny Handley (30), which strongly suggests that the linears are of the same likely date as the 'banjos'. Recent finds from between 'banjo' (7) a and b include plentiful Durotrigian material as well as Roman finds up to the 4th century (information Mr M T Green). Containment of stock is still the best explanation of the multiple linears and stock-processing of the 'banjos'. The apparent lack of 'Celtic' fields on the plan west of Gussage Hill could conceivably be partly connected with this interpretation but also may be related, again, to the effects of differential land use in later times. For instance, Colt Hoare's plan (Plate 1) shows the Cursus petering out as an earthwork west of the Hill, which shows that his quoted remarks about its 'perfectly distinguishable' course actually related to the area of the then new farm east of the Hill. In 1872 Warne also describes the Cursus as if it ran east only from the Hill.

Respect for round barrows is suggested by the apparent incorporation of a ring ditch (Gussage St Michael (a 36)) within Long Crichel (7) (Plate 19). (This linear is also now seen to have triple, not double, as formerly suggested, ditches alongside the Cursus until it actually elides with the north Cursus ditch and disappears 400 metres from its south-west end.) Similar concern for barrows occurs in the enclosure Gussage St Michael (8) east of Gussage Hill where, although air photographs show the barrows and the enclosure bank peripherally intersecting, it must be supposed that the enclosure is much the later and was built to take in, or at least avoid destruction of, the barrows (34) and (35).

The difference between the profuse and highly complex interrelated ritual, sepulchral and 'secular' monuments on Gussage Hill and the relatively isolated and uncomplicated Gussage All Saints (20) (grid reference 998101) (the only extensively excavated site shown on Area Plan 2, where there is no 'hidden' extra complexity) is more remarkable than ever. In its crowded and long history with religious and secular interrelation, the Gussage Hill area matches Oakley Down (see Area Plan 3), where, however, there is positively no comparable arrangement of linears, the double parallel ditches there all being tracks.

Variety in the form and lie of boundaries is widely demonstrated on Area Plan 2. Parish boundaries, for instance, may encapsulate ancient linears otherwise unrecognised. The apparent integration of the multiple dyke Long Crichel (7) with the Cursus at its south-west end emphasises the existence of a formidable land division cutting across the grain of the country, including small river valleys—and across a road of uncertain antiquity followed by the parish boundaries. The divergence of line in Long Crichel (7) on Thickthorn Down (Plate 19), although anticipated by a curve shortly south west of the Cursus, coincides with this north—south route. Outside the area under study, a small test excavation recently showed that the present A303 road goes through a gap in the developed 'Grim's Ditch' on Thruxton Hill north of Quarley (SU 247440). Such later use and disturbance, together with possible recutting or refurbishing of lines across a gap, generally make it impossible without excavation (and perhaps with) to be sure of the nature of an often complicated sequence. That rivers might contrariwise function as boundaries can be argued from a consideration of the Gussage brook in relation to Gussage All Saints (20) and (a 64), given the following premises. At some time in the Iron Age, probably early, there were similar establishments, representing similar seats of independent power.

PLATE 19 The south-west end of the Dorset Cursus: an oblique air photograph looking west. Ditches show as parch marks. Multiple parallel lines to the north include the Cursus ditch, indistinguishable in terms of width from the triple ditches of linear Long Crichel (7) beside it. The south, outer bank of this multiple linear was presumably here built partly over the filled Cursus ditch. A ring ditch, Gussage St Michael (a 36), interrupts the linear ditches and is probably, therefore, the vestige of an incorporated barrow (see Area Plan 2). (NMR OAP ST 9612/9; © John R Boyden)

49

PLATE 20 Gussage St Michael 7 (c) and (d): an oblique air photograph showing newly revealed 'banjo' enclosures (cf, Area Plan 2). Note the relatively slight ditches of the 'banjo' enclosures; these ditches are edged so closely by pits as to indicate external banks; the pits leave reserved patterns within (c) and (d). A few pits intersecting the ditches, as well as on the line of any external banks and, otherwise, outside the enclosures, suggest phases when the enclosures were not significant. (NMR OAP ST 9913/11/475)

The only possible attributable territories, since the sites are but half a mile apart, would then lie south west and north east from them, making the stream, with its desirable meadow ground, the likely dividing feature, the other bounds unknown. (The ultimate development of (a 64) into a morphologically different pattern and the excavated story of change in (20) might indicate an end to the old *status quo*.)

Finally, there is a curiosity possibly referable to the selection of a similar solution to a similar need but at widely disparate times; the area defined by recently extant boundaries and labelled 'Thickthorn enclosure' (9612) is remarkably similar, even to the disposition of the ponds, to Rockbourne (54) (*see* Area Plan 6).

Area Plan 3

Oakley Down, Dorset

The area from Ackling Dyke north to Chase Barn in Wiltshire has been replanned by the Royal Commission since the publication of RCHM 1975, by photogrammetric means, and has allowed the compilation of Area Plan 3. (The adjacent, northern part in Wiltshire is presented on a local plan (*see* Fig 49) to show the context of Martin (69) in the area of Great Ditch Banks.)

The tight concentration of settlement, fields and barrows crowding in on each other, partly intruded upon and confused by ridge-and-furrow ploughing, is remarkable for its intensity, its range of date, from Neolithic to post-Roman, and the nature of its components and their relationships. There is much new information, especially from air photography, but also new doubts about sequence.

Settlement enclosure Wimborne St Giles (36) is now seen to be of rare form and of noteworthy local importance. Its slight-ditched one-hectare (2½ acres) annexe to the north is devoid of signs of occupation in contrast to the tightly packed main, substantially ditched, enclosure (Plate 21 and oblique air photographs NMR SU 0217/2/100 and SU 0117/27/89 (false-colour infra-red)). Roads, formerly thought, on the north, to be 'boundary ditches', link it to at least three other settlements, Wimborne St Giles (a 142), Sixpenny Handley (21), Pentridge (a 40) and, possibly via a track at grid reference 020194 (Fig 1), Pentridge (15) (all of quite different form), as well as to the Roman road south of it. The roads are marked partly by side ditches (giving a frequent total width of around 11 metres) and by broad bands on the line of the tracks which, on the analogy of recent excavation near Winchester (Fasham 1979, 51), indicate hollowing by traffic. (For the area approaching Pentridge (a 40) from the south, cf, oblique air photographs NMR SU 0119/12/288 and SU 0119/7/292 for tracks, fields and ditches on an axis athwart the present field pattern.) These 'bands' enter the annexe on the north side of (36). The road continuing through the settlement is free of any sign of hollowing, whether due to control of traffic flow or, perhaps, a metalled surface. The double-lynchet track to the south is,

again, partly hollowed (oblique air photograph NMR SU 0217/3/98). The annexe mentioned above may be comparable, in some sense, with areas defined by 'antennae' outside the much smaller Gussage All Saints (20) and Gussage All Saints (a 63) (*see* Area Plan 2), but the slightness of its defining ditch, or palisade trench, is in marked contrast to the impressive size of the Gussage 'antennae'.

It is not known for how long the occupation of (36) continued. Pits are widespread, some known from excavation to be Iron Age. Recent surface finds by Mr P Kitching include Durotrigian coins and pottery; other finds extend over the Roman period. (This information was made available to the Royal Commission by Mr M T Green.)

There are numerous other signs of settlement or 'settlement activity' in the area. The incomplete 'enclosure' (a), intersecting — and probably cut by — the north ditch of (36), is of a pattern and size to invite comparison with the Middle Bronze Age 'Angle Ditch' (Sixpenny Handley (27)) just west of Wor Barrow. Plentiful Romano-British and 'British' pottery found by Pitt-Rivers was said to fill a 'drain', 3 feet (1 metre) wide and 1½ feet (0.5 metres) deep, intersecting the 'Angle

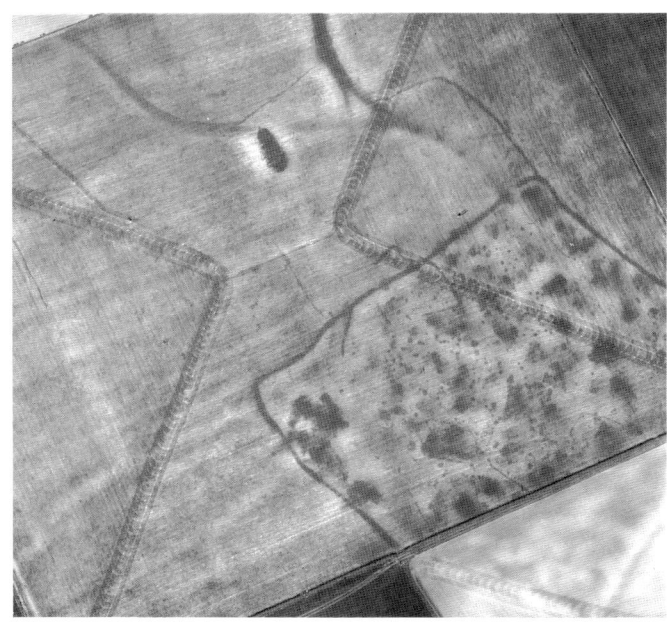

PLATE 21 Wimborne St Giles (36). An oblique air photograph of the greater part of the enclosure, looking north (cf, Area Plan 3). The north west of the enclosure is relatively free of pits (none of which can be seen outside the main enclosure), but a continuous spread of dark patches taking up much of this space also intersects the enclosure ditch. Narrow ditches within the enclosure include one bounding the 'reserved' line of the road south from the entrance at the north east. (For the abrupt end of the dark band of the road at the settlement, cf, Plate 31 of Rockbourne (53).) The annexe ditches can be seen to the north to link the ditches bounding the two approach roads. The elongated black patch with white halation cutting one of the roads within the annexe is a chalk ('marl') pit. The prominent ribbed lines seen as opposed triangles almost meeting below this marl pit are the result of modern cultivation. (NMR OAP SU 0117/24/297)

51

Ditch' (Pitt-Rivers 1898, Plate 248). This appears to have been part of a very irregular enclosure, (d), of some 7.3 hectares (18 acres), which itself presents a challenge to interpretation. The 'drain', because of its assumed nature (cf, page 5), was taken to be earlier than the much deeper 'Angle Ditch'. Its apparent late fill indicates otherwise. This is curious because the 'drain' seems to be part of the perimeter of enclosure (d) which might be thought of as earlier in date since it appears to antedate or be contemporary with 'Celtic' fields which abut its exterior but are absent from its interior.

The pattern of lynchets strongly suggests that enclosures other than arable fields were, or had been, in use in places. The trapezoid shape at (c) and the curving line by ring ditches Wimborne St Giles (a 140) and (a 141) are obvious examples; there is a close relationship between lynchets and barrows or ring ditches. Ring ditch (a 141) is probably on top of the curving line already referred to (oblique air photograph NMR SU 0117/10/111). A line of ring ditches is now seen to extend west as well as east of (114). Ring ditch (123) plainly transects an apparently ordinary field lynchet, though the actual sequence here, as elsewhere, because of the severe degradation by ploughing over a very long period, is uncertain. It may be noted how blocks of 'Celtic' fields are arranged on different axes.

An enigmatic 'parcel' of five close-set lines (?slight banks) at 'p' (grid reference 01671750) seems to be sliced across to the north by the ridge-and-furrow of medieval or later date (cf, oblique air photograph NMR SU 0117/24/298). There is no arrangement in 'furlongs' so the parcel, which might otherwise be taken for a small furlong, is most unlikely to be anything of the sort. Later historic ploughing had been extensive even before Pitt-Rivers' day. There can be little doubt that the scarp he dug, without result, south of his 'Angle Ditch', was a fragment of 'Celtic' field largely levelled by such ploughing.

Area Plan 4

Soldier's Ring and area, Damerham, Hampshire

This plan shows the setting of Damerham (18), a 'native' settlement of mainly Roman date, and of Soldier's Ring, (19), a remarkable and pretentious earthwork, probably late Roman, embracing most of an adjacent valley.

DAMERHAM

(18), *Settlement enclosures* (078178), Romano-British and, probably, prehistoric, almost totally levelled, lay with other features on the ridge of Top Down, east of Blackheath Down, here almost flat but with a moderate slope down 100 metres to the north west. They comprise (Fig 29):

A: 1.25 hectares (3 acres) in area, its north side curved, with signs of occupation overall;

B: 1300 square metres (⅓ acre), its north side also curved. It embodies

C: a ditched circle 23 metres across, containing a shallow circular depression 14 metres across, probably a house site.

Other features include: (16) (Tabulated Inventory, *see* Editorial Notes), an undated mound of uncertain nature lying across the line of ditch (d); three ditches radiating from C; ring ditch (17) within B just north of

C, either a barrow or settlement feature, and 'Celtic' fields (Figs 29 and 46c; Plate 22).

These features had all been substantially flattened before any planning took place by the Ordnance Survey; its large-scale maps show four mounds and a depression now identifiable as (16), C, 'x', another slight hump inside A and a scarp south of the hollow-way approaching A to the north west. The present plan was made on the ground when many ditches and pits showed as parch marks in grass at the end of the drought in 1976. Air photographs furnish evidence of further ditches to be added and suggest the pit total (not all plotted) to be up to three hundred (Plate 22). The south end of A is partly marked by a much-spread scarp. A scarp 0.75 metres high drops from B.

A sequence of development and relationships can be indicated. B is almost certainly later than C since its ditch intersects the ditches radiating from C and its bank, if internal, would have blocked the entrance gap in C. Enclosure A is later than the extension west of ditch (d), which would have blocked its entrance, and, inside, intersects storage pits. Ditch (d) is so precisely parallel to that radiating east from C as to indicate that it eventually formed with it a short stretch of 'broad way' continuous with the approach way (22), itself integrated with 'Celtic' fields.

Enclosure A appears to have been altered on its east side where two ditches exist, each apparently narrower than that on the west; the outer ditch diverges from a smooth curve to the north east and so is arguably an addition. The ditch apparently linking the two ditches north of the north-east entrance suggests the possibility of palisading. The ditches cut a low scarp (?'Celtic' field lynchet) midway along the east side. Redigging or re-use of parts of the ditch to the west and north may be suggested by irregularities along its line. The gap used by the hollow-way to the north west may be original. There are four pits indicated by parch marks outside the outer ditch on the east while air photographs suggest two or three more (oblique air photograph NMR SU 0717/19/279).

Dating depends largely on the surface collection of pottery organised by the South Wessex Archaeological Association, based at Christchurch, Dorset. The material recovered ranged from possibly prehistoric to 4th century AD, and included early 'black burnished' ware, Samian, New Forest and Oxford wares, with, in addition, pieces of quern, a hone-stone and iron slag. The large number of storage pits inside A indicates the probability of Iron Age origins. The very rare drought conditions of 1976 allowed precise identification on the ground which prompted an attempt to investigate by digging one pit, (x) on the Area Plan. It was found to be impossible to complete the work in the very short time available since other features, including flinty pavement, lay over the pit. Sealing layers included material debatably Roman or Iron Age. The pit appeared to be on a mound but this was found to be solid chalk, and its appearance was therefore due to the cutting away for platforms and so on around it.

(Further select air photographs: NMR OAP SU 0717/17/371−9; SU 0717/25, 26, 44; SU 0717/42/165; CUCAP VAP ANE 38−9: cf, Bowen 1975, air photograph on p 109.)

SOLDIER'S RING

(19), *Enclosure*, 'Soldier's Ring' (082175), undated, probably Romano-British, is a polygon of 10½ hectares (26 acres) with unequal sides but exceptional regularity of construction. It survives as a much-disturbed earthwork, its interior ploughed, embracing two re-entrants rising from the valley of the Allen stream in an area known as Allenford. A small enclosure, 'a', of unknown original form or attribution, now gone without trace, lay in the bottom of the north re-entrant (Fig 46k; Plate 23).

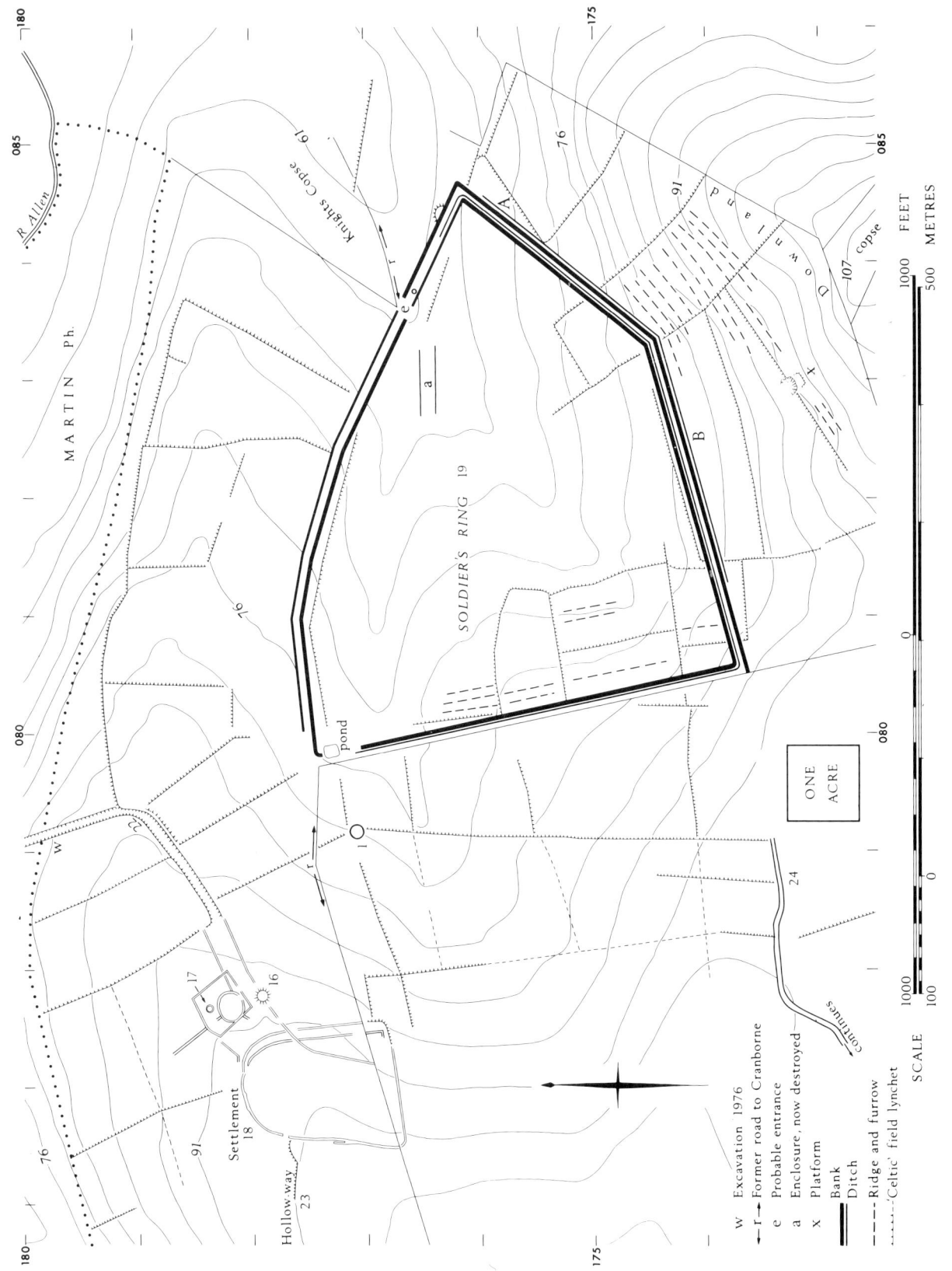

Area Plan 4 Soldier's Ring, Damerham, Hampshire (1:5,000)

w   Excavation 1976
r→ Former road to Cranborne
e   Probable entrance
a   Enclosure, now destroyed
x   Platform
━━━ Bank
─── Ditch
---- Ridge and furrow
····· 'Celtic' field lynchet

ONE ACRE

SCALE

SOLDIER'S RING 19

MARTIN Ph.

Knights Copse

R. Allen

Settlement 18

Hollow-way 23

Downland

107 copse

FEET
METRES

continues

pond

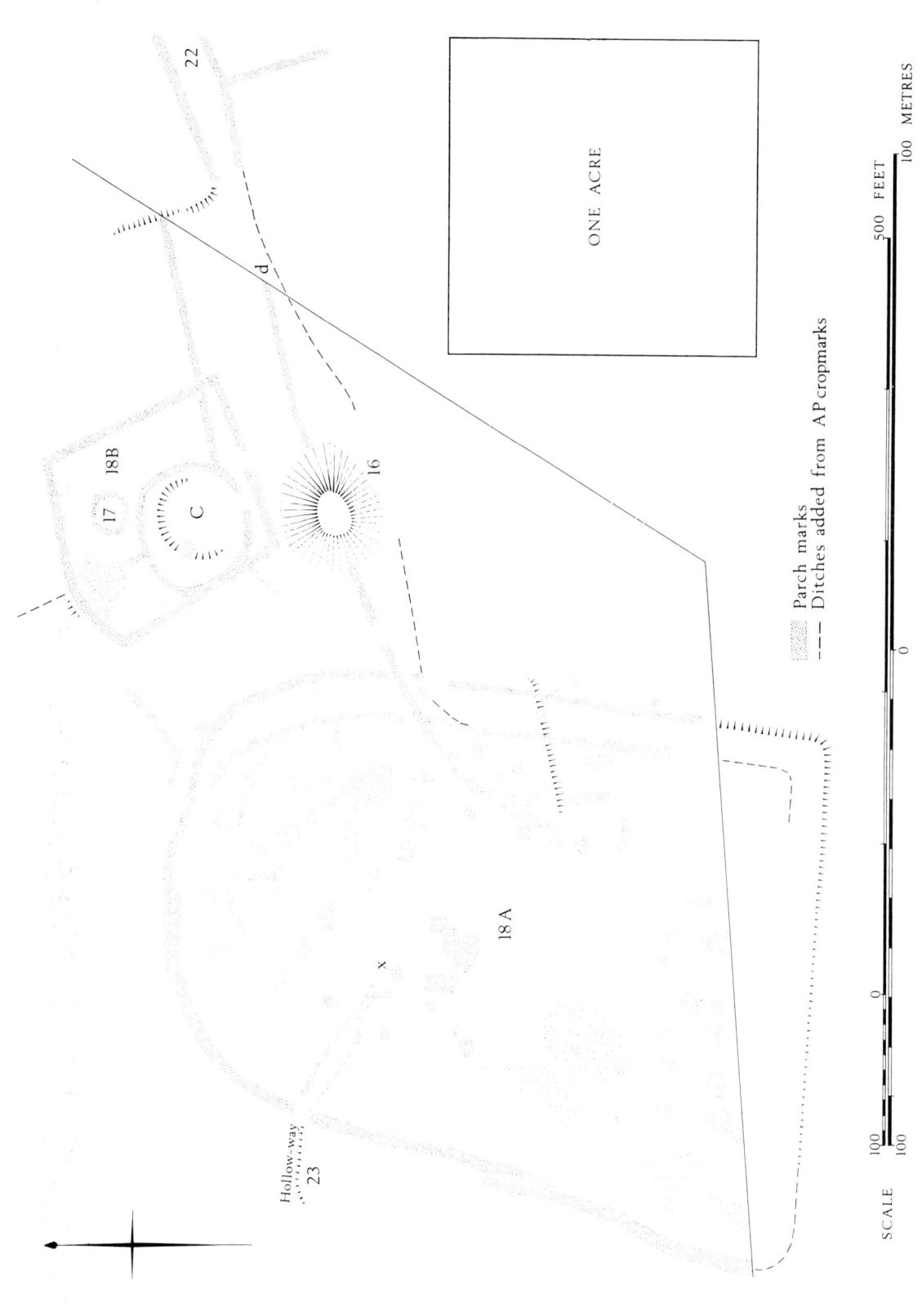

ONE ACRE

22

18B

17

C

16

d

18 A

x

Hollow-way
23

Parch marks
--- Ditches added from AP cropmarks

SCALE

100   0   100
100   0   500 FEET

0   100 METRES

FIG 29   Plan of Damerham (18) (1:1,250)

PLATE 22 Damerham (**18**). An oblique air photograph, under crop, extending left into fallow: linear hollow-way (**22**) is to the bottom right and part of Tidpit Common east of Martin (63) can be seen top right; 'Celtic' fields are widespread (cf, Area Plan 4 and Fig 29). A number of lines not included in the drawn figures probably relate to former hedges, tracks and cultivation patterns. Light-coloured blobs on the fallow are fodder. (NMR OAP SU 0717/42/164)

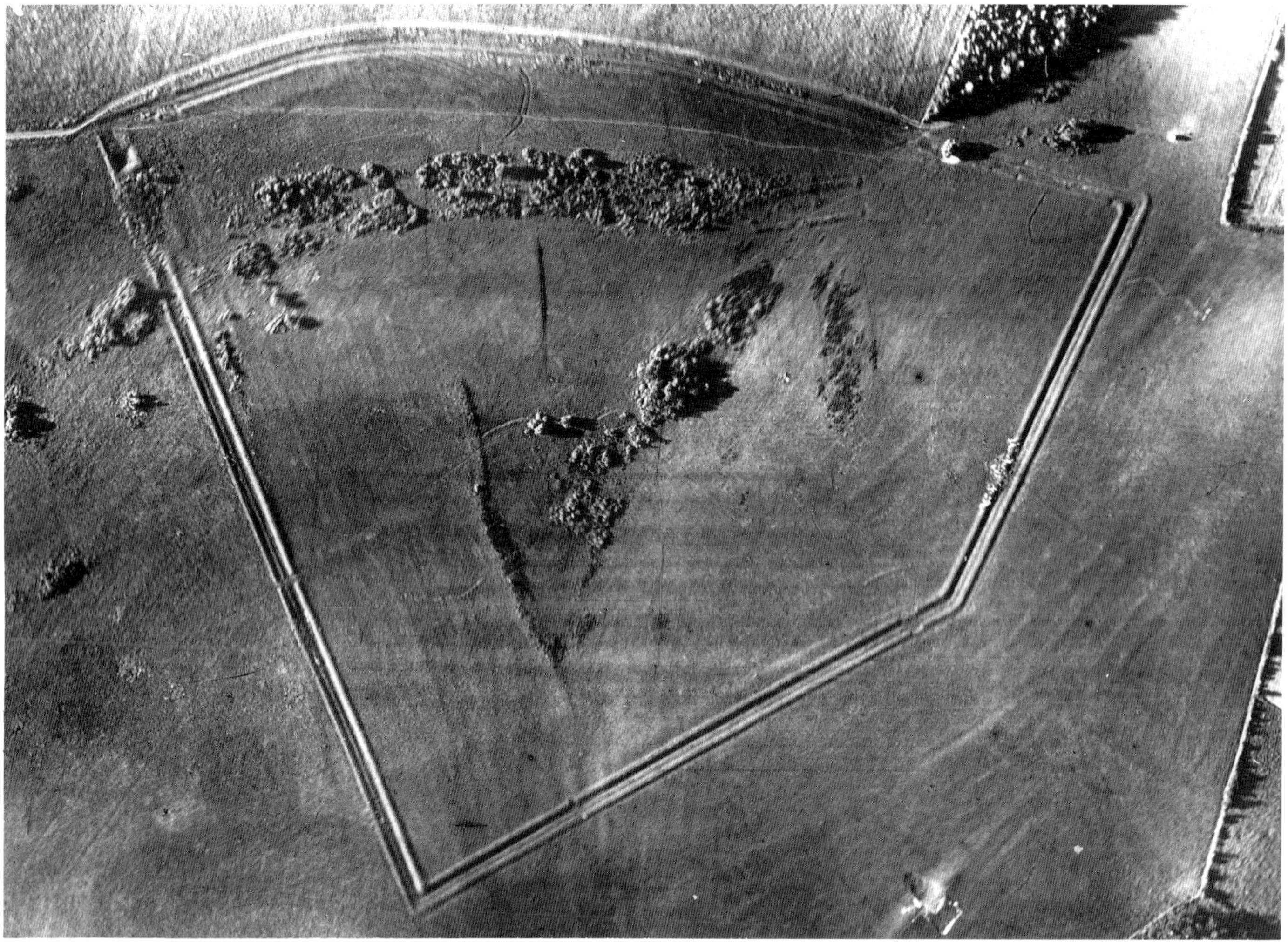

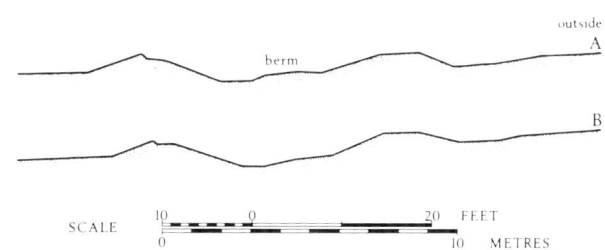

PLATE 23 Damerham (19): 'Soldier's Ring', with north to the top. The best air photograph of this site, taken in 1924, it is partly marred by ineradicable parallel stripes, due to photographic plate blemishes, left to right across top centre. Repeated here from the original negative after the illustration by Crawford and Keiller (1928, Plate XLIX), to show detail more closely. Note, for instance, the intermingling of 'Celtic' and 'medieval' lynchets in relation to the enclosure and lines of destructive ploughing of modern (?First World War) type right (east) of the enclosure. (NMR OAP SU 0817/6)

The first known detailed plan, already called 'Soldier's Ring', by Colt Hoare (Colt Hoare 1810, opp p 231), was approximate only in its proportions but was accurate in its presentation of the form of the main earthworks. It was drawn before the earthwork had suffered a variety of gross disturbance, including the construction of a square pond across the perimeter at the north west, and indicates only one entrance, at 'e', which is at the precise lowest point of the perimeter. Secondary gaps are ignored on Area Plan 4 but can be seen in the 1924 air photograph reproduced as Plate 23. Even at 'e', much of the 11-metre gap is due to disturbance. There are suggestions, too, on some early air photographs (eg, Crawford 1924, Plate IX) that ditches, narrower than those now seen immediately adjacent, formerly continued across the gap. The north side is damaged by a lane, set between the banks, which used to lead towards Cranborne. The form of the earthwork perimeter is a pair of banks separated by a berm and ditch (Fig 30). Grubbing by animals, and intrusion by the plough on the banks, have damaged substantial parts, but, where best preserved, an inner bank, 3.5 metres wide, is 0.8 metres above an external ditch 2.5 metres wide. Beyond

FIG 30 Damerham (19): profiles (1:250)

56

this is a flat space 1.5 metres wide, from which rises a low outer bank some 4 metres across. Beyond this again, now suggested on the east and south only, are faint traces of a second ditch 2.5 metres wide (originally noted by Williams-Freeman), the existence of which was confirmed by geophysical readings taken by the Royal Commission. Where cut, the inner bank displays copious flints. At the north east and south west the angles of the outer banks are higher than the sides, as Sumner noted. A small well with brick head 1.1 metres across is seen between the banks east of 'e'.

The interior had been much damaged by ploughing in different periods even before 1924 when air photographs (such as Plate 23) show some curious features, possibly referable to a nine-hole golf course locally reported to have existed there.

Enclosure 'a' is best seen in the same Plate. Colt Hoare shows a blocked-off west end which, allowing for his grossly wrong scale, might have been some 12 metres by 10 metres, with the entrance facing the long, narrow enclosure and continuous with it for some 40 metres to the east. There is now only a thick mat of flint slurry in the area.

Soldier's Ring lies over 'Celtic' fields. These were crossed over and much altered by ploughing with broad ridges. Ploughing of the interior since 1924 has made it impossible to see on the ground whether the enclosure crosses any of the long narrow plough marks as well as over the 'Celtic' fields. The available early air photographs are ambiguous.

There is no direct dating evidence. The form, and a very rough topographical likeness to the much larger Rockbourne (54), suggests it is late Roman (see page 68).

(Further select air photographs (all vertical): NMR OAP SU 0817, 2−5 (Crawford collection); RAF CPE UK 2150, 4133 (1947).)

(Bibliography for Soldier's Ring: Colt Hoare 1810, 234; Sumner 1913, 39; Williams-Freeman 1915, 409; Crawford 1924, Plate IX; Crawford and Keiller 1928, 252.)

Despite a likely overlap in date between (18) and (19) it can be shown that there was no formal route connecting them.

The linear (22), leading north east from (18), was the main approach to that settlement; the excavation across it at W (Area Plan 4) exposed a 'hollow-way', itself the product of heavy traffic. There may have been a ditched boundary earlier than, at least, (18) A. The hollow-way (23) west of (18) A is of unknown date and nature (cf, Plate 22). Some of it may be relatively recent. In 1924 a track ran immediately outside the north bank of (19), whereas today it runs between the banks on that side. This route continued on the west ('r' on Area Plan 4), is relatively modern, shown on early OS maps, and clearly ignores (18). Contrariwise, it is tempting to see the west side of Knights Copse, which joins the ancient line of the parish boundary to the probable entrance to (19), as the original direct route to a ford or watering place. Potential water supply is otherwise indicated by the modern insertion of a well into the valley bottom line of Soldier's Ring, just east of the entrance, and a 'dew-pond' into its highest part.

The right-angled arrangement of ditches at Y (grid reference 075172 on Fig 1; cf, oblique air photograph NMR SU 0717/17/372) is of unknown date or purpose but, like the 'Angle Ditch' (Sixpenny Handley (27)), is roughly aligned with 'Celtic' fields. The bow in linear (24) east of it, again ditch, track or both, is unexplained. Feature 'x', south of Soldier's Ring, is a small platformed area, partly quarried and undated.

'Celtic' fields are arranged conformably with linear (22), are earlier than (18) A and (19), and there is a change of axis at barrow (1). Subsequent ploughing has totally destroyed many lynchets. Broad ridge-and-furrow can still be seen across 'Celtic' field lynchets on the slope rising to the south east from (19). As already noted, destruction inside the enclosure makes it impossible to determine the relationship with certainty, but the disposition of the ridge-and-furrow parallel to the south side of (19) reinforces the strong probability of a considerably later date, although it is just feasible that some of the long, narrow elements might be 'parcels' of possible Roman date (cf, page 98).

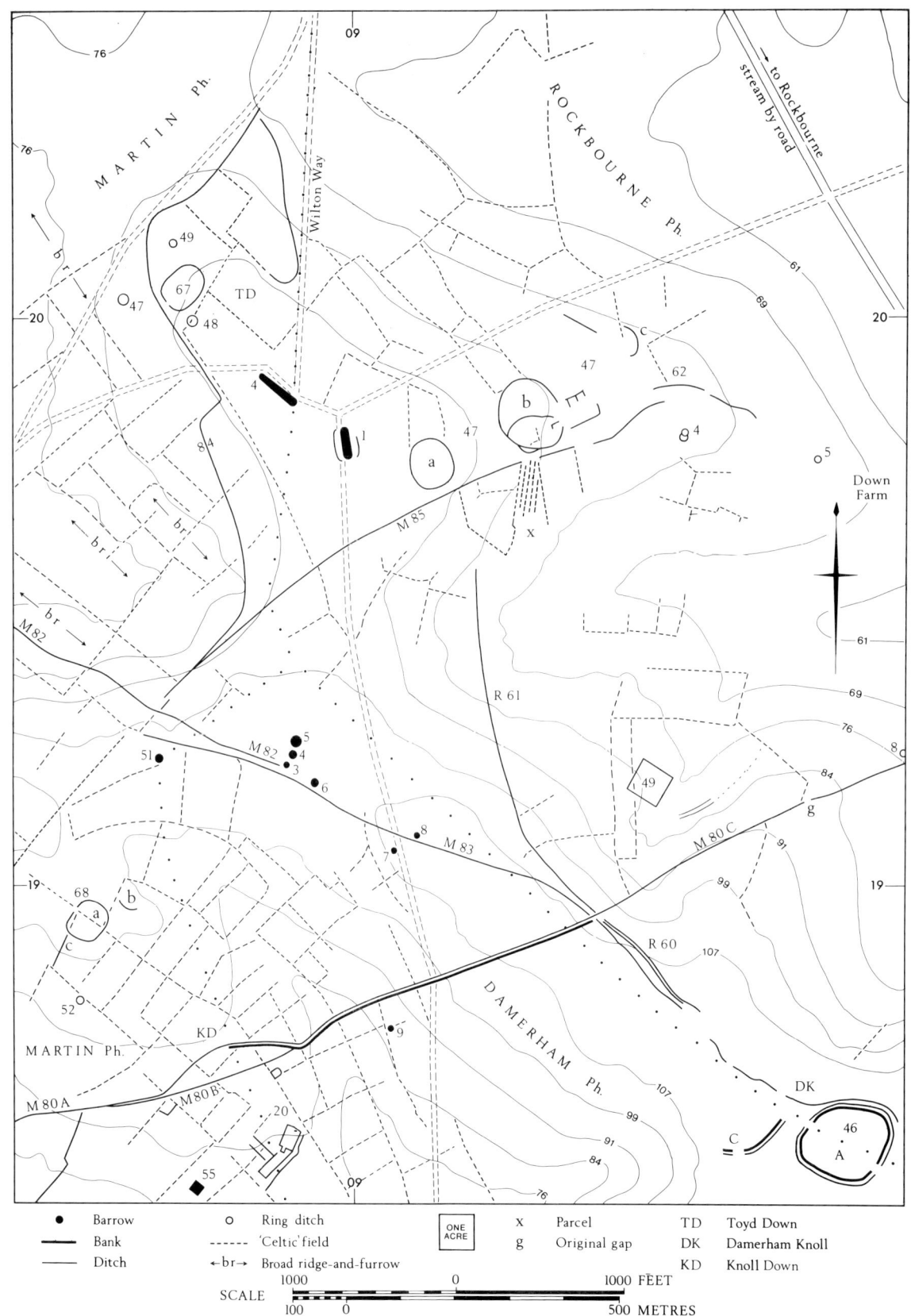

76

09

MARTIN Ph.

ROCKBOURNE Ph.

to Rockbourne
stream by road

61

76

br

20

○49

67   TD

○47

○48

4

61

69

20

47

c

47

62

b   E

4

a   4

○5

Down
Farm

M 85

x

61

R 61

69

76

8○

M 82

br

49

84

g

M 82   ●5
        ●4
51 ●   ●3
        ●6

M 80 C

91

●8   M 83

99

19

19

68

b
a
c

R 60   107

52 ○

KD

9

DAMERHAM Ph.

107

MARTIN Ph.

99

M 80 A

M 80 B

91

20

84

DK

C   46
     A

55

09

76

Area Plan 5 Knoll Down and area, Hampshire (1:10,560)

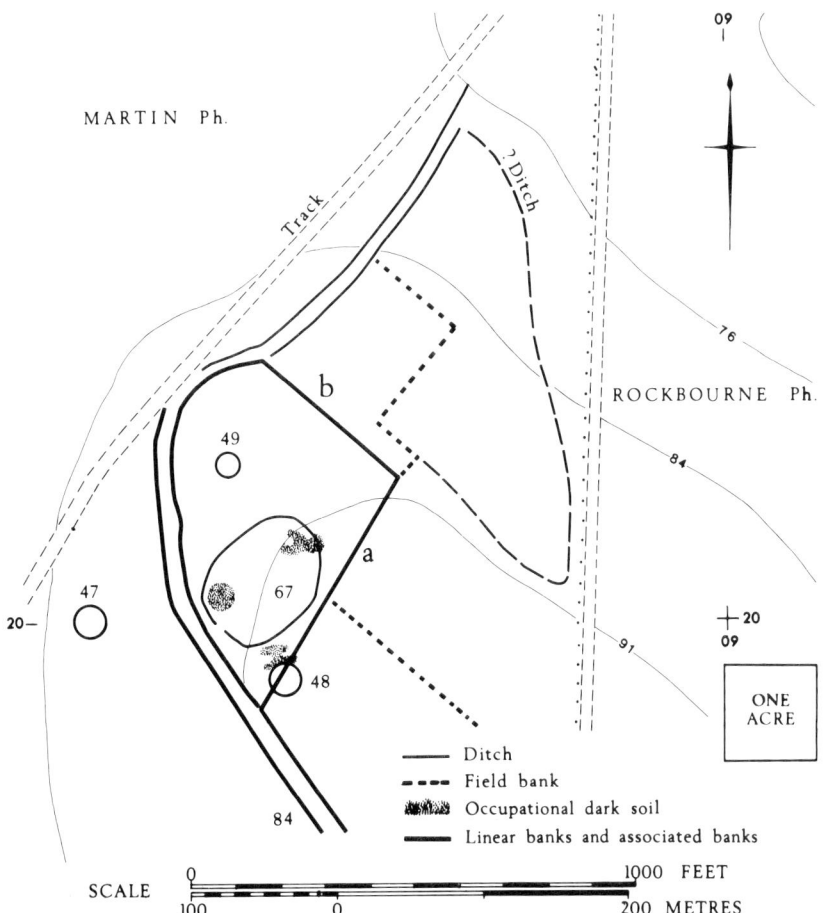

MARTIN Ph.

ROCKBOURNE Ph.

ONE ACRE

———— Ditch
- - - - Field bank
▩▩▩ Occupational dark soil
▬▬▬ Linear banks and associated banks

SCALE

FIG 31 Plan of Martin (67) with linear (84) and ring ditches (47), (48) and (49) (1:5,000)

Area Plan 5

Knoll Down and north, Hampshire

This is an area of 4 square kilometres taking in the remoter parts of three parishes, Martin, Damerham and Rockbourne, where detectable archaeological remains (including those, like 'Celtic' fields, not produced by cutting into the bedrock) are particularly profuse on air photographs taken since the war of 1939–45. Evidence for former strip ploughing is widespread, although, since almost the entire area is now arable, traces of earlier systems and earthworks are being rapidly obliterated. Exceptions are those few earthworks which have been scheduled, notably Knap (Martin (4)) and Grans (Rockbourne (1)) long barrows, one or two round barrows and parts of 'Grim's Ditch' (Martin (80)) and areas with tree cover, of which the only large stretch is that on Damerham Ridge. Apart from these earthworks, there is relatively little to be seen at ground level, where most of the actual surface remains are being so steadily spread or eroded that they will slowly become indistinguishable as relief features.

The area is geologically Upper Chalk, with parts capped by Tertiary gravels on Damerham Ridge. Broad, dry re-entrants penetrate the area from three 'river valleys', two still with streams (the River Allen (to the south and west of the Plan) and

the 'Rockbourne' stream) and the third, at East Martin and tributary to the Allen, occasionally wet. Two 'through' roads crossed the area in medieval and later times and are partly still in use as farm tracks: one from Martin continued eastwards to Downton and at Knap and Grans barrows intersects with the Wilton Way to Damerham, via Allenford, with a fork, leading along Damerham Ridge in the direction of Rockbourne. Both those important roads cross ancient fields and linear boundaries.

The pair of long barrows, Knap (Martin (4) on Area Plan 5) being the longest in Hampshire, betokens a considerable Neolithic presence (cf, page 79). Bronze Age settlements remain so far undiscovered. (Iron Age settlement might be equally unnoticed without the obtrusive enclosures.) Barrow Rockbourne (4) is a 'ring-and-tongue' barrow of a type so far found only east of Bokerley. Ring ditch Martin (48) intersects a lynchet or bank by settlement Martin (67), described below, itself probably associated with curious loops in linear Martin (84).

MARTIN

(67), *Settlement* (087200), prehistoric, Toyd Down, ploughed out, is seen on air photographs as an oval enclosure of about 0.5 hectares (1¼ acres) with a ditch 1.5 to 3 metres across, probably outside a bank (Figs 31, 46e; Plate 24). It lies at the top of a slope falling gently northwards. Its west end is hard against the east bank of linear Martin (84). There

59

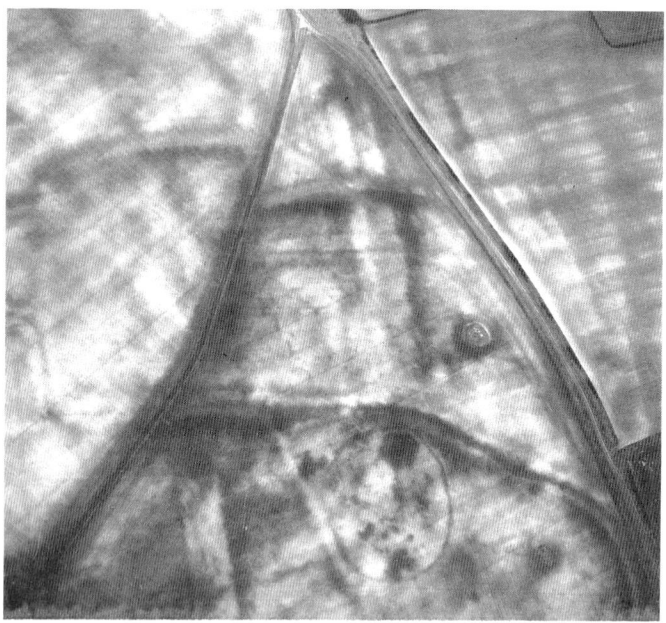

PLATE 24 Martin (67). An oblique air photograph looking south west (*see* Area Plan 5), emphasising the prominent circular patch, just inside the entrance gap to the north west, and strongly suggesting a ditched perimeter to the patch. (NMR OAP SU 0819/11/356)

is an entrance 3 metres wide to the enclosure just south of this conjunction. Another ploughed-down bank, (b), further to the north, extended south east from the linear to meet (a) (Fig 31).

The interior of the oval enclosure contains black occupational marks and, probably, pits. Immediately north east of the entrance there is a particularly regular, almost round, black patch up to 18 metres (60 feet) across, conceivably a house site, set narrowly apart from the enclosure ditch, suggesting an inner bank to the enclosure. The ditch is least distinct to the south. Black smears occur outside it here and also intersect its line to the north east, suggesting occupational activity independent of the enclosure.

(Further air photographs: NMR OAP SU 0819/11/353−5, 356 (plate 24), 357−8; CUCAP OAP ANE 46−8 and AQZ 15, 17.)

The ovoid enclosures Rockbourne (47) a (0.5 hectares (1¼ acres)) and b (1 hectare (2½ acres)), described below, mark a settlement apparently related to 'Celtic' fields and to linear Martin (85) (probably incorporating a track) which, in turn, flanks a 'parcel' of closely set parallel lines, (x), representing some sort of special land use adjacent to the settlement (cf, page 98). Rockbourne (47) c, an 'open' arcuate ditch, is matched by a similar feature at Martin (68), 1350 metres south west of it.

ROCKBOURNE

(47), *Enclosures and settlement* (093198), north west of Down Farm on a ridge sloping gently east towards the Rockbourne valley, its chalk blotched by scattered clayey patches.

It was possible to see and partly survey on the ground most of the circuit of (b). The ditch fill, up to 3 metres across, reached the precise

shoulder of the ridge to the north and extended a little below it to the south. It could not be detected visually on a massive natural mound of clayey pebbly material to the south east but, from gradiometer readings, certainly rose over it a little inward of the crest. This would have allowed a view to the south east otherwise blocked by the mound. It is the only section where a gap in the ditch might have existed. Enclosure (a) certainly displays no gap at all. There is no positive sign of a bank to either (a) or (b). Air photographs show a 'blister' consisting of a slighter ditch diverging outwards from the south-west section of (b), indicative of recutting.

Pits and smear marks in (a) and (b) are unevenly distributed, but a notably round patch near the centre of (a) suggests a particular feature, eg, a house or pond (Plate 25; cf, page 87), and a curving east−west ditch bisects (b). There are slight rectangular ditched arrangements immediately east of (b). A few pits occur also outside the enclosure (Fig 46e). In 1976 unabraded sherds of Middle Iron Age type, undecorated, were seen brought to the surface near the centre of (b). Patches of intense burning were due at least partly to relatively recent scrub clearance.

There are very faint suggestions that (a) and (b) were built over 'Celtic' fields of an earlier system.

(Further air photographs: CUCAP VAP RC8 X 104−7; NMR OAP SU 0819/12/151; SU 0819/24; SU 0919/38/139; SU 0919/43 and 0919/44 (Plate 25).)

'Celtic' fields are arranged in roughly axial blocks, one of them apparently determined by the lie of Knap Barrow (Martin (4)). Plate 26 shows two other blocks where a triangular gap has been spanned by presumably later lynchets. Enclosure Martin (68), described below, intersects, and probably overlies, 'Celtic' fields and part of the long, lynchetted boundary line also crossed by Martin (80) (Plate 27).

MARTIN

(68), *Settlement* (085189), prehistoric, just south of the ridge top east from Windmill Hill, seen in arable on air photographs.

There is a thin scatter of pits, suggesting Iron Age occupation, together with dark smears (complicated by natural patches of clay-with-flints) concentrated in the northern half of enclosure (a), which is of about 0.5 hectares (just over 1 acre). The apparently wider ditch round the south-west half reinforces the suggestion of a functional distinction. One certain entrance 3 metres wide opens to the north west. A straight ditch (c) coincides with the line of a 'Celtic' field lynchet south from (a) (Fig 46d). Some air photographs show 'Celtic' fields on a slightly different line just east of Martin (68) enclosure (a), but these would still intersect the curving ditch (b) (cf, page 97).

(Further air photographs: Plate 27 (NMR OAP SU 0918/8/120) ((a), with pits, and (b)); NMR OAP SU 0818/1 (suggests ridge-and-furrow formerly contributing to destruction to the south west); CUCAP VAP RC8 X 104−5 ((a) just visible with 'Celtic' fields).)

There is a ditched 'pen' integrated with fields at grid reference 087186. Linear Martin (80) slashes across 'Celtic' fields in the lower half of the area (cf, Plate 40), the bow on Knoll Down and the chord formed by Martin (80) B being equally over 'Celtic' fields (Evans and Vaughan 1985; *see also* page 12 above), as are elements of settlement Damerham (20).

DAMERHAM

(20), *Settlement* (088187), near the crest of a north−south ridge, is shown by ill-defined marks of small enclosures and other ditched

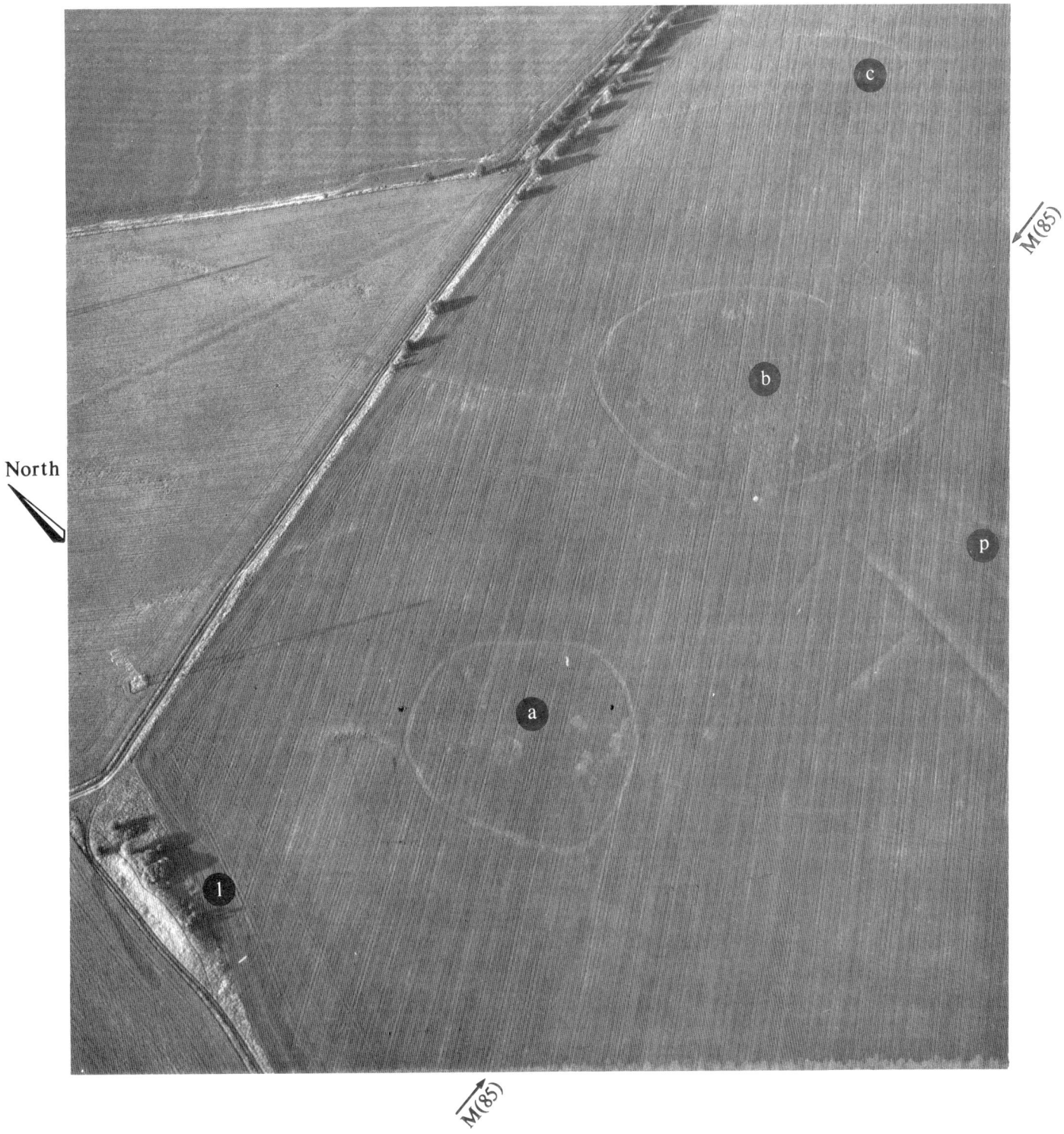

PLATE 25 Rockbourne (47). An oblique air photograph under crop, with north to the top left (cf, Area Plan 5). Both enclosure **a** in the foreground and **b** beyond show evidence of occupation. A prominent round patch 13 metres (40 feet) across in **a** probably marks a discrete feature, such as a house site or pond. There is no observable break in the ditch of **a**. The gap apparent south east of **b** is due to the presence of a substantial, natural sandy mound. Apparent pits can be seen in **b**, mostly in the southern half; there are a few very small patches, ie, pits, in **a**. There are probable pits outside the west, near, side of **b**. There is a parcel of close-packed parallel lines, **p**, of uncertain nature but probably agricultural, within a 'Celtic' field south west of **b**; the west side of the 'parcel' seems to correspond with a ditch and its north side to butt linear Martin (85) opposite apparent evidence for the recut of the ditch of **b**. The curving ditch **c** can just be seen to the top right. Bottom left, capped by trees, is Grans Barrow (Rockbourne (1)), the ditch along its west side prominent as a crop mark (cf, RCHM 1979, 52–3). (NMR OAP SU 0919/44)

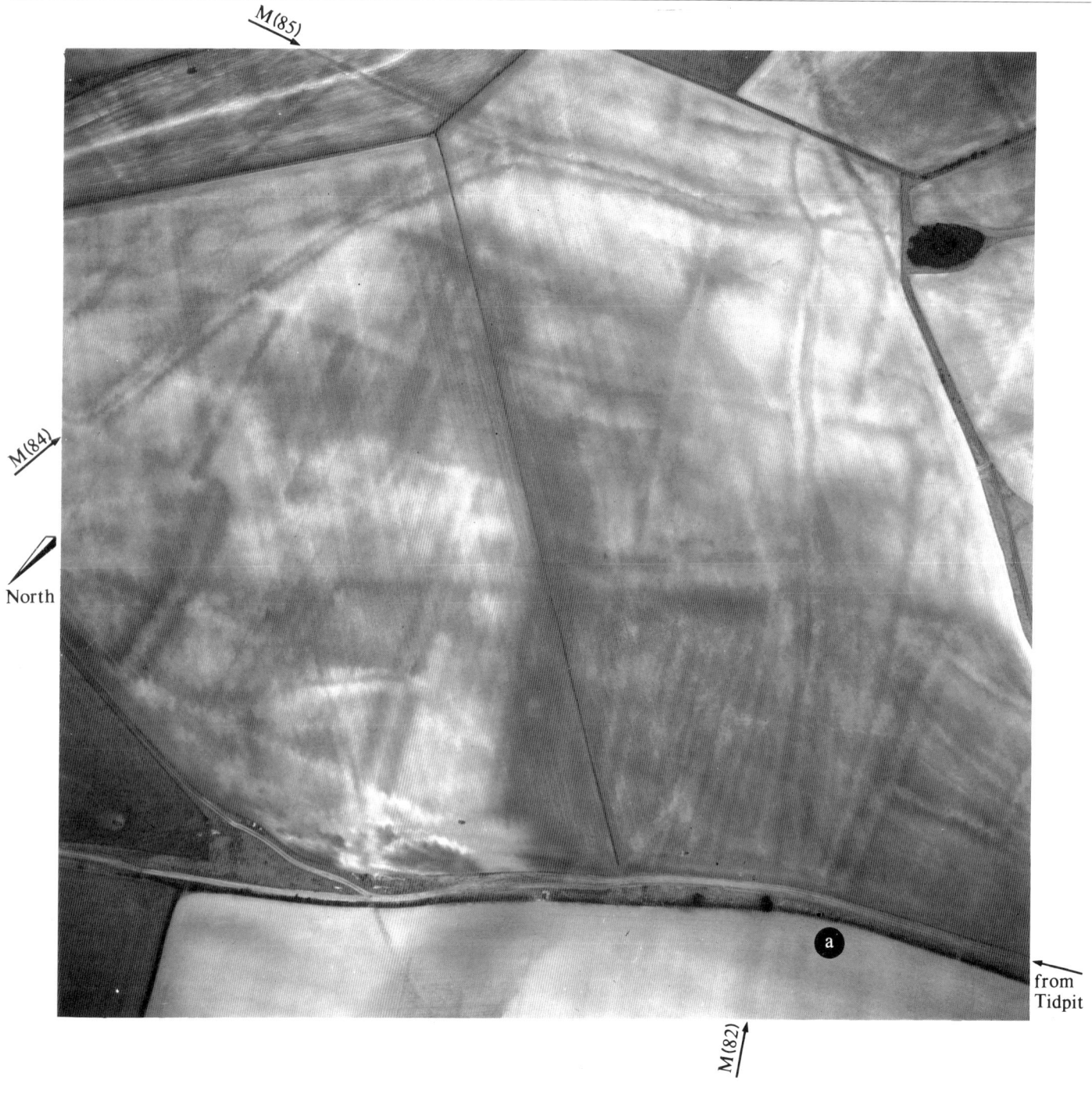

PLATE 26 'Martin', Toyd Down: linears and 'Celtic' fields overlaid by old plough ridges still clearly visible in modern arable. An oblique air photograph looking south east from about 084195 (part on Area Plan 5). **a** points to the narrow gap between two blocks of 'Celtic' fields. Linears (82) and (84) mostly run athwart 'Celtic' fields. Martin (85) fuses with Martin (84) but is itself a probable base for 'Celtic' fields. Martin (82) cuts deeply into 'Celtic' field lynchets and, with little doubt, was eventually used as a road which cut across (85) (cf, Plate 25 of Rockbourne (47)). (NMR OAP SU 0819/23/153)

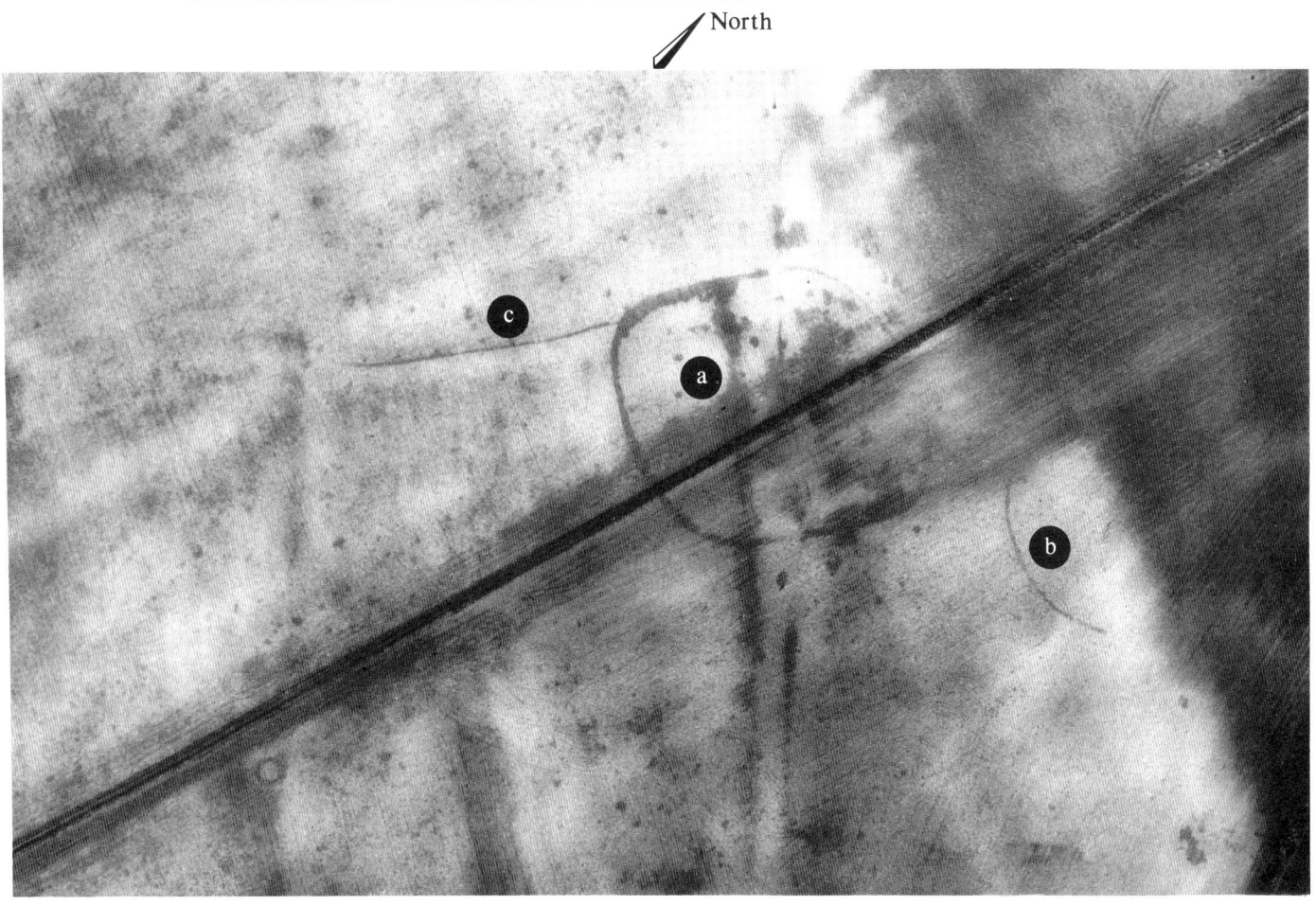

PLATE 27 Martin (68). A steep oblique air photograph with north to the top right: settlement enclosure, with entrance at the top, and associated ditches (**a**, **b** and **c**) (cf, Area Plan 5). (NMR OAP SU 0918/8/120)

arrangements (Plate 28). A small round-ended enclosure lies just downhill of a metre-high lynchet; south of it, and above a lynchet dropping south, is a larger, rectangular enclosure flanked by a track to the south east, and other ditched features to the south west, all athwart the parish boundary. The few finds noted suggest Iron Age origins for the settlement.

(Further air photographs: NMR OAP SU 0818/4 (Plate 40) and 122; SU 0819/10/340−1 and 342 (Plate 28).)

The main bend in Martin (80), as is seen on Fig 3, occurs at the bow and not on Damerham Ridge, east of which the linear Martin (80) C is probably a continuation of the B element underlying the A work. A clear gap through this, 'g' on the plan, is best seen on Plate 29. A quite unresolved point is the nature of linear Rockbourne (60) which might continue Martin (80) A − or two other linears − south east to skirt the probably Iron Age enclosure Rockbourne (46), described below. Its discontinuous line becomes intermingled with the remains of a skein of tracks on what was an important route. The ditched

loop round (46) A might be compared with the well-known example around what was to become a hill-fort on Ladle Hill in north Hampshire (Piggott 1931), but within this volume's area there are also examples of contemporary tracks making such deviations (cf, track skirting Wimborne St Giles (a 142) on Fig 1). The cross-ridge dyke − or incomplete enclosure Rockbourne (46) C − is just as puzzling in that it 'faces' (46) while being very close to it. Obvious questions are raised which may equally apply to Rockbourne (47) c or Martin (68). Linear Martin (82) cannot be traced east of barrow Damerham (3), but its line is continued by Martin (83) which, with little doubt, embodies a track. The enclosure Rockbourne (49) appears to overlie 'Celtic' fields which give the impression of having been much altered before that happened.

ROCKBOURNE

(46), *Enclosure* 'Rockbourne (or Damerham) Camp' on Damerham Knoll (SU 099185), (a) on Fig 32, is probably Iron Age; other, undated, earthworks (b) and (c) lie west of it. Enclosing some 1.3 hectares ($3\frac{1}{5}$ acres), it spans a narrow ridge of chalk, the highest part of which

63

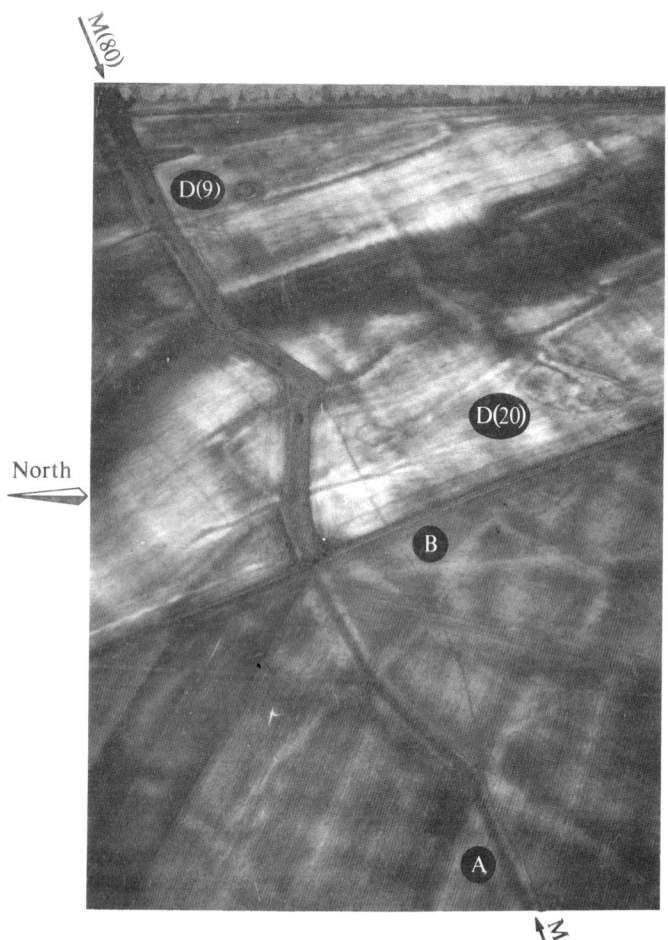

lies 250 metres to the west, capped by gravels and sands of the Reading Beds. A single bank, at most 1 metre above the ditch, with only traces of a counterscarp bank, is grossly disturbed on the north side where the linear Rockbourne (60) curves closely round it (Figs 32 and 46f).

When surveyed for this volume, the interior had been recently cleared of trees, prior to replanting, leaving only a few patches of impenetrable scrub and log piles. Hollowed tracks of a former main medieval route leading to the 'Wilton Way' cross the enclosure and cut the relatively slight perimeter works. Numerous small quarry pits prevent identification of any structural remains inside, but a probable original entrance through the southern part of the east side, just south of the parish boundary now bisecting the enclosure, interrupts the defences where they drop into the head of a narrow re-entrant from the south east.

An unexplained very slight bank, (b), barely 20 metres long with a ditch to the east, lies immediately against a slight constriction in the ditch of (a) on the west side of the enclosure (Fig 32). Some 25 metres further west, a rather more substantial, but now broken and much disturbed, bank (c), seems once to have crossed the ridge. Williams-Freeman (1915) showed a double bank of which there is no trace. The position of its ditch and its convexity towards the south east suggests that it was an entity separate from (a), possibly associated with (b), though the constriction of (a)'s ditch by (b) might otherwise suggest it intruded on, and was therefore later than, (a).

(Bibliography for Rockbourne (46): Sumner 1913, 28–9; Williams-Freeman 1915, 182–4, 400.)

(49), *Enclosure* (09541917), undated, visible on air photographs in arable on the north side of a gulley south east of Knoll Down (Damerham), is almost square, 0.2 hectares (½ acre) in area, with a narrow ditch demarcating the precisely straight sides and sharp angles. No entrance is apparent but the south side becomes vague where it meets the dark hill-wash of the gulley. It lies just outside the bounds of the medieval field system. There are no marks suggestive of settlement (Fig 46a).

(Further air photograph: NMR OAP SU 0919/37/116 (Plate 29).)

Most of the monuments, the majority flattened and only visible clearly on air photographs, occur in the north of the parish of Rockbourne and are illustrated on this Plan (5) and on Area Plan 6 (Rockbourne Down). Remarkably little appears in the area of open fields and historic development south of the east–west droveway skirting Duck's Nest (3) (Area Plan 6). That the imbalance must be quite unreal is indicated by chance finds both major, such as that of the Roman villa (57) in 1942, and lesser, such as that of the Brookheath Roman coin hoard (*see* Rockbourne (59) in the Tabulated Inventory, *see* Editorial Notes). Field walking and surface collections by the Avon Valley Archaeological Society and others are also exposing sites such as Rockbourne (59).

PLATE 28 Knoll Down, Damerham, around grid reference 087187. An oblique air photograph, with north to the left (*see* Area Plan 5). Linear Martin (**80**) here crosses a ridge, the axis of which is followed by the Damerham/Martin parish boundary, roughly bisecting the Plate horizontally. The linear's developed course, **A**, appears as an earthwork on the far side of the parish boundary. Its bank is right (south) of its ditch, which, west of the parish boundary, appears, ploughed, as a broad, dark line. The early, thin, line **B** of the linear is at first closely parallel to this (ie, under the bank of the refurbished **A** as seen in greater detail in Plate 40) and then continues across the chord of the bow, 270 metres long, which the final builders constructed north from the original line. 'Celtic' fields had been ploughed for a long time before the linear was first laid out, crossing them diagonally as if careless of their existence. Poorly defined enclosures of Damerham (**20**), probably Iron Age, lie apparently on the fields.

The mound of barrow Damerham (**9**) was respected by cultivation of the fields; whether it antedated Celtic cultivation is uncertain.

The straight line running from the right of the Plate to meet the junction of linear and parish boundary is the product of relatively modern cultivation. A hollow-way cuts clearly through the linear shortly east of the parish boundary and parallel with it. The difference in soil colour west and east of the parish boundary is a striking indication of different land treatments. The broad dark band of soil near the top of the Plate is valley soil wash. (NMR OAP SU 0819/10/342)

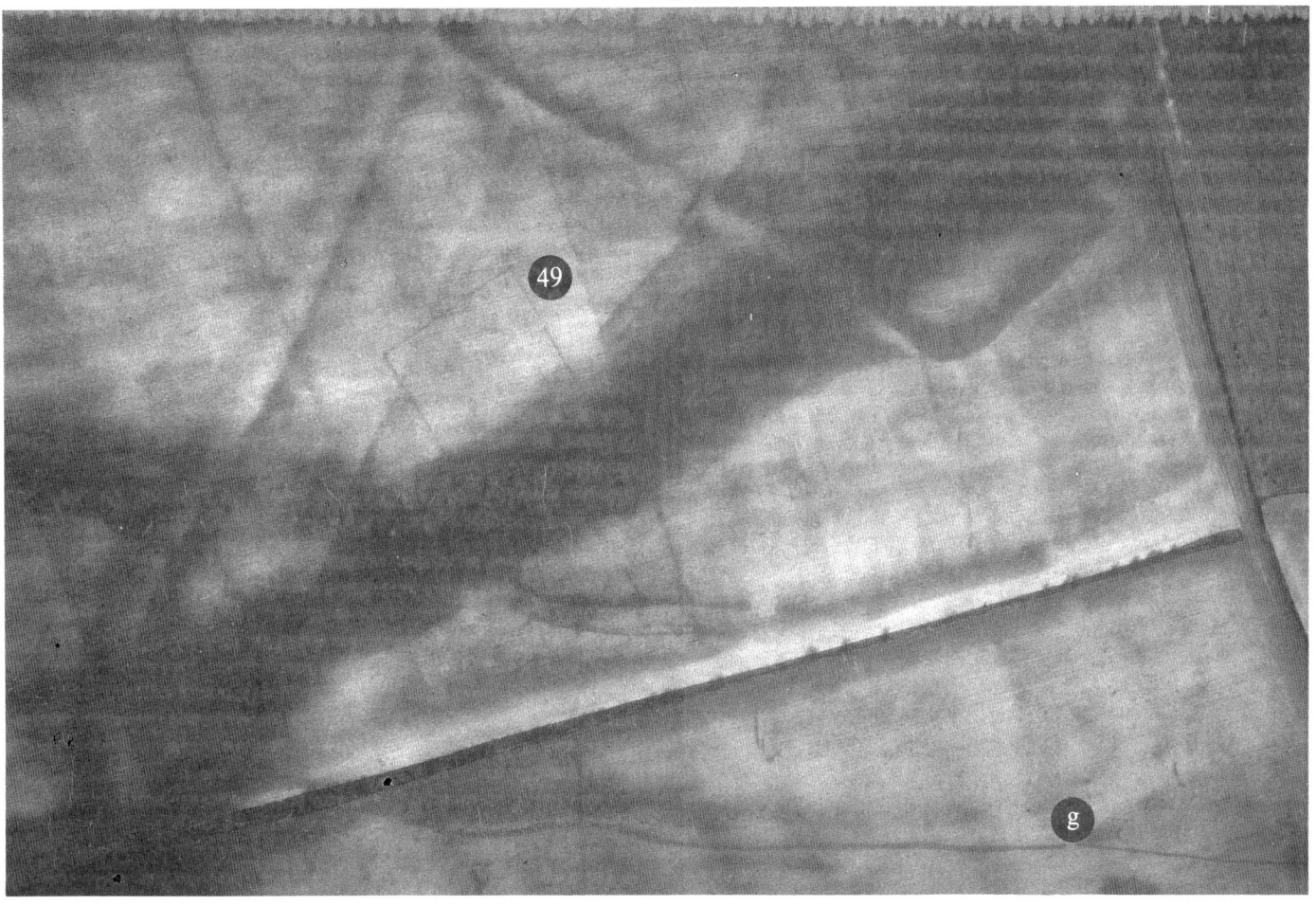

PLATE 29 Rockbourne, east of Damerham Ridge 0919. A near-vertical air photograph of crop, with north to the top. Linear Martin (80) C runs close, parallel to the bottom of the Plate. The square enclosure (49) is immediately west of a broad band of hill wash in a shallow valley bottom, apparently crossed, just south of the enclosure, by a partly ditched track. Roughly parallel south of this track is the linear. A narrow gap in its line, g, of about 4 metres separates ditches of different width, that to the west being almost twice that on the east side. In this area of extremely degraded remains the linear appears to cross 'Celtic' fields whose pattern had been greatly modified before enclosure (49) was built, with its west corner over one long lynchet line. (NMR OAP SU 0919/37/116)

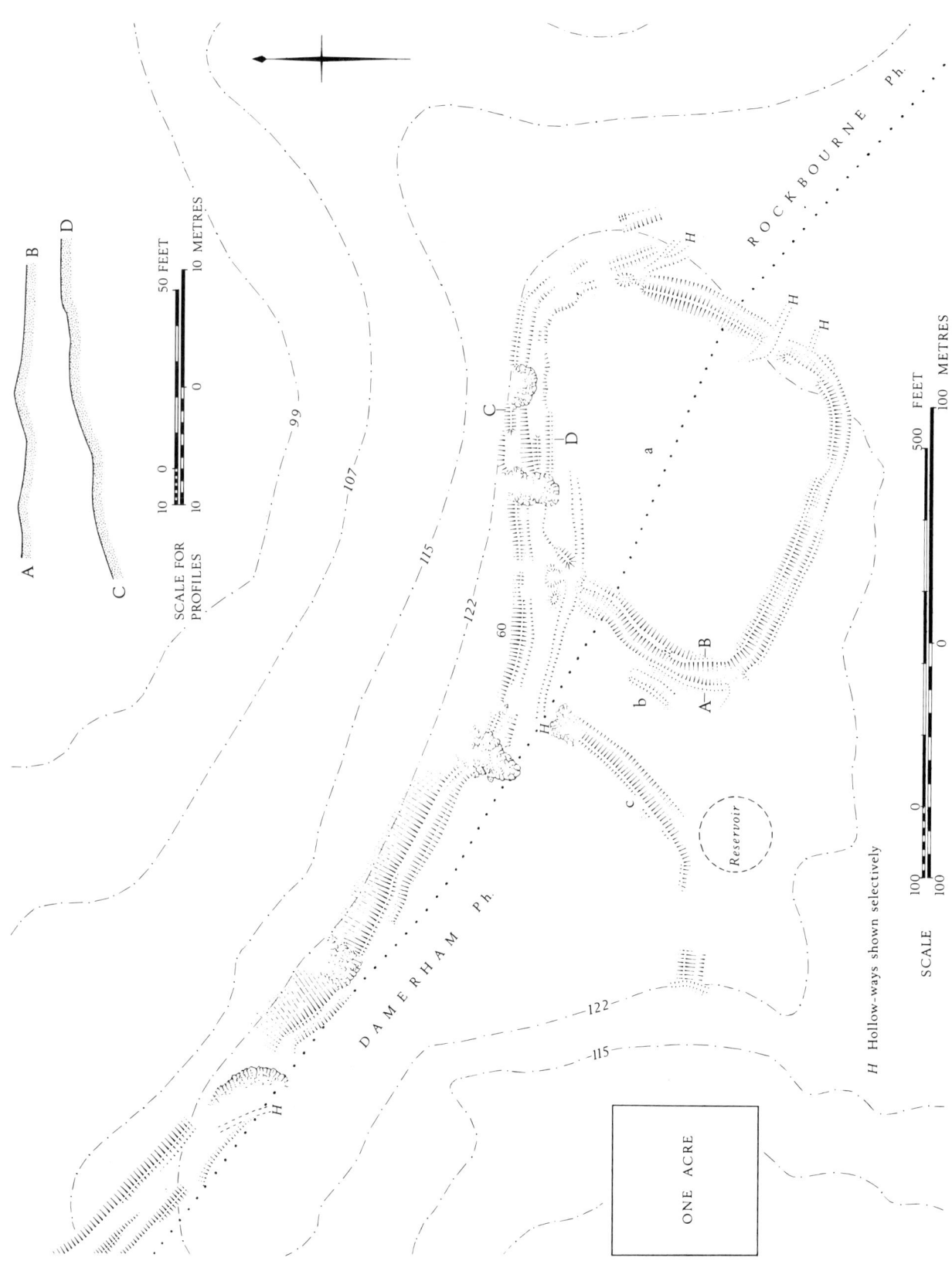

FIG 32 Plan of Rockbourne (46) with linear (60), and profiles A–B and C–D (1:2,500)

Area Plan 6

Rockbourne Down, Hampshire

Area Plan 6 is designed to show the setting, relationships and antecedent archaeology of the largest 'monument' described in this volume, Rockbourne (54). The area consists of a shallow basin at the head of a former feeder of the stream through Rockbourne village, 2.5 km to the south. There is patchy clay-with-flints evident almost everywhere. The remarkable 'Spring Pond', or the headwater springs in its immediate area, is arguably the *fons et origo* of ritual attraction for important barrow burials while of practical use for the much later stock farmers. Curiously, there may be a relatively modern counterpart to this arrangement in Long Crichel, Dorset ('Thickthorn enclosure' on Area Plan 2, *loose*).

Heywood Sumner's delightful account (Sumner 1914), embellished by drawings of notable use as well as beauty, is the starting point for any consideration of the archaeology of Rockbourne Down. After he had planned and carefully noted the form of the earthworks of the great enclosure (54), he carried

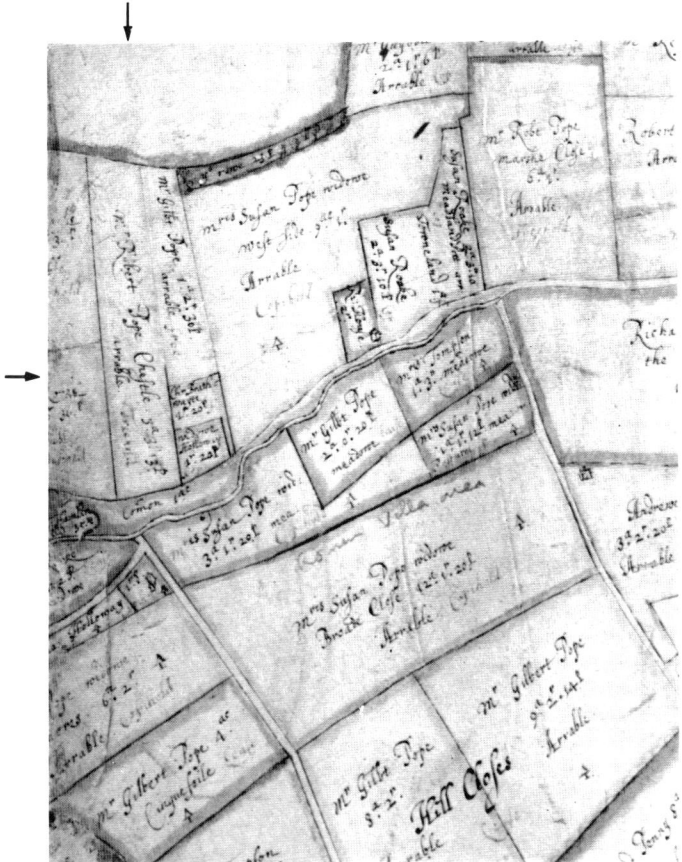

PLATE 30 Rockbourne (57): the stony area of the Roman villa, 'Chestle', otherwise unrecognised, on a 1671 estate map of Lord Shaftesbury's, the modern discovery being first made roughly where arrowed marginally. 'Roman villa area', written in a late hand, centre, is misleading (reproduced by permission of The Earl of Shaftesbury).

out select excavations on the enclosure works and other features which he took to be related. He concluded that the whole was a Romano-British 'Farm Settlement, occupied by poor labourers'. The disclosures of aerial photography in particular, re-interpretation of his 'hypocausts' as corn driers and the discovery of the Roman villa (57) (Plate 30, Fig 25) make it necessary to revise these views.

ROCKBOURNE

(54), *Enclosure* (108215), insecurely dated but probably late Roman (Figs 46a, c (Rockbourne (55)) and k and Fig 33 (profiles); Plates 31 and 32). It takes in a broad re-entrant valley of Upper Chalk, capped in places by clay-with-flints, with the remarkable Spring Pond now just outside its entrance on the valley floor. The enclosure is a pentagon with a rounded north-west side, enclosing some 35 hectares (86 acres). It is defined by a very unusual low bank with a ditch on either side, except at the east angle where the inner ditch, with an associated bank, separates to form the base of a triangle created by the continuation of the outer ditch and bank; at the south, a sharply angled trapezoidal enclosure of 0.6 hectares (1½ acres) is likewise formed by the divergence of the inner ditch, while the outer, single ditch, external to its bank, appears to be the sole perimeter feature. The only known original entrance is to the south south east. A causeway has been formed across the ditch to the north north east, immediately east of the barrow (42). The bank is of varying width; Heywood Sumner, who excavated it at the north west and north east, in 1911 and 1912, showed it to be 8 metres wide between ditches in the first instance and 4.6 metres wide in the second. Recent air photographs taken by the Royal Commission (cf, Plate 32) confirm this variation and indicate a degree of what appears to be recutting of the inner ditch at and just south west of the north angle, in particular. (Sumner should have had three ditches, therefore, in his section A–B, but he illustrated only two in profile.) Also apparent are newly visible features which require a reappraisal of the nature, origins and relationships of the whole monument.

There is another enclosure (55), described below, with indications of settlement, formally Iron Age, outside (54) but only 20 metres east of its north angle. There is also a strong suggestion of elements of a larger rounded enclosure inside, again seen on Plate 32 (e), just south of the north angle. This is crossed by what appears to be a road line, partly ditched and partly hollowed, extending from a point outside the enclosure on the north and meeting other tracks or roads from the west and south, near the centre of Romano-British settlement (53), described below, within and without the main large enclosure. The ditches of enclosure (54) cut across the settlement and 'Nothing was found in the filling of the ditches except potsherds, of the same type as those found in all other parts of this settlement . . . ' (Sumner 1914, 26); thus the finds in bank and ditches could be derived from earlier occupation. It is very possible, however, that limited occupation continued in the settlement area after the construction of the enclosure. Post-holes exposed at ground level cannot be taken as certainly to do with the enclosure bank since Sumner does not demonstrate that they pierce the build of that feature, and his 'stockade' post-holes are surely cut through by the inner ditch. The main enclosure remains thus technically undated. There can be little doubt that it superseded a settlement whose street system, in some sense linking it to other rural settlements, was blocked to at least the east and north west. It is therefore late Roman or later.

(53), *Settlement* (10852185), Romano-British, covered 2 hectares (5 acres). Humps and hollows, already much ploughed, at least in part, by 1911, have been severely ploughed since. The settlement is known

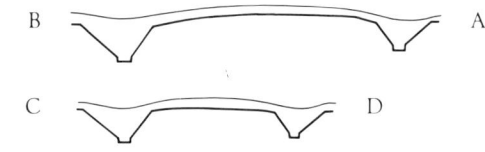

HEYWOOD SUMNER PROFILES

B ———————— A

C ———————— D

The interior is to the left in all profiles

RCHM PROFILES

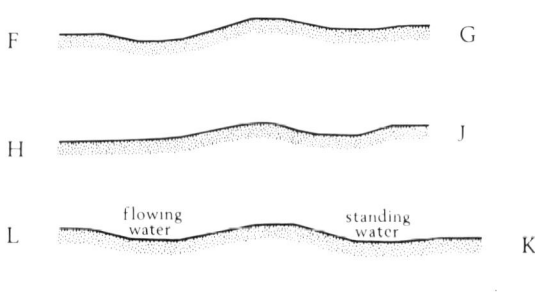

F ———————— G

H ———————— J

flowing water   standing water

L ———————— K

SCALE   10   0   20   FEET
        0   10   METRES

FIG 33 Rockbourne (54): profiles by Heywood Sumner (above) and the RCHME (below) (1:250)

from excavation and survey by Heywood Sumner in 1911 to 1913, and from recent air photographs which show a complex picture requiring modification of Sumner's interpretations (Plates 31, 32: NMR OAP SU 1021/18/403 (Plate 31) and detail in enlarged print NMR OAP SU 0921/8/189 (Plate 32)).

The developed settlement was disposed around a road junction just north of barrow (42). Sumner's excavation showed a narrow causeway of flints partly across the ditches of (54) just north east of this. Barrows were apparently (and most unusually) integrated into the south side of a trapezoidal enclosure, (b), contained in the west angle of the convergent roads. This belonged, on Sumner's evidence of Samian on the ditch floor, to the first half of the Roman occupation. Its north-east ditch only was largely filled with flints. A corn drier, prompting Sumner's term 'hypocaust quarter' for the area, eventually built across the ditch near the north-east angle of the enclosure suggests that its bank was external. 'Hypocausts' II and III ('d' on plan) were also corn driers. Two extended skeletons were found on III.

The settlement embodies a number of ditches, roughly consonant with an axis based on the roads, and a concentrated pattern of smear marks within them. Sumner's excavated finds at (d) were few and persuaded him that the site had been dismantled (Sumner 1914, 24). Small finds overall included bead-rimmed *pottery*, possibly some Iron Age, indeterminate 'coarse British', Samian and New Forest wares; a fragment of combed flue tile; *stone*: Purbeck 'marble' bowl or mortar;

querns, one of greensand; ten 'perfect' Purbeck roof tiles used in the upper 'floor' of corn drier III (inviting comparison with usage in Rockbourne (57) villa); nine *coins*, '3rd brass' from Gallienus (AD 253–68) to Valentinian I (AD 364–75) (others to House of Theodosius found by Mr M T Green); *metal* objects included iron arrow-heads; *Kimmeridge shale* spindle whorls and bracelet. Copious *animal bones* were mostly of ox but with considerable numbers of horse, a few sheep and at least five dogs.

The form of the enclosure of Rockbourne (54) has been compared (page 57) with the Soldier's Ring, also of probable late Roman date. Both, despite differences in detail, are formally more Roman than anything else that could possibly have appeared until, perhaps as a conceit, say, in the 16th century. The key to the Rockbourne date should lie in investigation of the trapezoidal and triangular enclosures, already referred to, which are an integral part of the design of (54). Fieldwalking over the former has produced no more than an odd sherd and there is with little doubt no Roman settlement there.

There are, otherwise, 'Celtic' field lynchets crossed by the bounding ditches and ridge-and-furrow of medieval type which lies over the ditches, as does a lynchet, probably post-Roman, just east of the entrance.

The size of the enclosure indicates large resources. The ditches excavated by Sumner (Fig 33) were each cut down to an 'ankle-breaking' slot, with steep scarps flanking the low bank. An inner ditch is conventionally regarded as most efficient for the containment of stock and therefore likely, as here, to be a token of such a use, while an outer ditch may have corresponding importance to keep out feral animals, particularly along a perimeter of 2.5 km. The two points at which the ditches generally defining the border actually diverge to form encapsulated enclosures should provide a clue as to how things were managed. It is most unlikely that stock would be driven along between the ditches in any numbers but, if the low, broad form of the contained bank is an original feature, then it seems possible that it was a raised road for mounted patrols, perhaps carrying a simple portable bridge to get into the interior when necessary (cf, page 87: enclosures with unbroken ditches). There would still be room for a quickset hedge on the outer side of the 'bank', or for any use of hurdles, but more excavation is needed before Sumner's dubious interpretation of a massive stockade can be accepted.

The two encapsulated enclosures offer only a little, otherwise, in terms of explanation. Though of different shape they are both about 0.6 hectares (1½ acres) in area; the trapezoid has a ditched sub-division. Neither seems to have had entrances into the big enclosure, though one could have existed at the south of the triangle. One reason for two possible pounds is that the great enclosure was at one time roughly bisected from the north, where a fragment of ditch springing from the innermost ditch just east of A–B, runs south and disappears on meeting the present strip of disturbed downland.

Apart from the Duck's Nest long barrow, (3), which most clearly presents itself towards the west (RCHM 1979, 51), the first obvious exploitation of the area is marked by a locally remarkable collection of round barrows grouped around or

PLATE 31 Rockbourne Down from the west, with Tenantry Farm in the foreground (cf, Area Plan 6). Settlement (**53**) is immediately beyond the broken long copse in the middle distance. Roads through the settlement are partly marked by broad dark bands; the band from the west stops abruptly in the settlement area (cf, Plate 21 and Area Plan 3). The ditches of enclosure (**54**) lie obliquely across the settlement (cf, Plate 32, a close-up of the detail described here). (NMR OAP SU 1021/18/403)

North

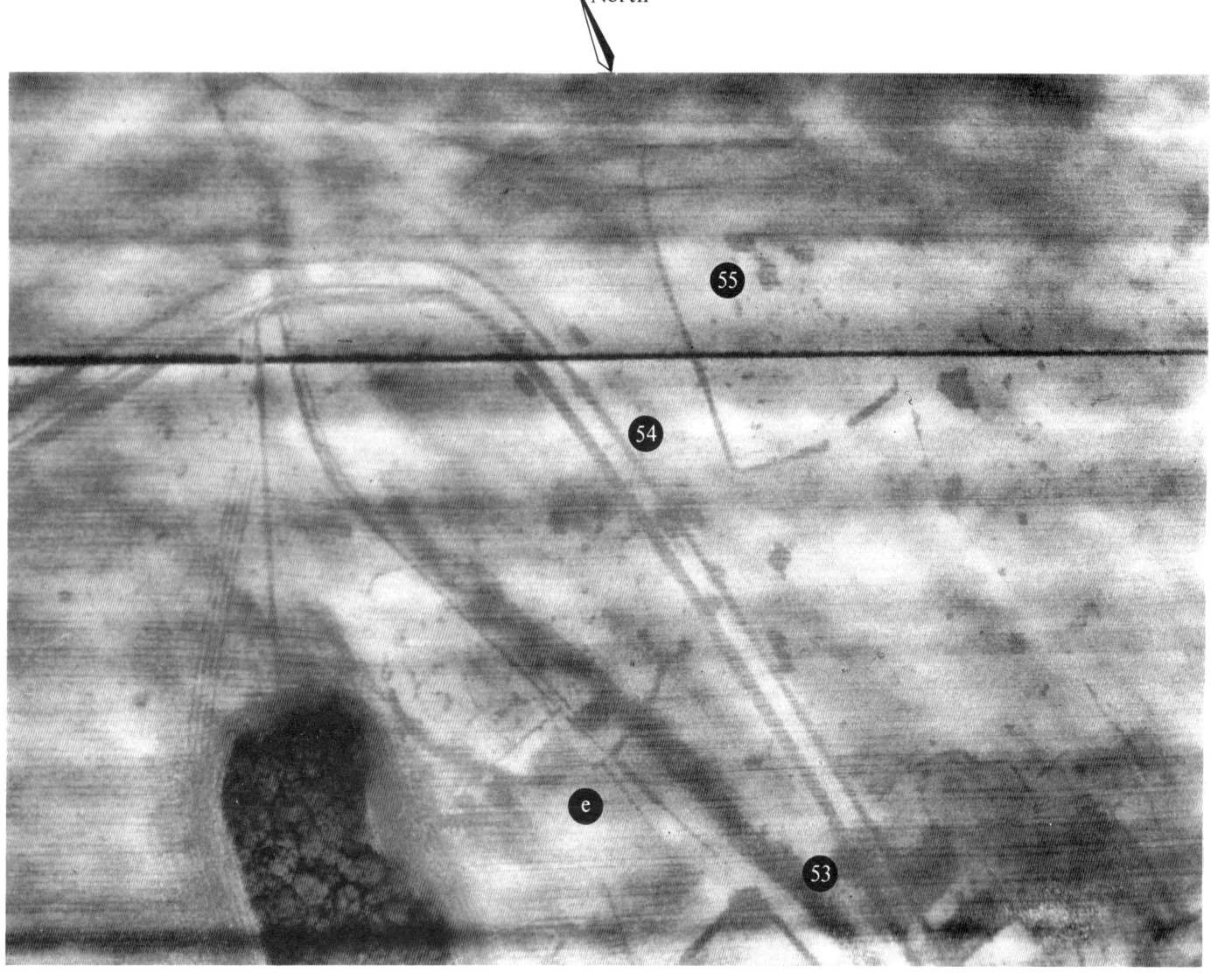

PLATE 32 Rockbourne Down looking north north east over the north angle of enclosure Rockbourne (54) (cf, Area Plan 6). The probably Iron Age 'enclosure' (55) shows very faint traces of a possible palisade trench parallel with its ditch west of the conspicuous entrance in the south side. Another incomplete but probable enclosure, ?ovoid, partially marked by curving ditches with gap (a possible entrance) at **e**, is overlaid by a broad band of probable Romano-British hollow-way following the line of sinuous ditches west of it. Just west of where these intersect (54) is the terminal of a ditch bisecting the enclosure. A few metres west of this, the innermost, narrow, ditch of (54) is apparently broken roughly at Sumner's cut A−B. Elements of (53), bottom right, include, prominently, the north-east angle of Sumner's 'Hypocaust Quarter' (trapezoidal enclosure). Halfway along the modern east−west hedge line (omitted from the Area Plan) are two unexplained bath-shaped patches, one on either side, obviously aligned with the ditches of (53). (NMR OAP SU 0921/8/189)

overlooking Spring Pond and the Winterbourne that rises in its immediate vicinity (cf, page 80). It is possible that ritual matters attracted the barrow makers into the valley bottom around the water source (cf, Ross 1967, 20). The barrows themselves vary from large and compound, (23), to very small. One ring ditch, (41), uncertainly a barrow, intersects (54). Another ring ditch, (34), lies immediately outside enclosure (56), intersecting a 'Celtic' field lynchet in a combination of relationships apparently similar to those adjacent to enclosure Martin (67). There were undoubtedly more barrows than already recorded. Some effects on air photographs may be discounted, however; for example, Plate 31 shows, bottom right, a pair of small trees within circles which are caused by ploughing around them.

The settlement enclosures (52), (55) and (56), all described below, are remarkably different in form, with (52) lacking any sign of an entrance and (55) any sign of a north-east side. Although the relationship with the 'Celtic' fields is evidently complex, all doubtless were served by fields, but the eastern extension of (52) may have encroached on former arable while (56) may lie on earlier fields.

(52), *Settlement* (10352045), Iron Age and Romano-British, on the summit and west shoulder of the ridge immediately north west of the Duck's Nest long barrow, (3), is detectable as a compound oval enclosure of 1.4 hectares (3½ acres) and abundant pits and smear marks (Fig 46d).

The ditch of the enclosure had been almost obliterated by ploughing before 1926 (ms letter to Williams-Freeman from O G S Crawford, 10 May 1926, in the NMR). Ditch 'f', which bisects the enclosure, is, on air photographs, little more than 1.2 metres across. It is best interpreted as the east side of an earlier enclosure, the ditch of which was otherwise enlarged to about 3 metres across and extended east from the north-east and south-east corners to create an addition which effectively doubled the original size. The western half lay on a slight ledge just west of the summit, the extension being taken up and over the crest.

In 1939 a trench ('e' on Plan) was cut across the ditch of the extension to the south east by Stuart Piggott. It was found to be V-shaped, about 3.5 metres across and 1 metre deep. Pottery found in the ditch, up to 0.3 metres from the top, was typologically (Middle) Iron Age 'exactly comparable with ... (Little) Woodbury' (Piggott 1941) (finds in Salisbury Museum). There was no apparent entrance break anywhere in the wider ditch, where it could still be seen as a distinctive mark in the downland grass in 1939, and none can be seen on air photographs of the crop or soil marks of this, or of ditch 'f'.

Air photographs of the area under arable show extensive smear marks of occupation throughout the enclosure, some intersecting line 'f'. Pottery gathered from the ploughed surface includes 1st to 4th-century AD Roman ware and none necessarily prehistoric.

The eastern half of the enclosure intersects a scarp, hollow-way or ditch, or all three, in part following the edges of 'Celtic' fields; other fields appear to be integrated into a settlement area roughly corresponding with the western half of the enclosure, but the ditch itself may lie over a 'Celtic' field edge. Broad ridge-and-furrow (marked 'br' on Area Plan 6) of medieval or later date is detectable over 'Celtic' fields east of the enclosure and intrudes on its ditch but does not go over it. Crawford (ms letter cited above) noted 'hollow tracks' leading into the enclosure from the north, almost certainly along the line just west of (e) referred to above.

(Further air photographs: NMR OAP SU 1020/4/198; 1020/5/392, 393.)

(55), *Enclosure* (108220), not visibly complete, undated, probably Iron Age, on the ridge top at the north of Rockbourne Down (Fig 46c; Plate 32), with ground falling gently to the south and east. It lies within 20 metres of the north angle of the great enclosure (54). There are no features in relief but ditches indicated by crop marks were confirmed in geophysical survey by Dr A J Clark, of the Geophysical Section of the Ancient Monuments Laboratory (English Heritage). These constitute the west and south sides only, of an enclosure of less than 0.4 hectares (1 acre) in area, the former completeness of which is suggested both by the shape and by the existence of an entrance about 6 metres wide in the south side. Some air photographs (cf, Plate 32) show a thin broken line inside and parallel to the ditch west of the entrance. The only surface finds are heat-affected flints and a few pieces of heathstone, which extend east (but not west) from the notional enclosure, as if occupation also occurred outside it on the unditched side.

(Further air photographs: NMR OAP SU 0921/8/189 (Plate 32), 190–1; SU 1021/18/403 (Plate 31).)

(56), *Enclosure* (11052105), probably prehistoric, known from air photographs only, lies on the shoulder of a gentle spur in a position 250 metres to the east of, and overlooking, Spring Pond (Plate 33: two air photographs, only one showing an entrance). A ditch about 3 metres across demarcates a rough D-shape of 0.4 hectares (1 acre), breached on the south by an entrance about 6 metres wide. The two almost straight sides of the enclosure, turning an ovoid into the 'D' shape, are probably due to construction along 'Celtic' field sides, the lynchets of which had presumably developed before the enclosure was built. Its position, however, so far as surviving signs of 'Celtic' fields indicate, was on the edge of a field system. A ring ditch (34) appears immediately adjacent, coinciding with the lynchet along the south east of the enclosure (Fig 46c).

(Further air photographs: CUCAP VAP RC8 BM 201 and NMR OAP SU 1121/1 (Plate 33); NMR OAP SU 1021/25/391.)

Linear (63), on the west of the plan, is unexplained and possibly incomplete. The very widespread superimposition of broad ridge-and-furrow, itself levelled by extensive later ploughing, adds to the problems of interpretation in other ways, too. Sumner seems to have been puzzled by the ridges, and, having excavated them in the area of settlement (53), declared them to be natural. The site of his excavation is within 'New Broke' on the Tithe Map, surely referable to a post-rig phase. With little doubt, the ridge-and-furrow went over the line of enclosure (54) in places, as in the vicinity of ring ditch (41), which could have accounted partly for the very low aspect of the enclosure bank. But an original relative flatness is still likely and would have encouraged, or at least not inhibited, the ploughing which, in any case, had to surmount 'Celtic' field lynchets.

There is a strong suggestion that the ridge-and-furrow respected the road leading north east past barrows (37) to (39). The road may well, therefore, have been used in medieval and later times, but the abrupt cessation of the dark band of hollowing at the east edge of settlement (53) strongly suggests an original connection with the Roman phase here (cf, note on Roman hollow-ways in Area Plan 3, *loose*).

Spring Pond was fully described and planned by Sumner (1914, 7–12, with contoured plan and section). It is about 60 metres long and 33 metres wide. ''Tis a ghastly place when 'tis

71

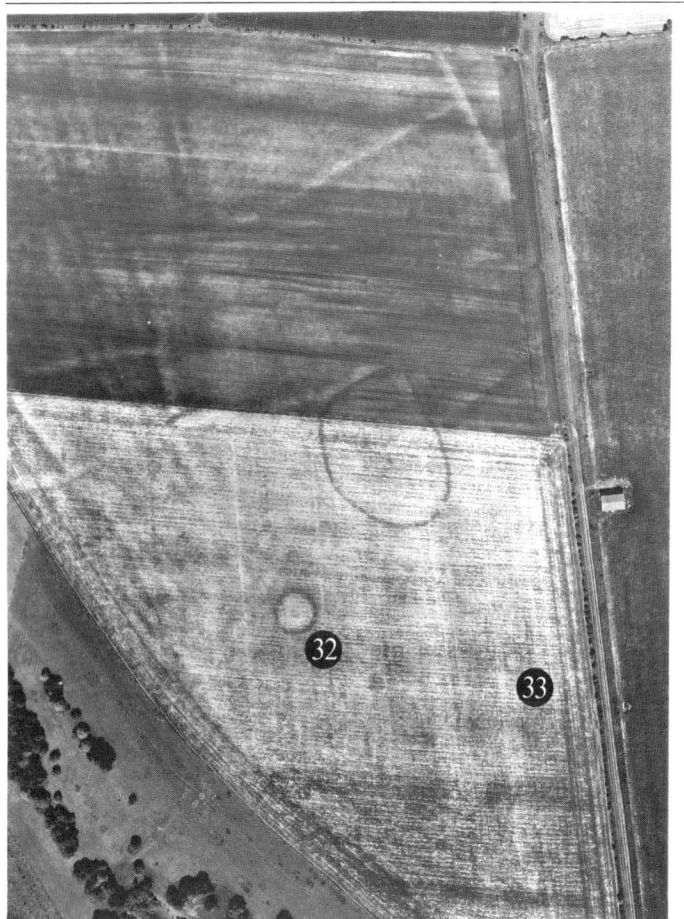
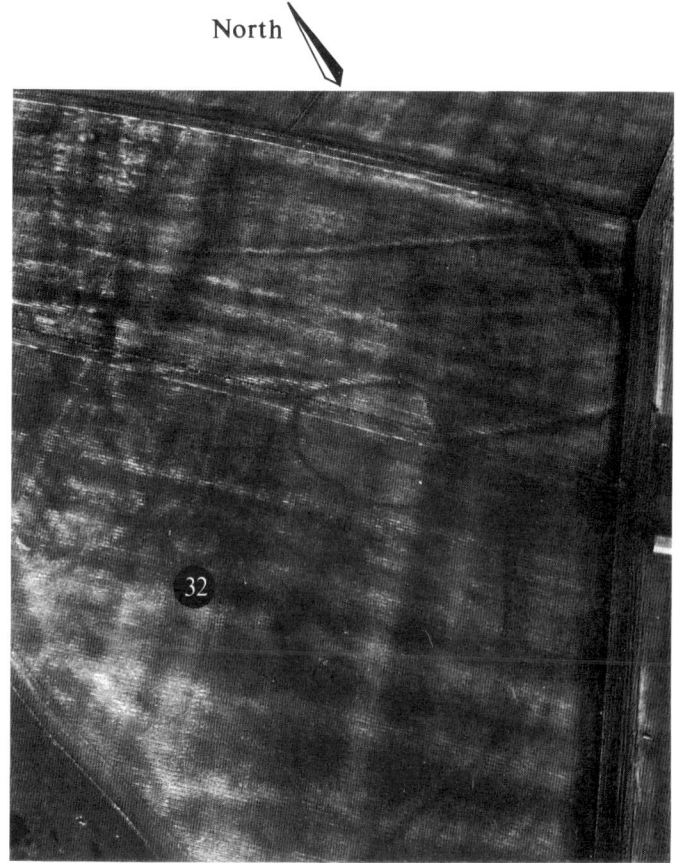

North

PLATE 33 Rockbourne (56): two views. To the left, a vertical air photograph under crop shows the entrance and true shape with ring ditches (**32**) and (**33**) and broad rig, centre and top left, over 'Celtic' fields. To the right, an oblique air photograph shows a distorted shape with no entrance apparent but with 'Celtic' fields clear to the top right and the broad rig in furlong arrangements at the bottom. The broad-rig ploughing has created a pair of lines along a headland skirting (**32**), falsely suggesting a track approach to the enclosure (cf, Area Plan 6). (Two photographs: CUCAP VAP RC8 BM 201 (left; Cambridge University Collection: copyright reserved) and NMR OAP SU 1121/1 (right))

full', he was told. It is remarkable, too, when it is empty, 8 metres deep at the northern end, shelving up to the south. The spoil around it is a testimony to successive deepenings, and since a rough estimate would match its bulk to the size of the hole, it is clear that this was no quarry in origin. The spoil lies partly over the bank of (54), at one point rising to 2 metres high. A short stretch of bank on either side of the entrance was noted by Sumner as being 'well defined', ie, higher and sharper than the low, broad profile visible elsewhere. The presence of Spring Pond, on the floor of a valley at its head, or the winter waterhead which it dramatically advertises, provides obvious practical advantages as well as problems for the stock farmer (such as was, surely, the creator of enclosure (54)).

The date of its first creation is unknown. A probable large pond is shown in the approximate position in 1671. It is said to have been deepened in the 19th century when the spoil was cast out to the south.

(Estate map (1671) in Shaftesbury Estate Office.)

Alleged county boundary in relation to Rockbourne (54) (Fig 34)

A feature itself datable that crossed the big enclosure (54), now technically undated, would provide a *terminus ante quem*. The possibility that a former county/parish boundary crossed it was raised by consideration of the 2-inch drawings for the First Edition of the OS 1-inch map. Enlargement of the OS First Edition, with the three long barrows of Duck's Nest, Rockbourne Down and Round Clump as controls (which prevented correlations with possibly changed boundaries or tracks), shows that the alleged county boundary bisected enclosure (54), extending from the long barrow Rockbourne (1) (where a bank noted elsewhere moves south from it on the assumed line) and across the long copse now seen west of (53).

Greenwood's map of 1826 shows the same line as the OS drawings; it is possible that the map of Isaac Taylor (1759) does, too. There is, however, no sign of a ditch or any other boundary on any air photographs, including those showing even slight ditches. Mr J R S Booth (OS Boundary Division), in a personal communication, noted that the 1807/8 drawings did follow an aberrant line and that Greenwood followed it. He is inclined to think that it was an error (possibly by contractors). It is a pity that the Wiltshire County map by Andrews and Dury (1773) is not more accurately to scale in order to check this.

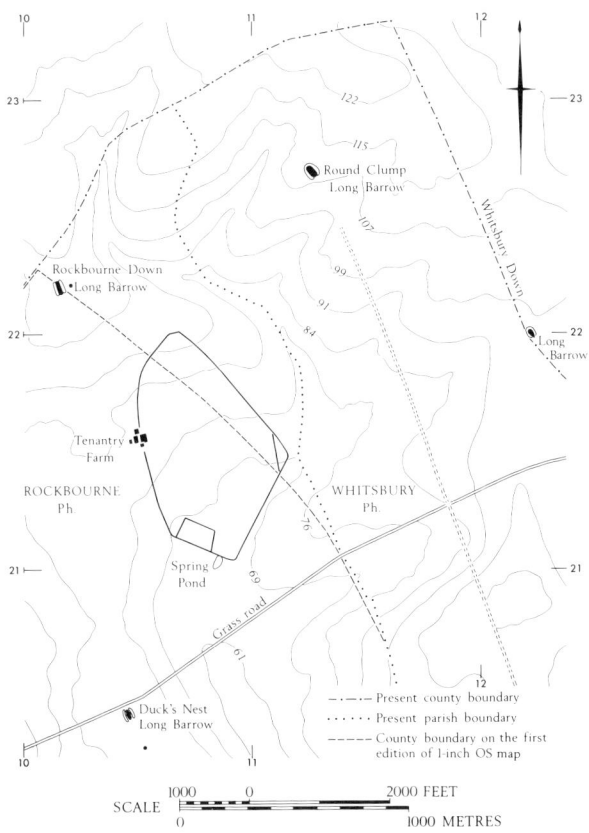

FIG 34 Rockbourne and Whitsbury parishes, showing alleged old county boundary. Only long barrows and round barrows nearby are shown (1:190,000)

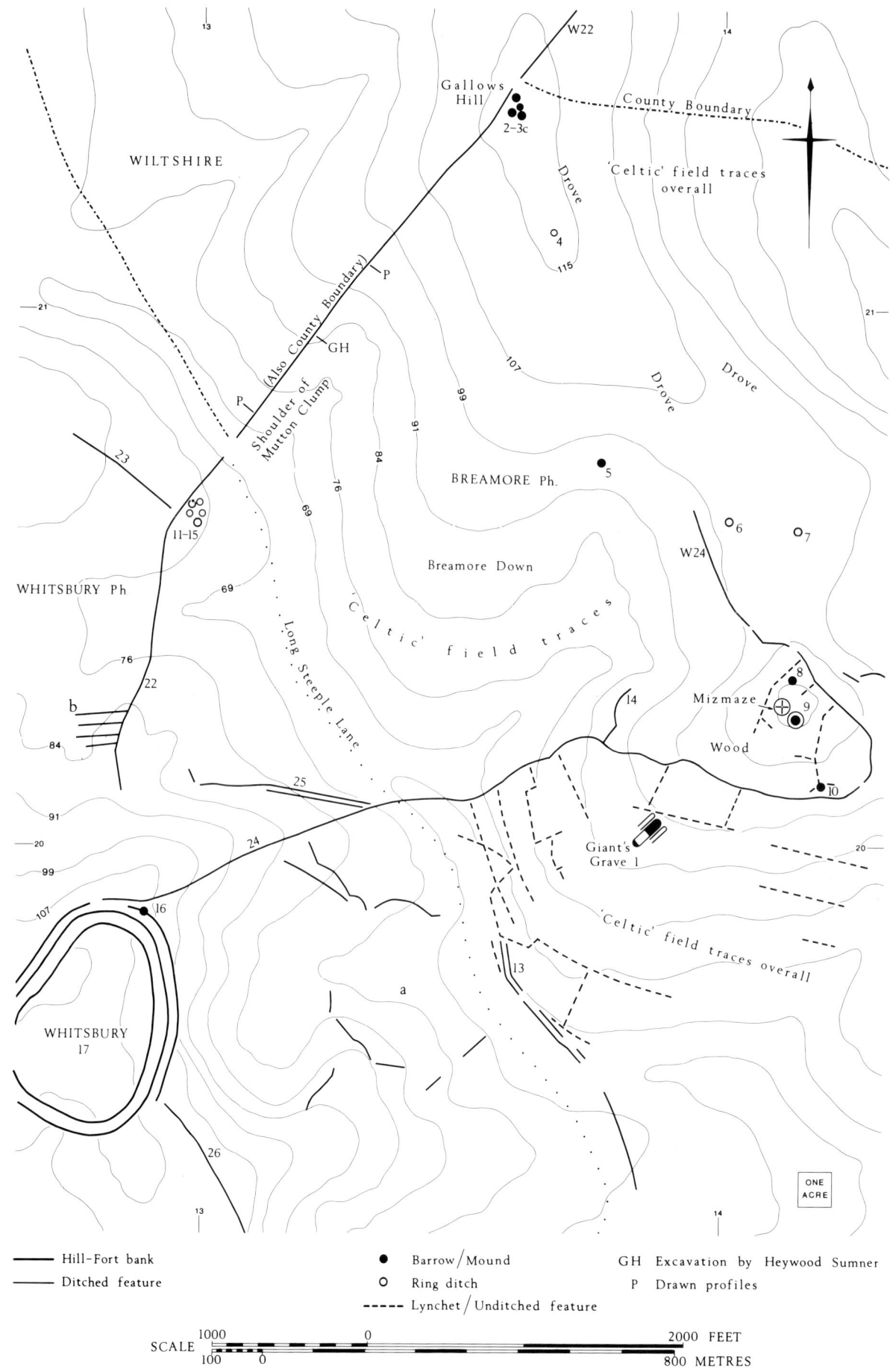

WILTSHIRE

W22

Gallows Hill

2–3c

County Boundary

'Celtic' field traces overall

Drove

○4

115

(Also County Boundary)

P

GH

Shoulder of Mutton Clump

P

107

99

91

84

76

Drove

Drove

BREAMORE Ph.

●5

○6   ○7

21   21

23

Breamore Down

W24

○○○
○○
11–15

'Celtic' field traces

WHITSBURY Ph

69

69

Long Steeple Lane

Mizmaze

8 ●
⊕
● 9

76

b

22

Wood

84

25

14

10 ●

91

24

Giant's Grave 1

'Celtic' field traces overall

20   20

99

107

●16

13

a

13

WHITSBURY
17

26

13   14

ONE
ACRE

—— Hill-Fort bank   ● Barrow/Mound   GH Excavation by Heywood Sumner
— Ditched feature   ○ Ring ditch   P Drawn profiles
- - - Lynchet/Unditched feature

SCALE   1000   0   2000 FEET
         100   0   800 METRES

Area Plan 7 Whitsbury and Breamore, Hampshire (1:10,560)

Area Plan 7

Whitsbury and Breamore, Hampshire

This plan is included to show how, if at all, Whitsbury and Mizmaze Hill are focal to the pattern of linears in the area.

(17), *Whitsbury hill-fort* (128197), although relatively unobtrusive in today's landscape, has massive multivallate defences enclosing 6 hectares (15 acres) on the highest local summit, the southern end of a chalk ridge which is here capped by Tertiary gravel, clay and sand (Fig 35). In its early days it must have made a strikingly white hill, especially from the east. The ground falls from it in medium slopes on the north and west, very gently to the south while on the east the outer defences dip deep into the corrie-like head of a re-entrant penetrating the hill from that side. There are panoramic views to the north but visibility to the east is severely limited by Mizmaze Hill. A gap of 50

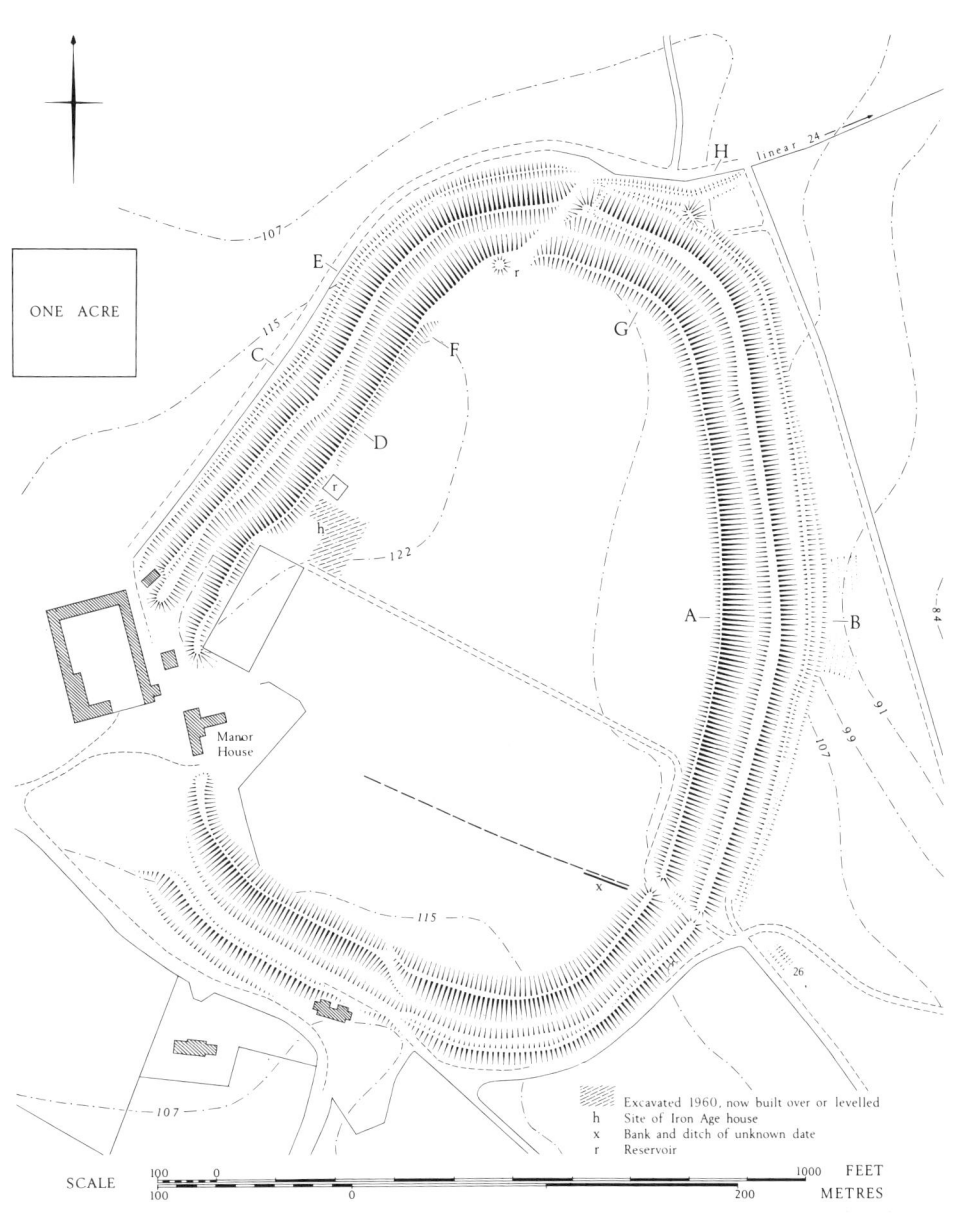

ONE ACRE

Manor House

Excavated 1960, now built over or levelled
h Site of Iron Age house
x Bank and ditch of unknown date
r Reservoir

SCALE 100 0   1000 FEET
       100   0   200   METRES

FIG 35 Plan of the hill-fort Whitsbury (17) (1:3,750)

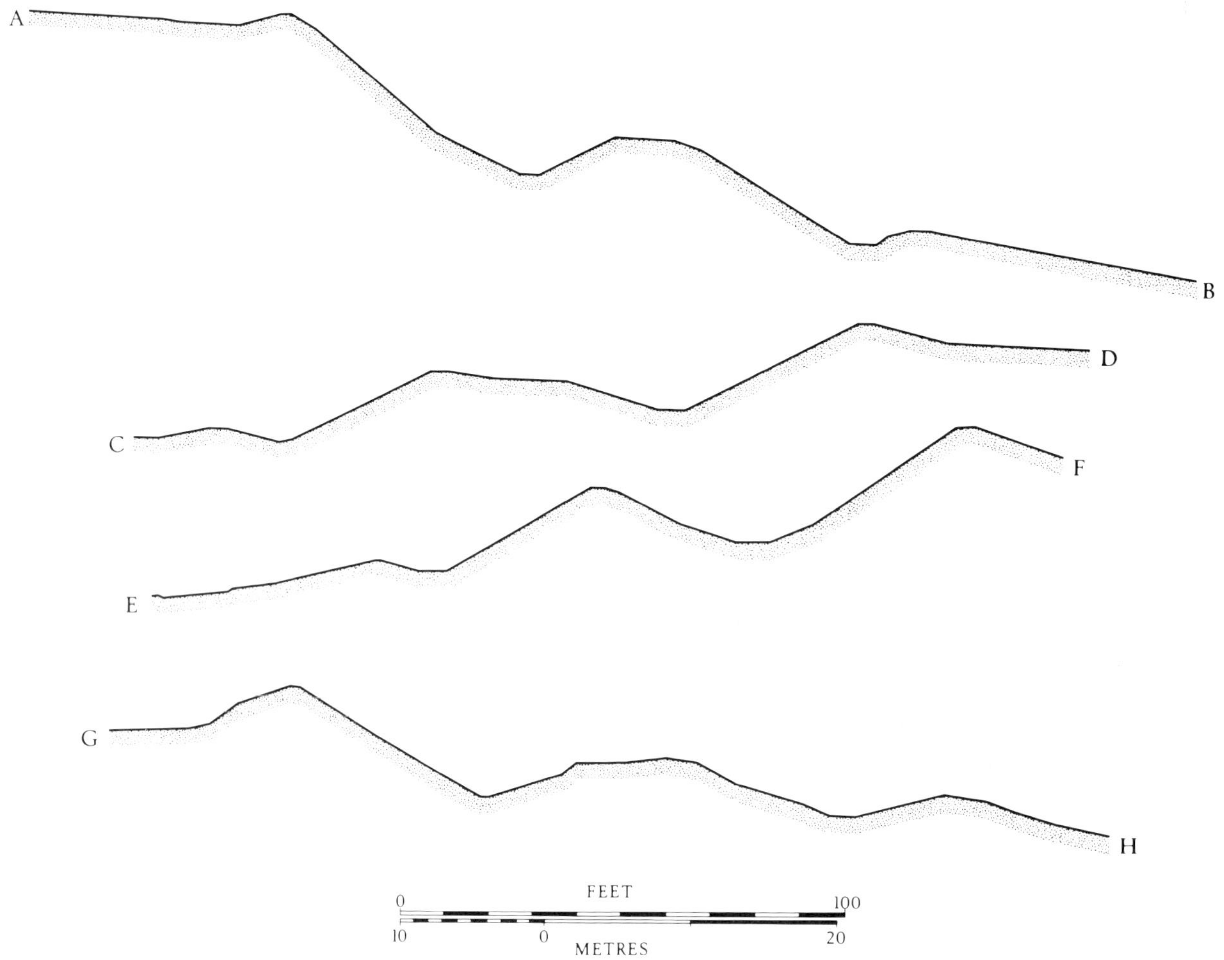

A
B
C
D
E
F
G
H
0
FEET
100
10
0
METRES
20

FIG 36 Whitsbury (17): profiles (1:500)

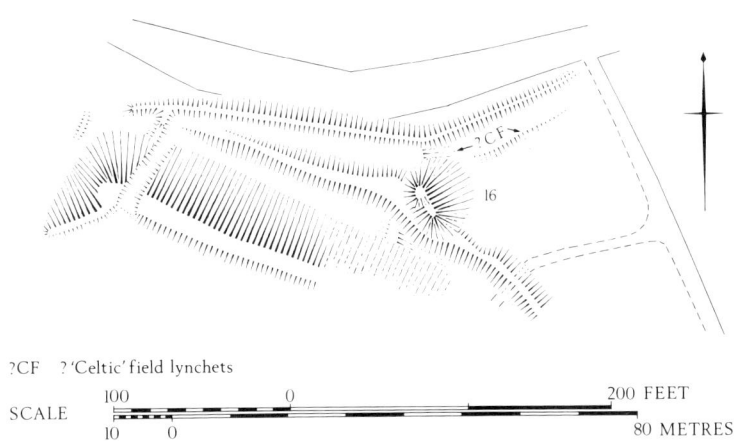

?CF
16
?CF ?'Celtic' field lynchets
SCALE
100
0
200 FEET
10
0
80 METRES

FIG 37 Plan of Whitsbury (16) (1:1,250)

metres in the south west of the defences is occupied by the Manor House and outbuildings, presumably covering the site of the original entrance, breaks at the north and south east being secondary; trees otherwise mask the whole perimeter. In 1810 Colt Hoare had noted it to be 'much obscured by copse wood'.

The defences are regularly disposed except about 100 metres north of the Manor House, where a sharp bend in the inner bank and ditch is not matched in the straight run of the outer ditch. This is the only apparent pointer to phases in the construction of the hill-fort. There is no direct correlation apparent between the steepness of the natural slope and the overall width of the defences; thus, in Fig 35, E−F has a considerably narrower spread than A−B, where the total drop is 6 metres more. On the east, the defences drop impressively down a steep natural slope. Near its foot the outer main rampart falls in great steps to the re-entrant head hachured at B on Fig 35. It is notably flat-topped and broad along this entire side, and becomes so again on the west side, south of C−D. The profiles (Fig 36) suggest that the flat tops of this rampart are close to the position of the old ground surface. Tracks follow the course of the outer ditch. The counterscarp bank is of very varied size, from puny to 8 metres wide and 1.4 metres high. On the east side, a scarp up to 0.6 metres high, just beyond the counterscarp bank, has probably been created by ploughing.

The interior has been ploughed (as can be seen on air photographs (CUCAP OAP NM 73−5) taken in 1954) but is now pasture. It has been variously subdivided in the past; there are traces of a bank and ditch ((x) on Fig 35) of unknown date, but possibly associated with a former drive to the Manor House, extending north west from just south of the south-south-east entrance. An excavation by Professor Rahtz for the MoW in 1960, prior to building works at (h) on Fig 35, the highest part of the interior, disclosed a complete, apparently D-shaped Iron Age hut with a rammed chalk floor and a central clay hearth, with which were associated pottery of the Yarnbury−Highfield group of saucepan-pot styles, part of a bone weaving comb, a possible chalk loomweight and two iron staples. Above this was a scatter of Roman pottery (1st to 4th-century AD). A narrow, steep-sided trench contained the upper part of a post-Roman grass-tempered vessel, burnt daub and charcoal. There was also evidence for some possible post-Roman refurbishment of the inner rampart (Ellison and Rahtz 1987).

Varied destruction, as well as planting and hedging, make it impossible to decide whether the outermost bank of the hill-fort has incorporated any element of the approaching linears (22), (24), and (26). To the north, the nature of the connection between hill-fort and linear (24) is now possibly recoverable only by excavation. West of the point at which (24) changes direction, opposite (16), it is probable that some of the visible remains crossing the hill-fort ditch belong to hedges, one of which has roughly followed the line of the linear bank from the east (Fig 37). Whatever the actual story, it is probable that, in the Iron Age, a continuous bank and ditch extended east from the hill-fort to, and round, the Mizmaze Hill. A suggestion has been made that a further linear extended south west from the hill-fort. This is regarded as unproven, though possible, and is illustrated (Fig 64), with a note, on page 118.

(Bibliography: Colt Hoare 1810, 231; Sumner 1913, 20−2; Williams-Freeman 1915, 177−9, 418.)

Three linears approach Whitsbury. That from the north, Whitsbury (22), of 'spinal' type, is first seen 0.8 km south east of Clearbury, almost 5 km distant, but has not been aligned on that hill-fort. It has not been traced closer than a point 200 metres distant from Whitsbury, partly because a mixed clayey cover masks any soil marks and prevents geophysical determination and partly because of degradation associated with tracks through and around the ramparts. This second factor makes it impossible to see the relationship between linear Whitsbury (24) and the much more massive counterscarp bank of the hill-fort. Linear (24) changes direction when it passes probable barrow (16), which interrupts the counterscarp. It is quite possible that the barrow was an earlier target for the linears. Similarly, there is no visible link between Whitsbury (26), to the south, and the hill-fort's counterscarp bank. Lack of counterscarp west of the linear could be due to differential destruction in land once arable.

The 'spinal' linear Martin (80) is last seen on air photographs to the west 1 km away from Whitsbury, apparently making for a point some 600 metres north of it, close to the cluster of barrows (11) to (15), around which linear Whitsbury (22) bends. The only ditch meeting here is the slight Whitsbury (23), and the fact of this being visible makes it less likely that Martin (80) has been missed. The nature of the grassy interior of Whitsbury, once ploughed, but now pasture, adds to the difficulty of determining how the hill-fort, the hill itself, or some 'lost' feature on the site might have been associated with the linears (perhaps variously at different stages).

East of Whitsbury (Fig 38) a series of problems present themselves. Linear Whitsbury (24) at first runs almost straight, crossing Long Steeple Lane, but then ripples in a series of undulating curves, matched in the short ditch Breamore (14) abutting it, and loops round the foot of the higher reaches of the hill capped by barrow Breamore (9) with the Mizmaze beside it (Fig 39), which, together with the siting of the long barrow Breamore (1), Giant's Grave, suggests that the hill had some special significance. Relationship with 'Celtic' fields is not clearly determinable as the linear climbs from Long Steeple Lane. The sinuous course of Whitsbury (24) indicates that it was probably not intended to bound arable fields. There is a strong suggestion in the pattern of the 'Celtic' field arrangements of more than one phase. Destruction has gone so far that it is not now certain whether those west of Breamore (14) had once extended north and were subsequently cut by the linear. Similar questions of sequence obviously arise north of Giant's Grave. The long barrow's ditches are, or were until recently, still clearly to be seen so these were not absorbed into the surrounding arable arrangements (cf, Whitsbury (1) in the Tabulated Inventory, see Editorial Notes). Its alignment could fit into the 'Celtic' fields discussed above but not with those locally ending on the massive lynchet skirting it to the north, which must be entirely positive.

Some of the features shown east of Whitsbury defy categorisation (Area Plan 7). On air photographs these include discrete series of arcing lines, apparently ditches in the area of (a). The 'parcel' of thin parallel lines north of Whitsbury (b) is also of uncertain nature and attribution but can be discussed in relation to other 'parcels' (page 98). The lines appear to abut and join the ditch of linear (22), which would be unlikely were they furrows.

Linear (13) could be a track parallel with and uphill of the potentially wet Long Steeple Lane. Whitsbury (25) also suggests a ditched track.

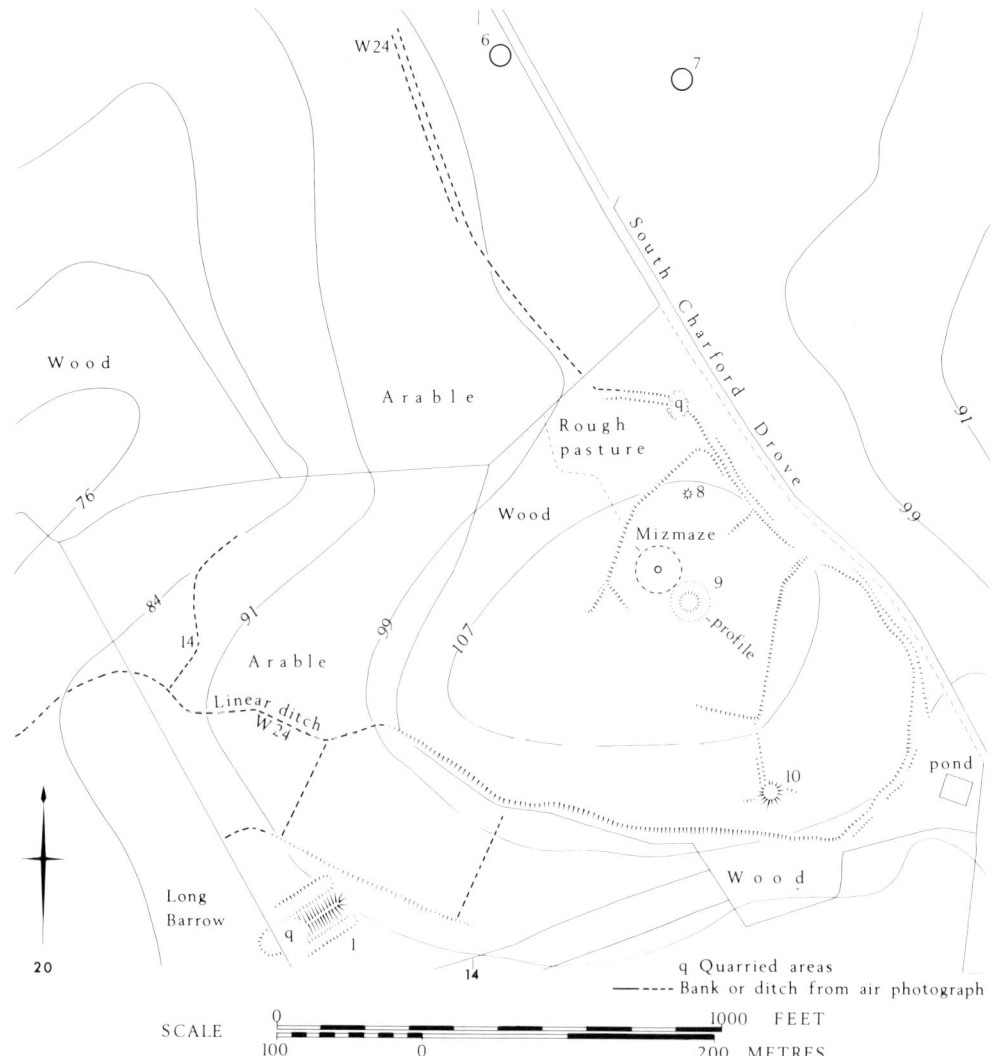

FIG 38 Plan of Breamore, Mizmaze Hill (1:5,000)

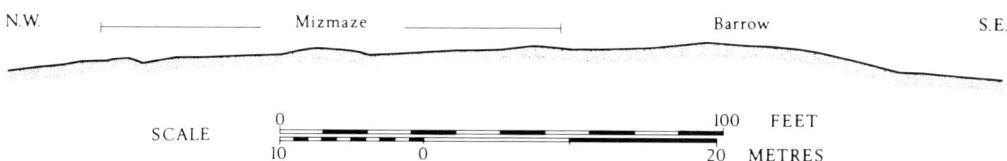

FIG 39 Breamore: profile across Mizmaze and barrow (1:500)

A REVIEW OF MONUMENTS EAST AND WEST OF BOKERLEY DYKE

Long barrows and long mounds

The long barrows in Hampshire have been described and discussed, against a wider background, in RCHM 1979, while the Dorset long barrows are inventorised in RCHM 1970a and b, 1972 and 1975. There is a marked concentration clearly associated with the Dorset Cursus and for a similar distance beyond either end, taking up the area between the River Stour in Dorset and the Hampshire River Avon. This zone is later split by Bokerley Dyke (Fig 2). The inferred disruption of an earlier Neolithic continuum is lent weight by the seeming independence of distribution demonstrated by the round barrows (see below). Some long mounds are probably not barrows (cf, page 87).

A later Neolithic flint cairn is associated with a long, natural mound in Farnham parish (Dorset). A mound of impressively 'long barrow' proportions east of Bokerley is more likely to be an unexplained part of the settlement with which it is described (Martin (66)).

Round barrows, ring ditches and round mounds

Unbroken ring ditches are, in most cases, where unassociated with settlement, the surviving evidence for barrows or cognate structures, although excavation may occasionally fail to disclose any burial (cf, RCHM 1960, 16–23, for discussion).

As anticipated in RCHM 1975 (page xxvii), aerial reconnaissance has revealed many more ring ditches than then known: well over a hundred, including sites exposed by parch marks in grass during the late part of the drought in 1976. The overall grouping has, however, been emphasised rather than altered and large areas remain 'blank'. A 46% increase in the barrows known around the Knowlton Circles both stresses the way in which funerary monuments can be crowded around presumed religious centres and, in this instance, indicates a break with the older tradition widely marked by long barrows (Fig 40). Whether round barrow groups are 'clearly associated' with the Cursus (RCHM 1975, xxviii) is therefore that much less clear. There is indeed a concentration roughly following the Cursus which does not maintain its density to the north-east (later) end, but continues in a thick spread for over a mile

beyond the south-west end and at one point, just short of the end of phase 1 below Bottlebush Down, seems to sprawl across the Cursus (RCHM 1975, Plate 48). Nor is there any clear association of round barrow groups with long barrows (such as was apparent in places in south-east Dorset (RCHM 1970a)), though isolated round barrows are repeatedly found fairly close to long barrows. Wor Barrow (Sixpenny Handley (29)), for instance, close to a major group of round barrows, though still some 200 metres distant from the nearest point of the main concentration, has two small barrows, one (40) with an 'irregular ditch', immediately adjacent (Area Plan 3). The distancing of the Duck's Nest long barrow, Rockbourne (3),

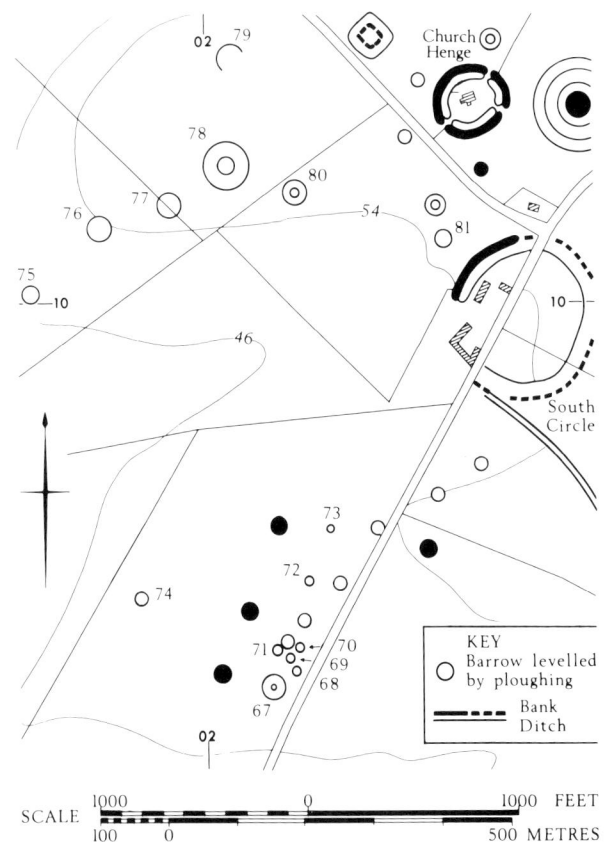

FIG 40 Distribution of barrows round Knowlton Circles, Woodlands, Dorset (1:10,560)

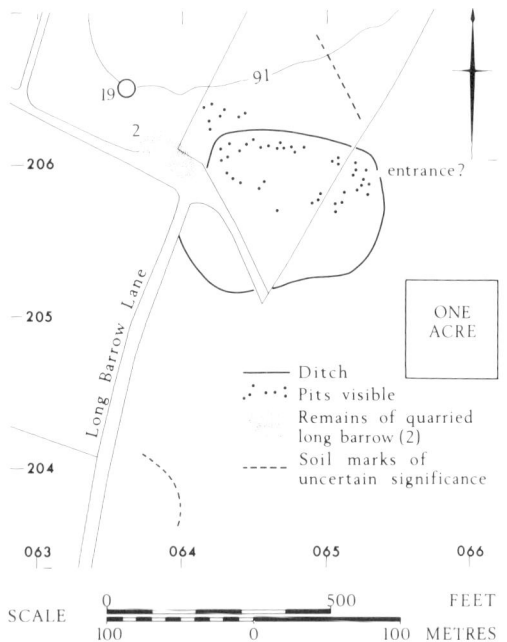

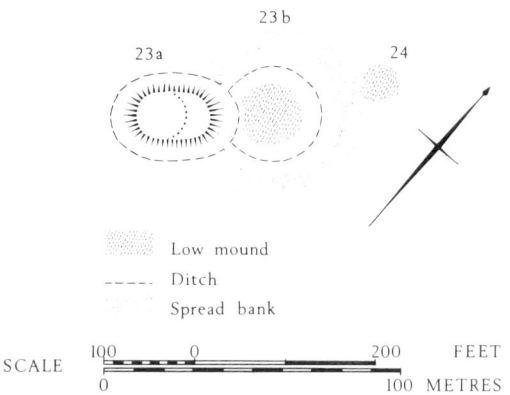

FIG 41   Plan of Martin (65), with long barrow (2) and ring ditch (19) (1:5,000)

FIG 42   Plan of barrows Rockbourne (23) and (24) (1:2,500)

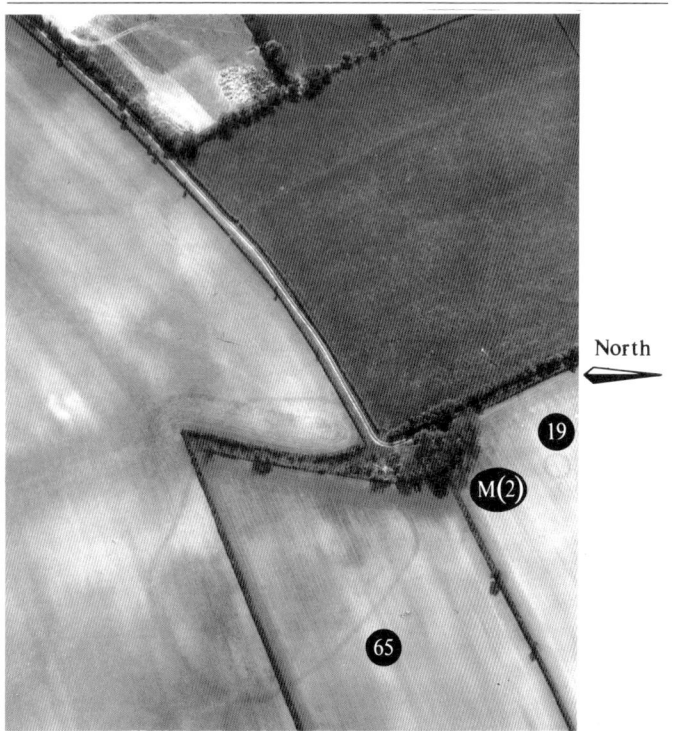

PLATE 34   Martin (65). An oblique air photograph looking west, with entrance gap in the near end of the ditched enclosure; long barrow Martin (2) is in the clump of trees outside the far end; ring ditch (19) is to the right of this. There is an unexplained curving ditch apparent south west of (65), on the near side of Long Barrow Lane opposite the field with white rectangles. (NMR OAP SU 0620/17/21)

from the low-lying Rockbourne Down southern group of round barrows, the only major group in the study area east of Bokerley, and set, perhaps significantly, around Spring Pond, is more extreme. This time there is a lone round barrow (Rockbourne (12)) on the same ridge not far to the south (Area Plan 6). (The skyline view is much more frequently and clearly displayed by the long than by the round barrows, which latter are not infrequently found in relatively depressed situations.) Newly discovered isolated ring ditches lie close by long barrow Martin (2) (Fig 41; Plate 34, with Martin (65)) and Rockbourne (45) by Rockbourne (2), the latter so insignificant that, although it can just be seen on Plate 35 in RCHM 1979, it was unnoticed. (For its position, cf, Fig 34.)

Most barrow types are found throughout the area under study but large barrows are rare east of the Bokerley Line. Round barrows with irregularly dug or interrupted ditches are found on both sides of Bokerley (cf, Sixpenny Handley (40), cited above, to the west, and Martin (39) and (45) to the east). Two differences can be tentatively noted. There are no clear disc barrows east of Bokerley (Rockbourne (23) (Fig 42) being considered a 'saucer' barrow; cf, Grinsell 1940, 13 and 221, his barrow number 54 NW), a local difference, and – so far – no

PLATE 35 Damerham (2). An oblique air photograph of this compound barrow from the west. (CUCAP OAP BHK 9; Cambridge University Collection: copyright reserved)

Ring ditches, almost certainly barrows, are seen in or by settlements both east and west of the Bokerley Line but seem particularly obtrusive on the Hampshire side. There is one extreme example where a cluster of three (Rockbourne (42)–(44), see Area Plan 6), one of which was demonstrated to be a round barrow, was virtually integrated in the structure of a small trapezoidal enclosure, apparently Roman in date and part of settlement Rockbourne (54) (Area Plan 6). Others, eg, Martin (16)–(18), are immediately adjacent to settlement (58) (see Fig 44). It is tempting to think that, for the settlements concerned, such conjunctions may sometimes point to Bronze Age antecedents otherwise missed. For the relationship with 'Celtic' fields, see, for example, page 52 above.

Some round or irregular mounds which are apparently not barrows (two at Woodcutts excavated, for instance, by Pitt-Rivers) occur in or near settlements and are discussed below, on page 87. One barrow labelled 'disc' in *Dorset IV* (RCHM 1972), Tarrant Launceston (46), might be reconsidered as an incomplete enclosure, cognate in form with some occasionally found near settlements.

Small square enclosures (probable Iron Age barrows)

These structures are characterised by a roughly square plan with continuous ditched sides of no more than about 21 metres (Plates 38, 39 and 40), two of them only about half that. Some are seen to have enclosed mounds or pits. They occur in the area under study both east and west of Bokerley (Fig 43). The distribution shown is remarkably sparse, suggesting some function of more general consequence than simple burial of an individual or, conceivably, just burial according to an imported rite rare in the area. Those known so far are, however, probably well short of the actual numbers. The only excavated example, Sixpenny Handley (30), had a mound, plotted by Colt Hoare as one of a pair of mounds (Area Plan 2, cf, Plate 1; cf, Area Plan 2 and description on page 49), but the square ditch around it was found during the excavation (White 1970) and is not seen on air photographs. Its late Iron Age date tallies with the probable date of the multiple ditches against which it lay. (Both would be more at home in Yorkshire.) Conversely, barrow Wimborne St Giles (87), formerly described as a bowl barrow, is now seen on air photographs to be surrounded by a square ditch not visible on ground inspection (Plate 38). There is no consistent orientation.

An enclosure, Wimborne St Giles (125), whose importance is enhanced by surviving as an earthwork, is of similar size and shape but with a suggestion of an entrance: it appears on Fig 46a. The ditched 'square' excavated by Pitt-Rivers near Bokerley Junction (see Pentridge (15) and page 24), probably a late Roman cemetery, had sides approximately 34 metres long.

The Tabulated Inventory (available on request from the Royal Commission, see Editorial Notes) includes all examples so far recognised in Dorset and in the small area of Hampshire dealt with in this volume.

recognised pairings of elongated and round barrow, a sort of 'ring-and-tongue' (Plates 35, 36 and 37), west of the line, though there are good examples of elongated compound barrows apparently embodying round elements (cf, RCHM 1972, Pimperne (22) and Plate 55). It is the ring 'clamped' on to the elongated element which provides the distinction. There is only one in the area under study surviving at all as an earthwork, though even this is severely degraded and regularly ploughed (Rockbourne (23) (Plate 37)).

The oval ditch enclosing the two or more round structures often detectable in elongated barrows emphasises the apparent intention to stress some sort of connection, and this is presumably also to be seen in the frequently found pairs or threes set tight together (eight sets in Martin alone) on both sides of Bokerley, not infrequently against linears (cf, page 11 for a discussion of all relationships with barrows).

Whether these clusters, where not – as sometimes – incorporated in groups, are to be regarded as in some sense nodal to a territory, is unknowable, but the small numbers relative to the population and the time span envisaged makes it highly likely that they were placed very deliberately and formally for specific purposes not entirely funerary.

M(85)

PLATE 36 Rockbourne (4), an elongated compound barrow (ring-and-tongue), can be seen to the bottom left. The ring ditch Rockbourne (5) is to the top right, with linear Martin (85) extending into the area from the left. (NMR OAP SU 0919/1/390)

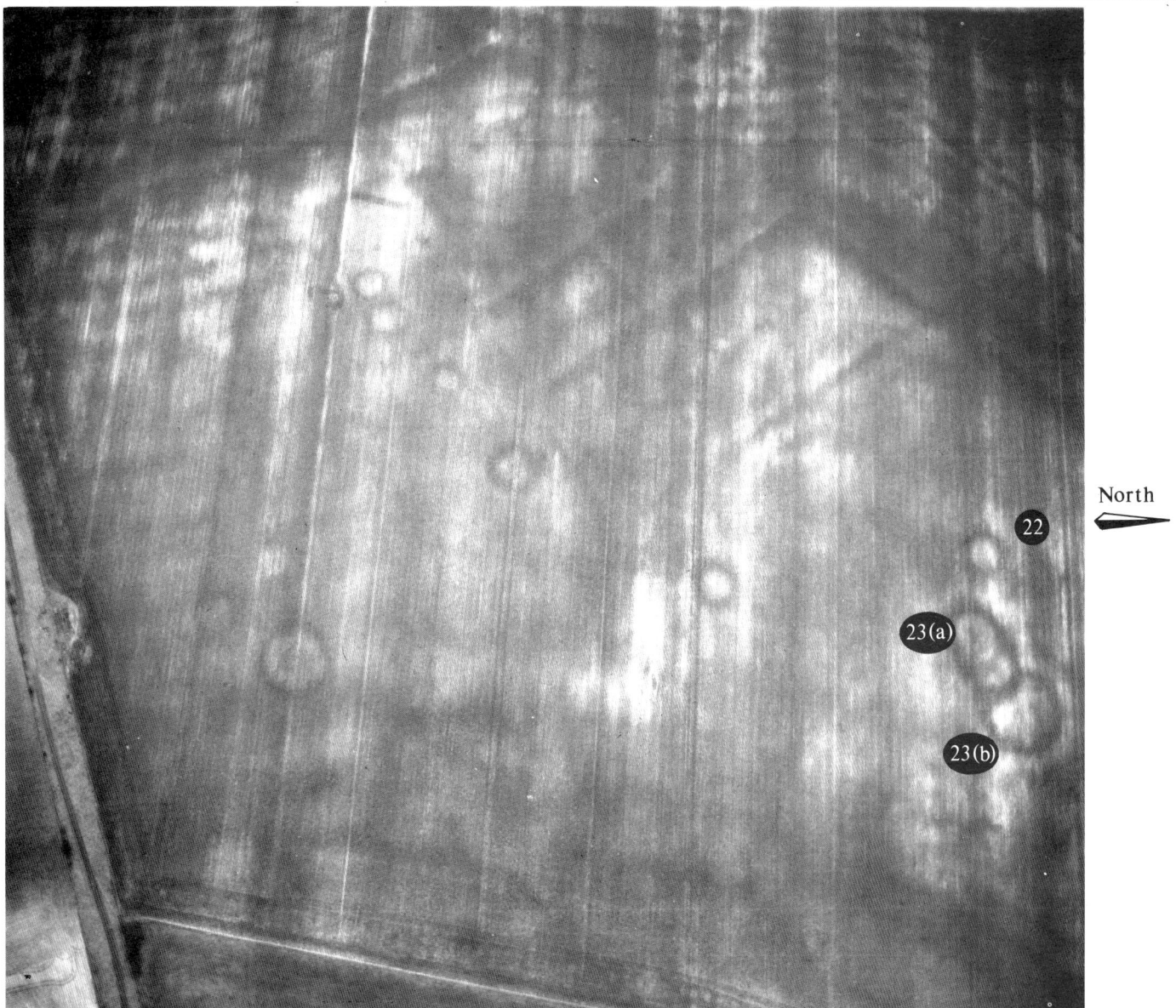

North

PLATE 37 Rockbourne, Tenantry Down. An oblique air photograph (*see* Area Plan 6) looking west. The compound barrow (**23**) **a** and **b** can be seen to the right, suggesting that (**23**) **a** incorporates at least two round mounds. Barrow (21) is immediately adjacent to the left of (**22**) but does not show clearly because it has an unditched, presumably scraped-up, mound. 'Celtic' fields are outside the barrow area and are partly overlaid by broad ridge-and-furrow, which also lies over some barrows. (NMR OAP SU 1020/6/396)

PLATE 38   Wimborne St Giles, Dorset: barrow (87), now seen to have a square ditch around the mound. Two close barrows in the foreground have been preserved from the plough, giving a misleading pear shape. The oblique line across the photograph beyond the barrows is the Roman road with a ditch and ?associated string of small quarry pits along it. (NMR OAP SU 0116/11)

Enclosures and settlements

The following account, with accompanying illustration (Fig 46), displays what is so far known to exist in the area covered by this volume in terms of enclosure shapes, features and attributes; it comments on some recurrent elements and makes suggestions on the interpretation of the relevant air photographs, some used as Plates in this volume. This section has a secondary purpose beyond that of following the Royal Commission's customary practice of inventorising sites in an area: it is intended to indicate what may be distinct or particularly significant on each side of the Bokerley Line and thus contribute to an assessment of its status as a major boundary.

In more general terms, it provides an opportunity of considering what use, however tentative, may be made of

comparative plans of shapes, features and dimensions; it is desirable to exploit to the full the information offered by this array of patterns, largely derived from air photographs, because adequate excavation, as known today, is never likely to be carried out on the great majority of sites. There are caveats, some obvious, largely to do with ignorance of dates and of what was in contemporary use. To these cautions can be added two others not usually much stressed but very important: first, since many features evade detection from the air, particularly if not ditched, enclosures may just signal the presence of settlement activity but not reveal either its full nature or necessarily reflect its range in space and time. Also, as is statistically evident, large numbers of settlements have entirely escaped notice, while many will continue to evade detection however much fieldwalking and geophysical examination may help to fill the

PLATE 39 Lower Whatcombe, Winterborne Whitechurch parish, Dorset. An oblique air photograph looking south east with small, square enclosure, possibly around a burial mound (a 29) adjacent to the wood. Traces of larger enclosures and a rectangular pattern of ditches partly along the lynchets suggest a nearby settlement. (NMR OAP ST 8400/1/78)

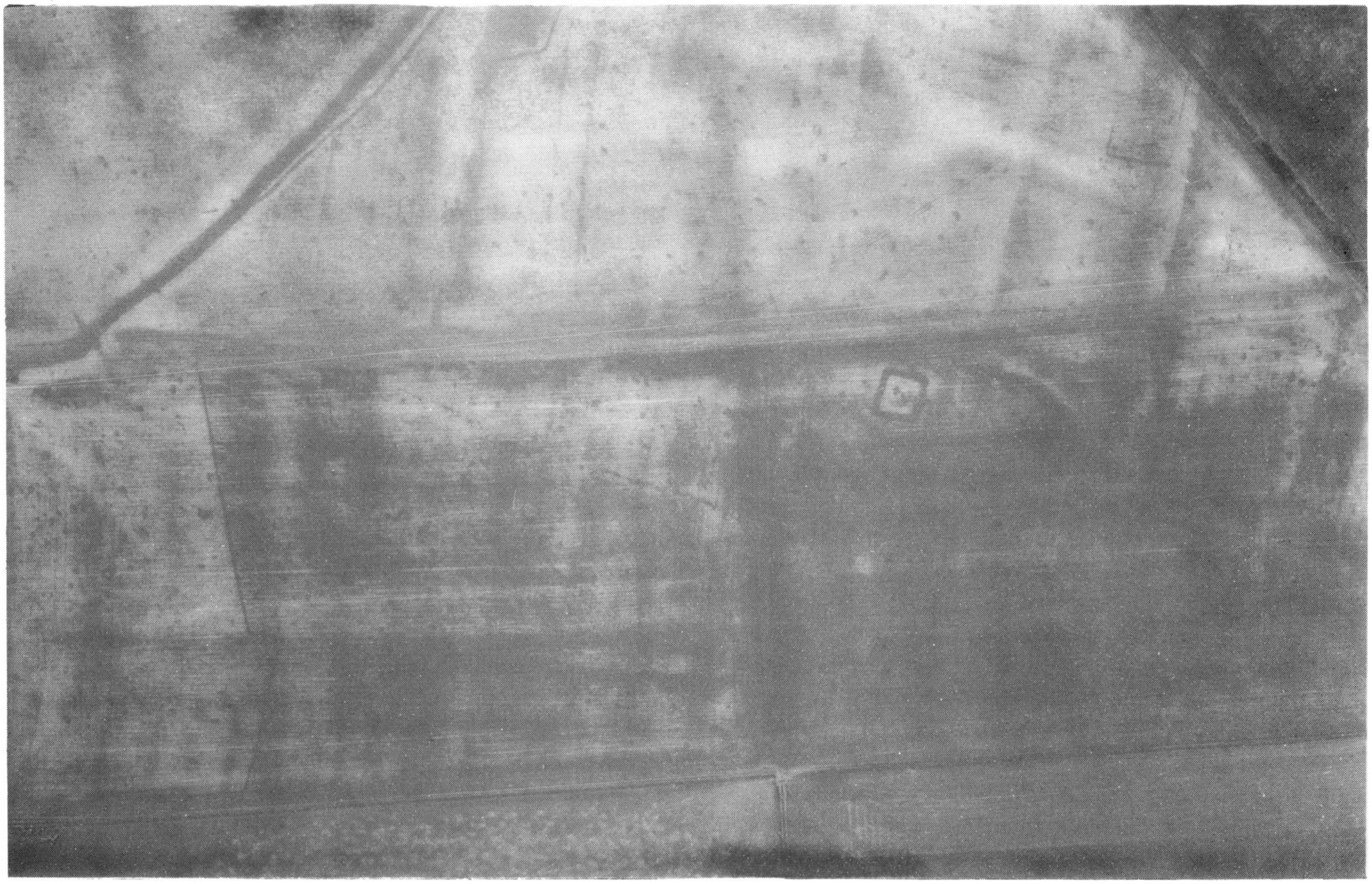

PLATE 40 Martin (55), a probable Iron Age barrow, to the right of the centre of the photograph. An oblique air photograph looking north east. Linear Martin (80) A is prominent at the top left, with linear (80) B emerging from it and closely parallel under the position of the bank of linear (80) A (cf, Plate 28). A partial enclosure ditch is close to (80) B at the top of the photograph, and a rectangular pattern of ditches extends over 'Celtic' fields diagonally across the parish boundary, forming part of Damerham (20). The undated straight lines connected by a stagger, bottom left, extended towards North Allenford (cf, p 117). (NMR OAP SU 0818/4)

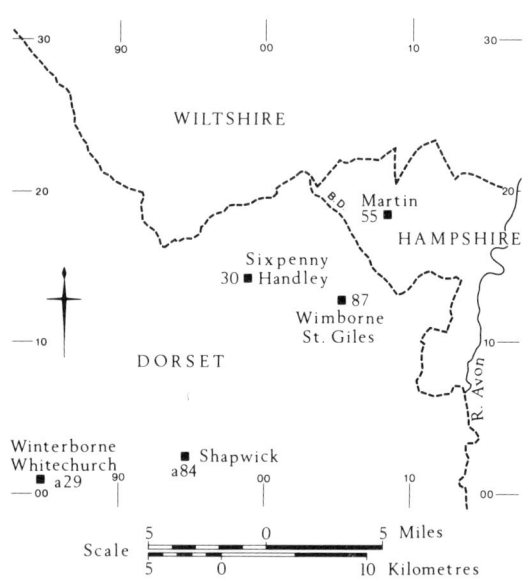

FIG 43 Distribution of some probable Iron Age barrows in Hampshire and Dorset (1:500,000)

gaps (cf, pages 7–8). Second, even though abandoned, levelled and possibly built over, ditches will generally remain the most prominent feature on air photographs while, conversely, the larger of them can have caused the total destruction of earlier, slighter features on the same line.

Definition precedes recognition. An enclosure is clearly a bounded area, most of those known about in this area being ditched; frequently, all traces of banks have disappeared and any that might have been defined by no more than scraped-up banks will almost all have been ploughed out of existence. In normal archaeological parlance, an enclosure will be intended to contain human habitation, stock or small-scale crops, as in the equivalent of gardens or orchards. It might be for burial or ritual, though the term will normally exclude some relatively small features (already defined, like ditches girdling barrows), arable systems such as 'Celtic' fields and some very large areas that become 'enclosed' because bounded by linear ditches. Occasionally there will be doubt as to whether a ditched surround belongs to a barrow or to some enclosure of a different date put around it. Ditches of different date may, of course, link up to form totally 'false' enclosures (as, probably, some in Pentridge (15)).

Unless there is obvious surface debris, excavation alone can adequately prove that an otherwise featureless enclosure was a settlement, ie, primarily for human habitation. Allowance has to be made for such compounds as rick and stockyards built in certain areas specifically because the managing settlements were so distant; also for quickly abandoned features, built for *ad hoc* purposes – a category which includes emergency military works – of all periods. There is little doubt that most enclosures were either part of a settlement or lie so close to it that the distinction is immaterial. Size is at least as important as shape, and the illustrations to this discussion are divided into groups

first by shape and then further subdivided by area (acreage). The details are given in the captions to Fig 46 (*see* page 91). The information, it must again be stressed, is incomplete in almost every sense, but insofar as the visible enclosures are concerned, certain observations can be made.

Shape

Shape (and size) are important because they reflect some sort of original intention to answer a particular need or needs in a way likely to follow the custom within a particular group or tradition.

It is not always clear, however, what the true shape was, and for this there may be a number of reasons apart from differences in modern treatment of the ground or in air photographic performance (as noted, pages 6–8 above). The clearest problem is set by incompleteness. The enclosure may have been unfinished, as surely the Mistleberry hill-fort (Sixpenny Handley (25)), or never meant to be more than partly bounded by a ditch; in the latter case, the remainder may have been fenced, as shown by Mr M T Green in Gussage St Michael (a 49) (Green 1979; *see also* Tabulated Inventory available from the Royal Commission), but perhaps elsewhere so impermanently with *ad hoc* arrangements of wattle hurdles as to leave no detectable trace whatsoever (and cf the gaps in Martin (62) a, Fig 44). The ditched arcs in Martin (68) or Rockbourne (47) and the 'angle ditches' like Pitt-Rivers' prototype by Wor Barrow (Sixpenny Handley (29)) might have been either, but the unexcavated and very curious pattern on Muston Down (Winterborne Whitechurch) (RCHM 1970b, 343: 'Celtic' field group 66) suggests something more permanent there. The most challenging fourth side in the area is the line of three barrows completing the trapezoidal enclosure Rockbourne (54) b. Scraped-up banks (such as that noted by Mrs Molly Cotton around part of 'Robin Hood's Arbour' in Berkshire (Cotton 1961)), totally removable in time by ploughing and so on, might sometimes have been used. Nothing was found by Pitt-Rivers to account for the gaps in Martin (56). A more complex problem arises with enclosures displaying more than one 'compartment'. Rockbourne (52), by 'Duck's Nest', is one such. The overall shape is parallel-sided with two rounded ends. If the ditch bisecting the enclosure marked the limit of an original enclosure, before it was extended, then it was of a different, almost 'tombstone' form. But, conceivably, it was intended from the start to have two compartments; there, as in so many other instances, excavation might provide an answer. Some enclosures, as noted in the analysis of types (pages 88–96 below), were certainly, whether from first origins or not, provided with complementary parts.

Size

The size of the enclosed area and of the bounding feature clearly relates to purpose as well as to scale. For instance, a small enclosure of 1 hectare (almost 2½ acres) like Mistleberry was intended to have true defences of hill-fort proportions, while the largest of all enclosures in our area, Rockbourne (54), had

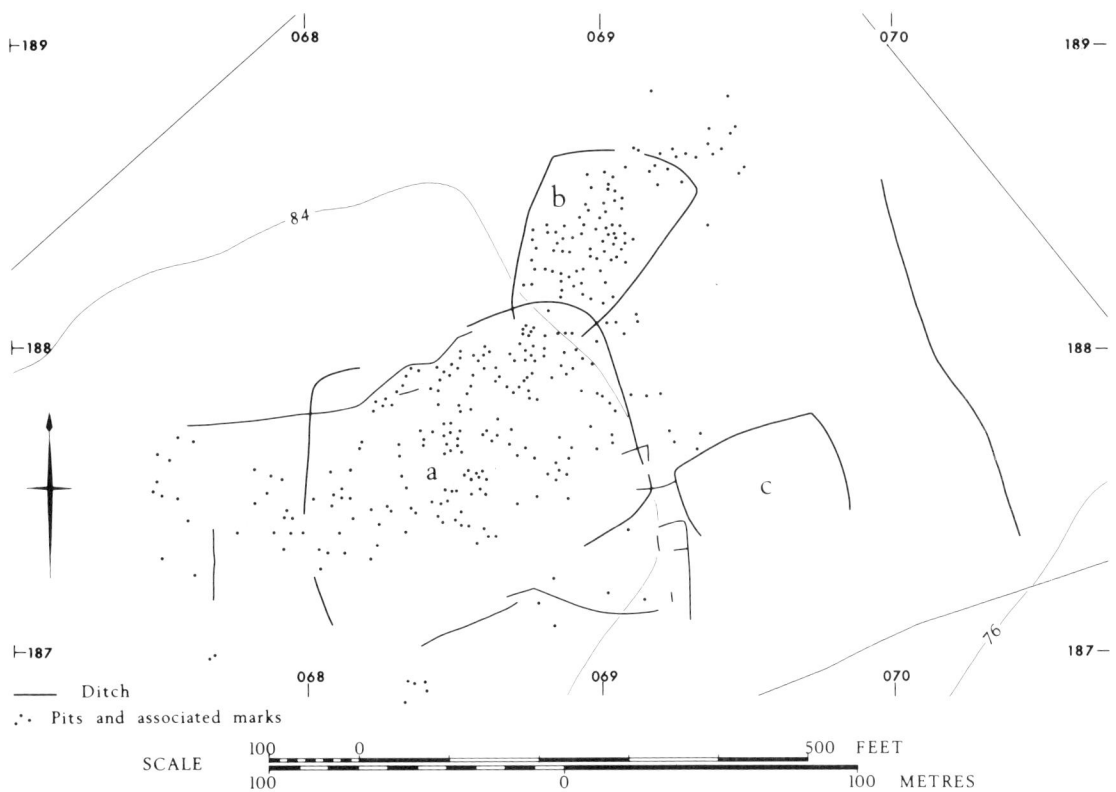

FIG 44   Plan of Martin (62) (1:2,500)

relatively slight but interestingly complex bounds, conjecturally best suitable for the containment of animals; its overall shape is likely to be connected to its purpose since it, like Damerham (19), was presumably arranged (as were some medieval deer pales) to take in the valley head as well as parts of the surrounding higher ground.

Features

These may occur and recur but only in a few instances (such as the 'necked' entrances to 'banjo' enclosures) can they be built in to a scheme of 'types'. As curious as the wide gaps already referred to is the quite certain lack of any break on some perimeter ditches (cf, Rockbourne (47) A), while remembering that impeccable air photographic evidence is needed to be sure of the absence of a gap (cf, Plate 33, Rockbourne (56)). It might be suggested that in those instances there was a bridge, possibly a cattle grid, at the entrance, in which case a break in the pattern of any occupation marks, pits and the like, might suggest its position. Alternatively, it could, presumably, be a moveable – or multiple – feature. The important question of the position of bank or banks relative to ditch is one that frequently cannot be resolved but, again, the distribution of pits (always allowing for intersection with features of an earlier or late 'open' settlement) can sometimes point to it.

Some features may not be homogeneous. The long, narrow enclosures 'tacked' on to enclosures of medium size, around 1.5

hectares (3½ acres) (Tarrant Hinton (20), Martin (58) (Fig 45) or Martin (66)) may be quite different in nature, but – allowing for the fact that some long narrow features might represent straightforward enlargement (for example, Damerham (18) A (*see* Fig 29)) – they suggest that there could be a common function. An apparent example recently excavated in Northamptonshire was suggested to have been for ritual (*Current Archaeology* 1984, 199). Test excavation of the extraordinary long mound associated with Martin (66) would help in this area. It would be tempting to suggest that these were the sites of rubbish tips (since pits were presumably filled from rubbish dumps) were the mound not on the prevalently windward side of the settlement. The odd, amorphous, mound on the north edge of Martin (63) on Tidpit Common, apparently not ditched, similarly merits a test excavation. (Some round mounds could perhaps be associated with settlement activities (eg, at Woodcutts, Sixpenny Handley (19) or, possibly, Damerham (16)).) The dark smears on air photographs, apart from those due to a patchy spread of natural clay or gravel, could mark rubbish spreads, the detritus from stacks or miskins or working areas or, occasionally, the sites of houses. Discs up to 3 metres or so across usually represent pits, mostly for storage. There are also very regular round discs, some of them 10 metres across; that in Martin (67) appears additionally to be ditched (cf, the 'house' in Damerham (18) B). Such relatively large solid discs could otherwise, for instance, perhaps be the sites of ponds (Rockbourne (47) A has relatively

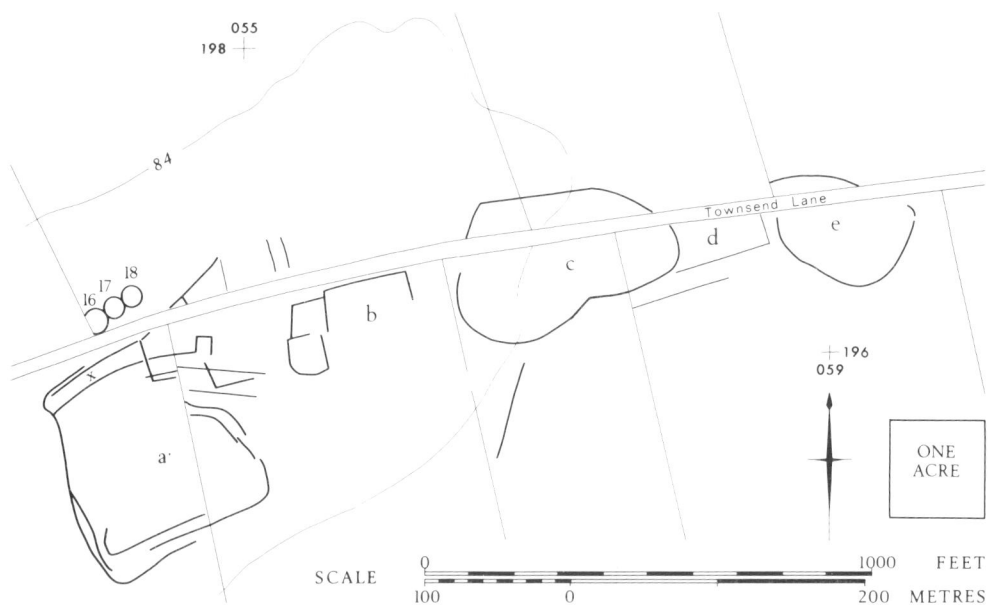

FIG 45 Plan of Martin (58) with round barrows (16), (17) and (18) (1:5,000)

few pits, perhaps suggesting a stock enclosure complementing the Roman settlement more apparent in (47) B, but pits do not necessarily rule out stock, cf, 'banjo' enclosures, page 99 below). All such marks may occur with or without enclosures, or overlap them. A concentration inside an enclosure suggests a rough contemporaneity.

Other features associated with enclosures (and linears) include protuberances (Tarrant Hinton (19)), and these are presumably related to huts or pounds of some sort. More puzzling is the apparent need for curved or straight sides noted in the types suggested below. Annexes are otherwise also noted. One particular suggestion is ventured here: Gussage All Saints (20) certainly had 'antennae' with ditches considerably greater than the settlement behind; some air photographs suggest a similar situation in Gussage All Saints (a 64) (Plate 41). The barricade of sharply angular triple ditches fronting Gussage All Saints (a 65) (Plate 42) suggests that an impressive façade was the ruling motive there too, but this time conceived in quite a different form.

Shape types

In the following discussion, topography or geology are not much considered, and Fig 46 (concerned only with morphology) which complements this account shows no contours.

The angle of a corner, sharp or rounded, and the lie of a side, the position of an entrance, was a matter of choice. Certain shapes and sizes thus suggest themselves by repetition to be deliberate and to have a meaning worth looking for, though not pursued far in this volume. Acknowledgement of a type or characteristic form can also lead to recognition where otherwise it might be missed or not further investigated (*see*, for instance, 'banjo' enclosures below). Categorisation is by shape:

differences in size may be critical but cannot be explained. The less regular examples are placed at the end of a given category. Even some of these display curiously repeated features (eg, Pimperne (17) and Martin (58) C). The following rough grouping is suggested.

a) *Rectangular and trapezoidal* enclosures which, with few exceptions, are of small size (Fig 46a). The notable exceptions are Hod hill-fort, Stourpaine (11), covering 21 hectares (52 acres) and the largest hill-fort in Dorset, whose shape is at least partly determined by the configuration of the hill it surrounds, and the 3.75-hectare (9-acre) enclosure on Oakley Down, Wimborne St Giles (36), Iron Age and Roman, only roughly rectangular but sufficiently so to make it stand out. Its undoubtedly integral annexe increases its area to almost 5 hectares (12 acres). Three in Dorset are linked to local linears. Martin (56) and Gussage St Michael (a 49) are Middle Bronze Age, as is the not distant 'South Lodge' enclosure, just in Wiltshire (SU 954174), so there must now be a suspicion, here as elsewhere, that smaller rectangular enclosures are quite likely to be Bronze Age (Sixpenny Handley (18) reminding us that this is not a rule).

b) *Small polygons* of 0.4 hectares (1 acre) or less (Fig 46b). (Two very large ones, 'kites', embodying angles and curves, are noted at the end of this Section (Fig 46k).)

c) *Tombstone or D-shaped* enclosures have a 'flat' (straight) 'base', parallel sides and a gently rounded (segmental) head, perfectly expressed in Gussage St Michael (7) h and only roughly so in others put into this category (Fig 46c). The 'D' shape is only ever approximate. The essential features are seen in large and small examples, eg, Damerham (18) A and B. Rockbourne (55) is assumed to have been complete (or 'completable') in some form partly because of this model. The

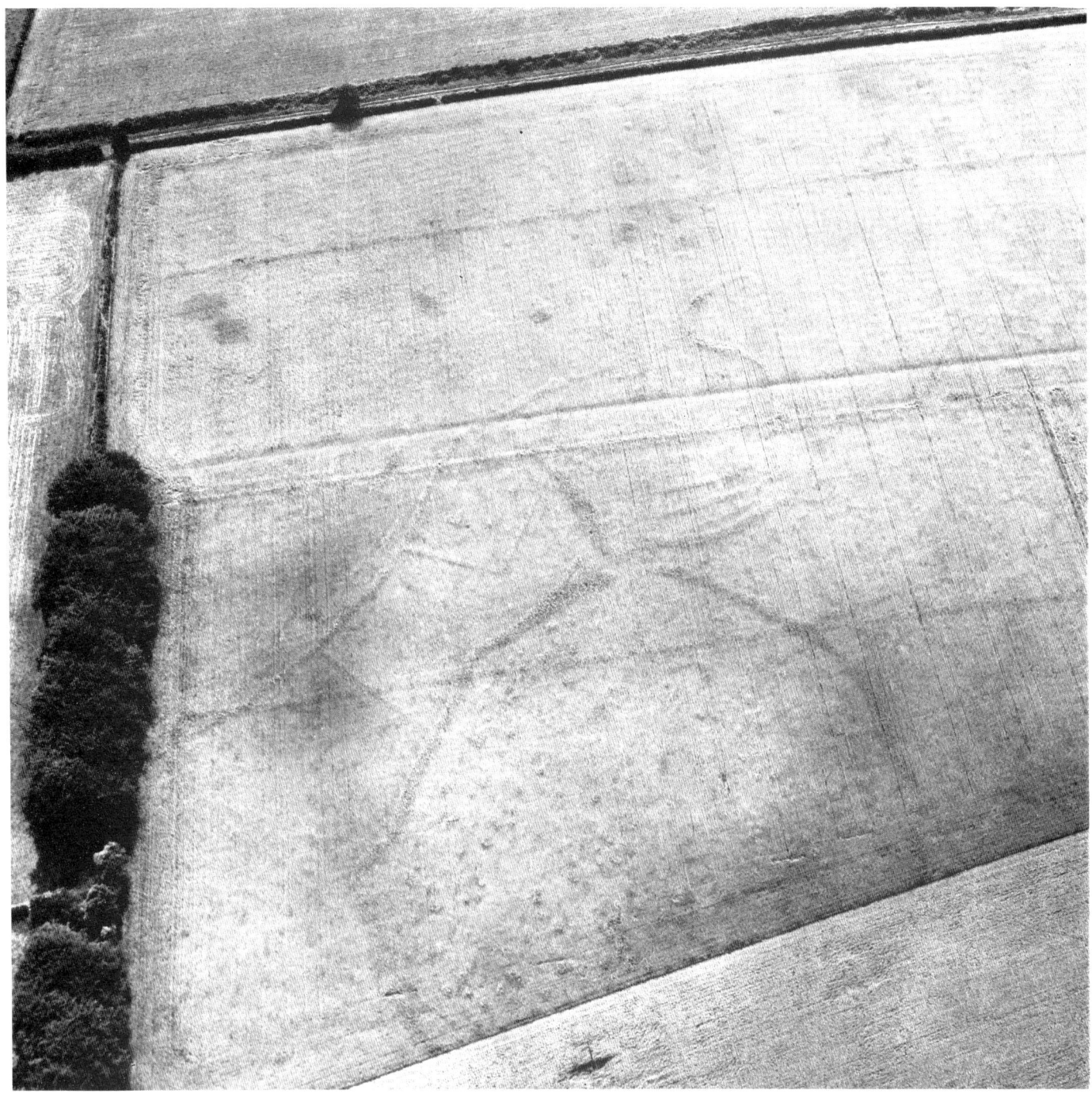

PLATE 41 Gussage All Saints (a 64) under crop. An oblique air photograph from the north west, showing 'antennae' from the entrance (cf, Gussage All Saints (20)), clearly distinguishable from the later rectilinear pattern of ditches (cf, Area Plan 2). (NMR OAP SU 0011/11; © John R Boyden)

PLATE 42 Gussage All Saints (a 65). An oblique air photograph from the east, taken by Mr M T Green and showing detail of the elaborate 'façade' (reproduced by permission of Martin T Green: copyright reserved).

probable first stage of Rockbourne (52) would have fitted the category.

A kindred type has one straight flat side and is very roughly semi-circular otherwise, sometimes called D-shaped. Another similar type of enclosure is:

d) *parallel-sided and double round-ended* (Fig 46d).

e) *Ovoid* enclosures markedly narrower than long: numbers are around 0.4 hectares (1 acre) in size, others up to 5 hectares (12 acres) (Fig 46e). Some contain pits, showing an Iron Age phase, and one large excavated example, Pimperne (15), contained a big house of that period.

f) There are many *sub-circular* enclosures, or enclosures of more or less consistent diameter covering between 0.8 and 2 hectares (2 and 5 acres), to some of which there are special reasons for

attaching particular importance (Fig 46f). They include Gussage All Saints (20), (a 64) and (a 65) with 'antennae' (*see* below), Penbury Knoll (Pentridge (18)), Tidpit Common (Martin (63)), Damerham Knoll (Rockbourne (46)) (these last three in relatively dominant positions) and the probably unfinished defensive works Mistleberry Wood (Sixpenny Handley (25)) and Spetisbury Rings (Spetisbury (30)).

At least two curiosities occur in this small display: the irregular and seemingly asymmetric east side of Gussage All Saints (20), possibly at one time enlarged to near-circular shape by much slighter bounds, and the extraordinary ditched façade to the otherwise irregular (a 65), inviting comparison, for this reason only, with the 'antennaed' (20) and (a 64).

g) *'Banjo' enclosures* are the most obvious of the repeated forms. Their particular size (small enclosures about 50 metres to 90

90

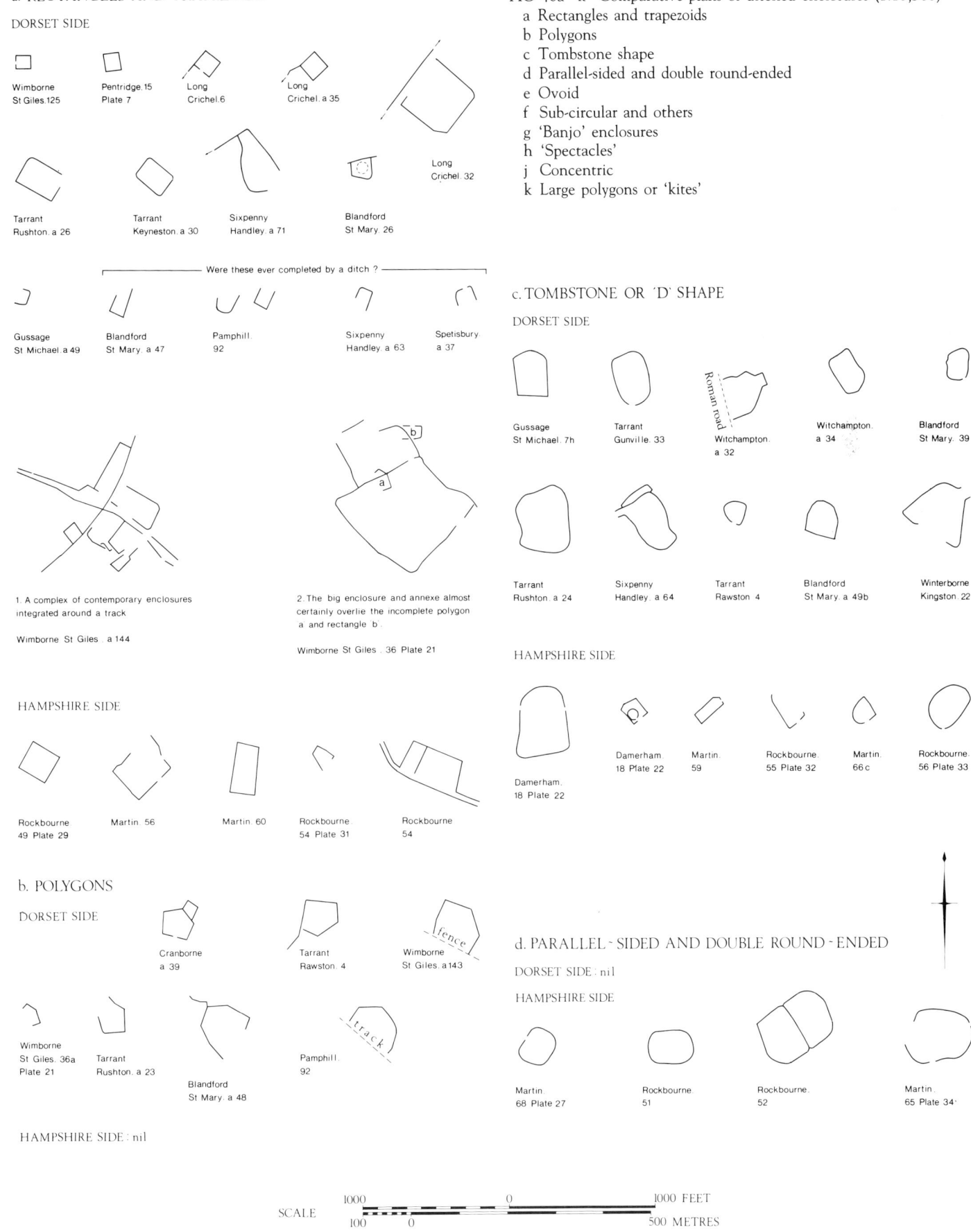

a. RECTANGLES AND TRAPEZOIDS

DORSET SIDE

Wimborne
St Giles.125

Pentridge.15
Plate 7

Long
Crichel.6

Long
Crichel. a 35

Long
Crichel. 32

Tarrant
Rushton. a 26

Tarrant
Keyneston. a 30

Sixpenny
Handley. a 71

Blandford
St Mary. 26

Were these ever completed by a ditch ?

Gussage
St Michael. a 49

Blandford
St Mary. a 47

Pamphill.
92

Sixpenny
Handley. a 63

Spetisbury.
a 37

1. A complex of contemporary enclosures
integrated around a track

Wimborne St Giles . a 144

2. The big enclosure and annexe almost
certainly overlie the incomplete polygon
a and rectangle b .

Wimborne St Giles . 36 Plate 21

HAMPSHIRE SIDE

Rockbourne
49 Plate 29

Martin. 56

Martin. 60

Rockbourne.
54 Plate 31

Rockbourne.
54

b. POLYGONS

DORSET SIDE

Cranborne
a 39

Tarrant
Rawston. 4

Wimborne
St Giles. a143

Wimborne
St Giles. 36a
Plate 21

Tarrant
Rushton. a 23

Blandford
St Mary. a 48

Pamphill.
92

HAMPSHIRE SIDE : nil

FIG 46a–k Comparative plans of ditched enclosures (1:10,560)

a Rectangles and trapezoids
b Polygons
c Tombstone shape
d Parallel-sided and double round-ended
e Ovoid
f Sub-circular and others
g 'Banjo' enclosures
h 'Spectacles'
j Concentric
k Large polygons or 'kites'

c. TOMBSTONE OR 'D' SHAPE

DORSET SIDE

Gussage
St Michael. 7h

Tarrant
Gunville. 33

Roman road

Witchampton.
a 32

Witchampton.
a 34

Blandford
St Mary. 39

Tarrant
Rushton. a 24

Sixpenny
Handley. a 64

Tarrant
Rawston 4

Blandford
St Mary. a 49b

Winterborne
Kingston. 22

HAMPSHIRE SIDE

Damerham.
18 Plate 22

Damerham.
18 Plate 22

Martin.
59

Rockbourne.
55 Plate 32

Martin.
66 c

Rockbourne.
56 Plate 33

d. PARALLEL - SIDED AND DOUBLE ROUND - ENDED

DORSET SIDE : nil

HAMPSHIRE SIDE

Martin
68 Plate 27

Rockbourne.
51

Rockbourne.
52

Martin.
65 Plate 34

SCALE

1000   0   1000 FEET

100   0   500 METRES

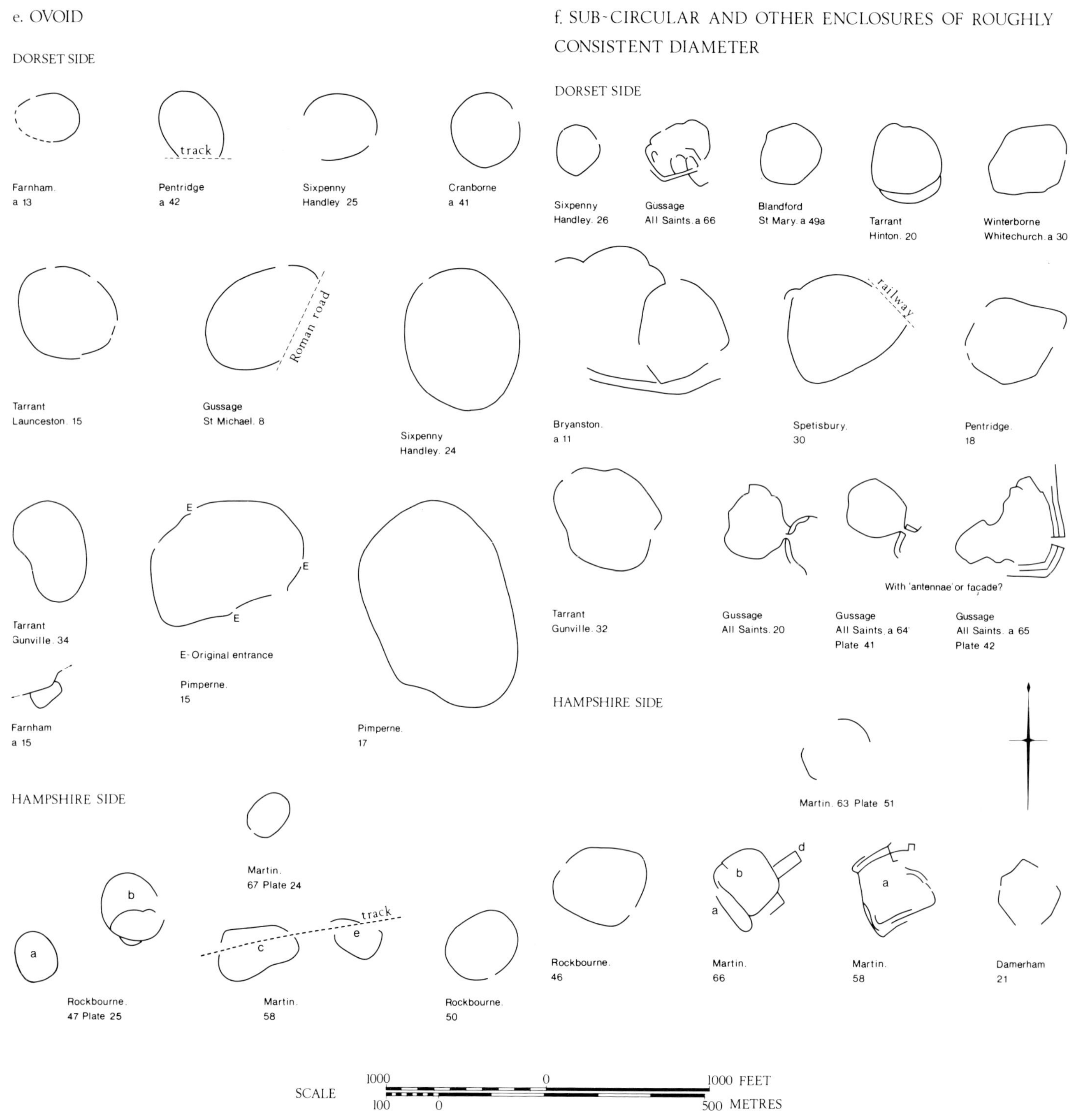

e. OVOID

DORSET SIDE

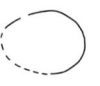

Farnham.
a 13

Pentridge
a 42

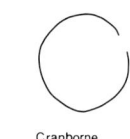

Sixpenny
Handley 25

Cranborne
a 41

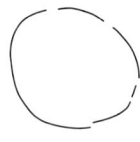

Tarrant
Launceston. 15

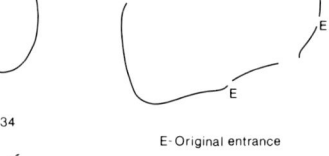

Gussage
St Michael. 8

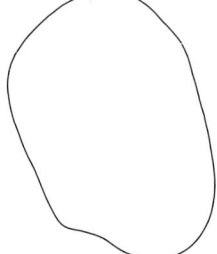

Sixpenny
Handley. 24

Tarrant
Gunville. 34

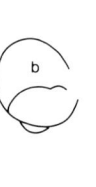

Farnham
a 15

E- Original entrance

Pimperne.
15

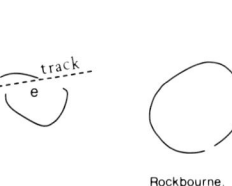

Pimperne.
17

HAMPSHIRE SIDE

Martin.
67 Plate 24

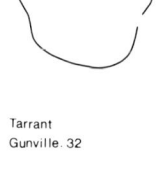

b

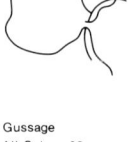

a

Rockbourne.
47 Plate 25

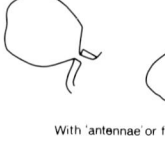

c

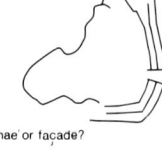

e

track

Martin.
58

Rockbourne.
50

f. SUB-CIRCULAR AND OTHER ENCLOSURES OF ROUGHLY CONSISTENT DIAMETER

DORSET SIDE

Sixpenny
Handley. 26

Gussage
All Saints.a 66

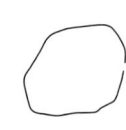

Blandford
St Mary. a 49a

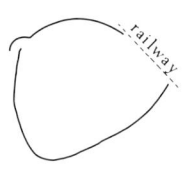

Tarrant
Hinton. 20

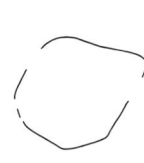

Winterborne
Whitechurch.a 30

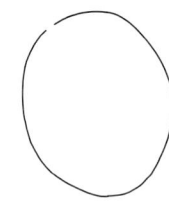

Bryanston.
a 11

railway

Spetisbury.
30

Pentridge.
18

Tarrant
Gunville. 32

Gussage
All Saints. 20

Gussage
All Saints. a 64
Plate 41

With 'antennae' or façade?

Gussage
All Saints. a 65
Plate 42

HAMPSHIRE SIDE

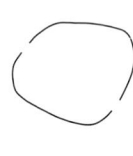

Martin. 63 Plate 51

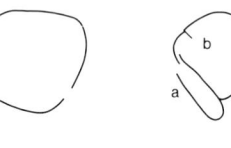

Rockbourne.
46

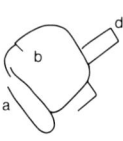

d
b
a

Martin.
66

a

Martin.
58

Damerham
21

SCALE

| 1000 | 0 | 1000 FEET |
| 100 | 0 | 500 METRES |

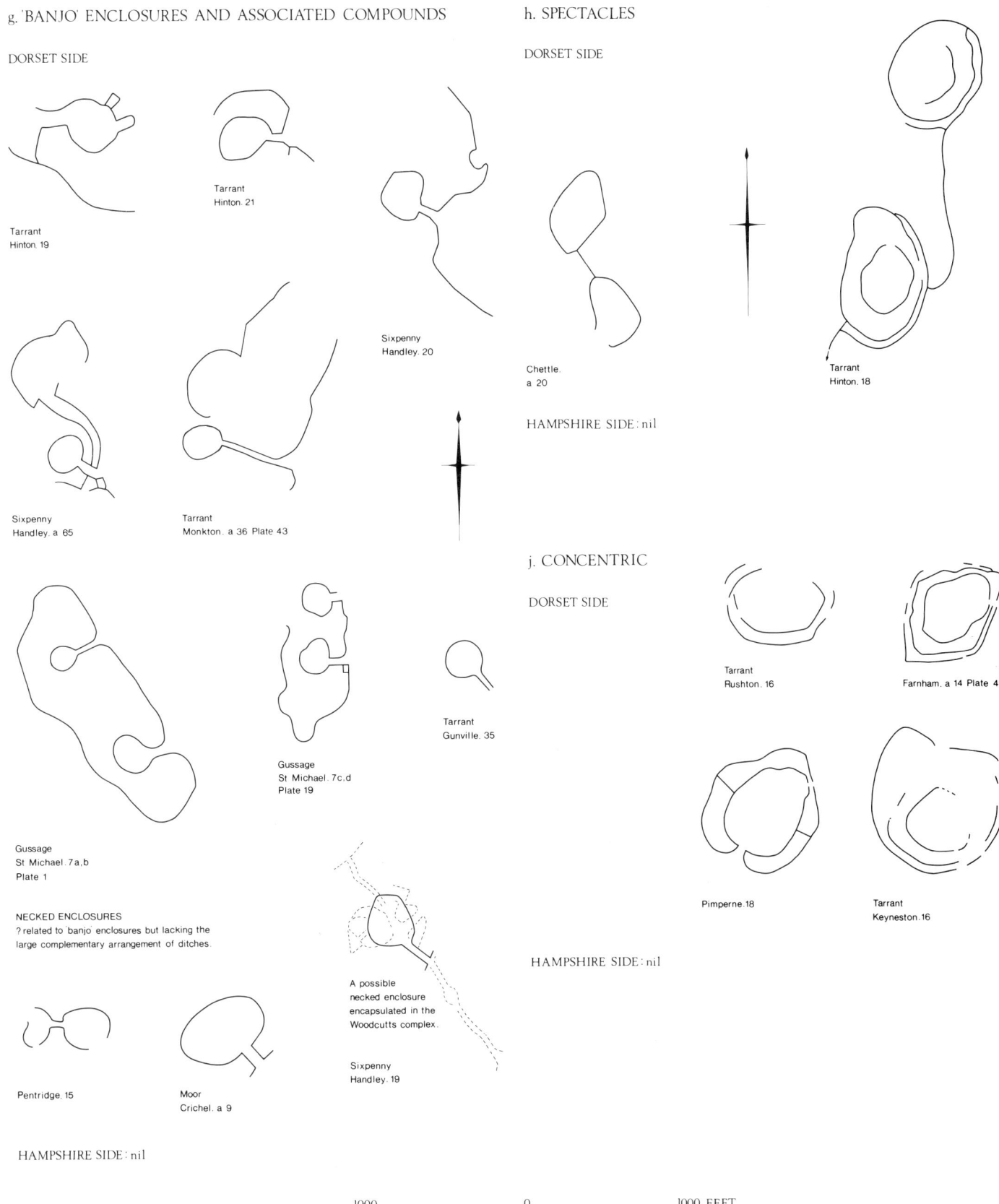

g. 'BANJO' ENCLOSURES AND ASSOCIATED COMPOUNDS

DORSET SIDE

Tarrant
Hinton. 19

Tarrant
Hinton. 21

Sixpenny
Handley. 20

Sixpenny
Handley. a 65

Tarrant
Monkton. a 36 Plate 43

Gussage
St Michael. 7a,b
Plate 1

Gussage
St Michael. 7c,d
Plate 19

Tarrant
Gunville. 35

NECKED ENCLOSURES
? related to 'banjo' enclosures but lacking the
large complementary arrangement of ditches.

Pentridge. 15

Moor
Crichel. a 9

A possible
necked enclosure
encapsulated in the
Woodcutts complex.

Sixpenny
Handley. 19

HAMPSHIRE SIDE : nil

h. SPECTACLES

DORSET SIDE

Chettle.
a 20

Tarrant
Hinton. 18

HAMPSHIRE SIDE : nil

j. CONCENTRIC

DORSET SIDE

Tarrant
Rushton. 16

Farnham. a 14 Plate 45

Pimperne. 18

Tarrant
Keyneston. 16

HAMPSHIRE SIDE : nil

SCALE

| 1000 | 0 | 1000 FEET |
| 100 | 0 | 500 METRES |

k. LARGE POLYGONS

DORSET SIDE: nil

HAMPSHIRE SIDE

(Hill-fort for comparison of size only)

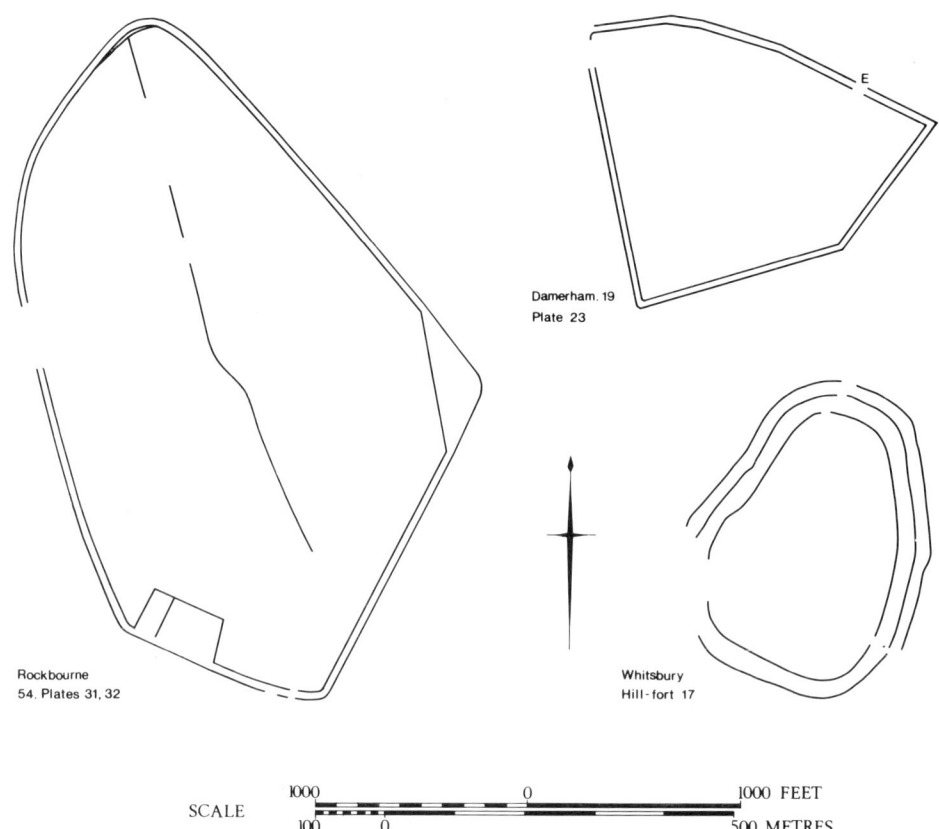

Damerham. 19
Plate 23

Rockbourne
54. Plates 31, 32

Whitsbury
Hill-fort 17

SCALE

1000   0   1000 FEET

100   0   500 METRES

metres in diameter) seems to be important or, it may be argued, they would not appear in pairs (Fig 46g). Similarly, the long, relatively narrow ('necked') approach way is surely functional and the great length of Tarrant Monkton (a 36) should help to resolve what it was (Plate 43). The shape and size together suggest, indeed, a use for stock processing of some sort. They are always, in this definition, associated with local ditch systems usually forming irregular enclosures; Gussage St Michael (7) provides a clear example. Other enclosures are, of course, frequently tacked on to others. 'Banjos' are frequently adjacent to, or overlain by, Roman settlement.

A 'necked' form roughly recalling the 'banjo' shape is also found, but it lacks the associated complex of recurved ditches and is, like Moor Crichel (a 9), generally larger.

The form of the small enclosure is variable but rounded in all certain examples. (The very small lozenge shape in Pentridge (14) (Plate 44), West Woodyates, is exceptional in all ways but has to be regarded as 'necked'.)

Recognition of the 'banjo' feature Tarrant Monkton (a 36) depends on the predetermined view of its character. Whether a 'necked' enclosure can be made of part of Pitt-Rivers' complex at Woodcutts, Sixpenny Handley (19), is a suggestion made graphically (in Fig 46g) at the end of this category.

h) *'Spectacles'* were first named by O G S Crawford to describe a site at Pewsey, north Wiltshire (Crawford and Keiller 1928, 224–6). The essence is a ligature connecting two rounded enclosures (Fig 46h). The complex Tarrant Hinton (18) is complicated by having both 'spectacles' and possibly concentric enclosures (Fig 47 and caption).

j) *Concentric*: the contemporaneity of the encircling bounds is reasonably indicated by the correspondence of entrances (Fig 46j). Pimperne (18) is further integrated by transverse ditches subdividing the outer space. Farnham (a 14) (Plate 45) is a telling example with a well, discovered by Mr M T Green, in the area compounded between the two ditches.

k) *Large polygons or 'kites'* There are two large enclosures in the part of Hampshire under study, 'Soldier's Ring', Damerham (19), and the 'Rockbourne Down Roman farm', Rockbourne (54), which Crawford included in his list of 'kite-shaped enclosures' (Crawford and Keiller 1928, 255–6). The comparable size, shape and situation of Soldier's Ring and an undated Wiltshire enclosure (SU 090382), which Crawford called the 'South Kite', are striking. Both, moreover, lie over 'Celtic' fields, but the bounding features are quite different in form. Rockbourne (54) has a similar kite shape but of three times the size. In all these instances it can be argued that the shape is the result of an intention to enclose a valley head or heads and low ground with water source(s) rather than to impose a geometric pattern on a piece of ground. The Rockbourne enclosure has a pair of parallel, wide-spaced ditches tucked against either side of a broad, low bank, giving quite a different profile from Soldier's Ring, although the actual ditch

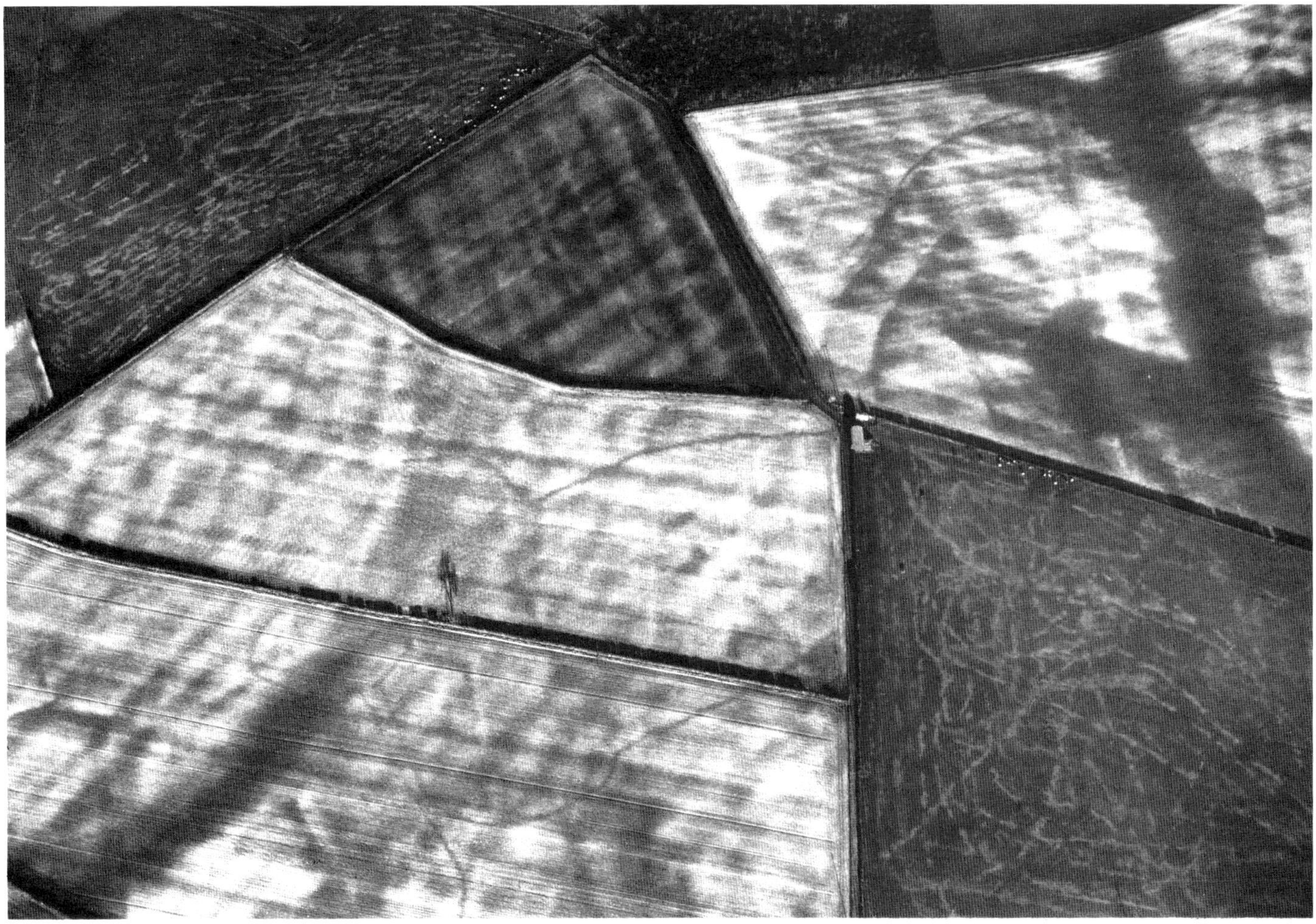

PLATE 44 Pentridge (14) adjacent to West Woodyates Manor. An oblique air photograph, with north to the left. The small, irregular quadrilateral enclosure, bottom left, has a long entrance way ('necked') recalling 'banjo' types. (NMR OAP SU 0119/22)

North

spacing is very similar. Technically, even the Rockbourne enclosure has now to be regarded as undated, since the Roman material found by Heywood Sumner could all have come from the substantial Romano-British settlement (53) which was crossed by the enclosure's ditches. The best working hypothesis, however, is still that 'Soldier's Ring' and 'Rockbourne Down' are of a very late date in the Roman period, the blocking of the local road system suggesting a depopulation of the countryside here.

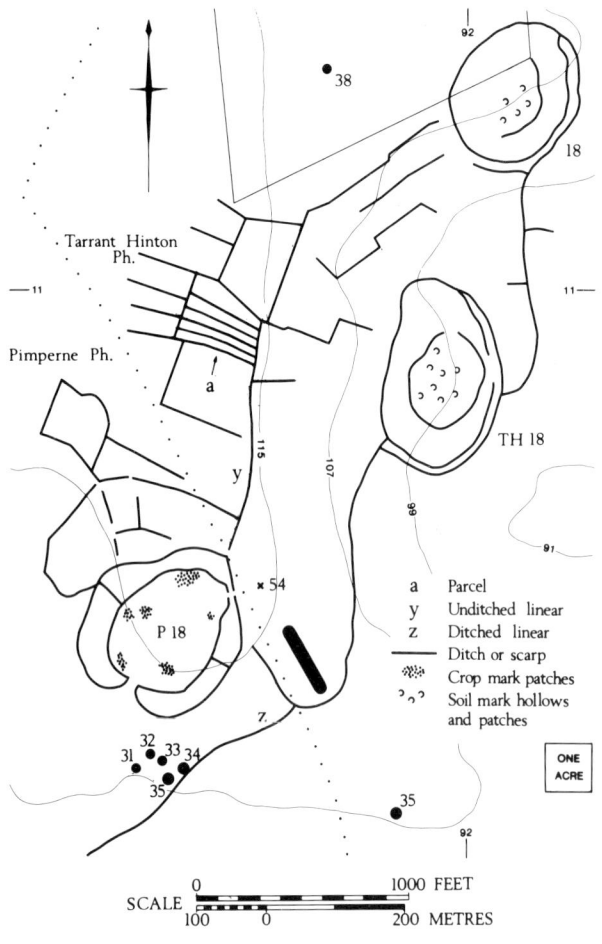

Tarrant Hinton Ph.

Pimperne Ph.

a   Parcel
y   Unditched linear
z   Ditched linear
—   Ditch or scarp
Crop mark patches
Soil mark hollows and patches

ONE ACRE

SCALE

0   1000 FEET
100   0   200 METRES

FIG 47 Tarrant Hinton and Pimperne Down (Tarrant Hinton (18) and Pimperne (18)). A revision of former plans, based on a close scrutiny of many air photographs, this plan is provided particularly to demonstrate a notable and subtle complexity that could too easily be dismissed as an area of 'Celtic' fields around a settlement.

Pimperne (18) appears to have become an integrated concentric enclosure with rare subdivisions while the ovals of Tarrant Hinton (18) may be enlargements from earlier enclosures markedly defined by zones of occupation: the ditched ligatures between all three enclosures may be related to the apparently unditched linear extending north from Pimperne (18), so forming a larger, irregular enclosure (possibly pastoral) (cf, Tabulated Inventory, see Editorial Notes). The 'parcel' of lines at 'a' was, at least partly, lynchetted (1:10,560)

There are no 'banjos', 'spectacles', concentric enclosures or multiple ditch runs in the area of Hampshire east of the Bokerley Line. That these features tend to go together as part of an economic, cultural package is strongly suggested, for instance, by the finding of multiple dykes and 'banjos' on the Grovely ridge in Wiltshire and the existence of concentric enclosures and 'banjos' north east of Winchester, much further away in Hampshire (Fig 48).

Some very small enclosures present particular problems. 'Small square enclosures' are discussed separately as possible Iron Age barrows (page 81). One, the 'square' in Pentridge (15), was apparently a late Roman burial compound. Others, roughly rectangular, occur among or near Bronze Age barrow groups (cf, Woodlands (23), Pamphill (a 105) or Wimborne St Giles (43)). Small clusters may be associated with settlement (Shapwick (a 87)). There are examples of small circular enclosures, plausibly each around a single house, either discrete before incorporation in a larger enclosure (Damerham (18) B) or independent after the apparent abandonment of a larger enclosure (Gussage All Saints (20)).

In contrast, there are some very large areas of settlement remains, the contemporaneity of which cannot be demonstrated but where the total size presumably reflects the suitability and therefore the probable long life and importance of the site. Martin (58) is a prime example. Pamphill (72) is another very large area but one where the components are much less clear.

Even more confusing are 'dispersed' enclosures where there is no obvious focus and where the enclosures themselves may be only partially exposed and not necessarily related.

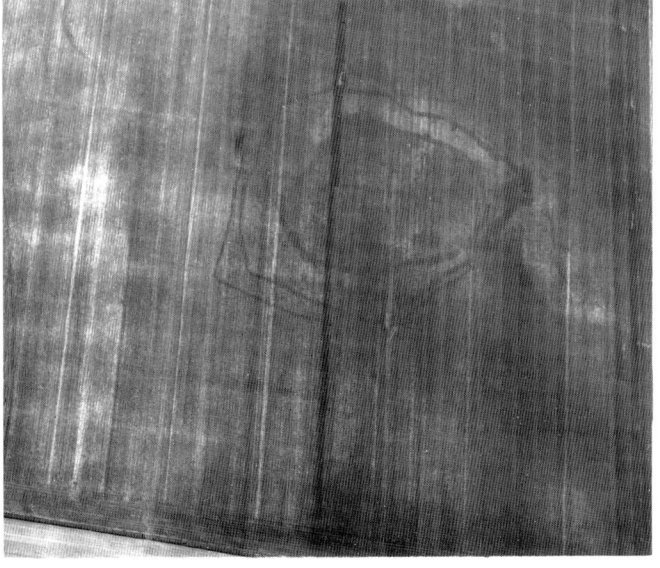

PLATE 45 Farnham (a 14): a concentric enclosure. An oblique air photograph looking north west. The inner enclosure has dark soil overall, with pits and other darker patches. A Roman well was discovered and dug by Mr Martin Green within the light-coloured band between the two further ditches on the photograph. The contemporary use of the inner and outer ditches is indicated by the coincidence of the entrance gaps. The outermost ditch, bottom left, with a notably angular bend opposite a more obtuse one in the second ditch, can just be seen, very faintly, continuing around at the top left. There are further thin ditches, apparently related to the outer ditch, to the top right. (NMR OAP ST 9515/6/274)

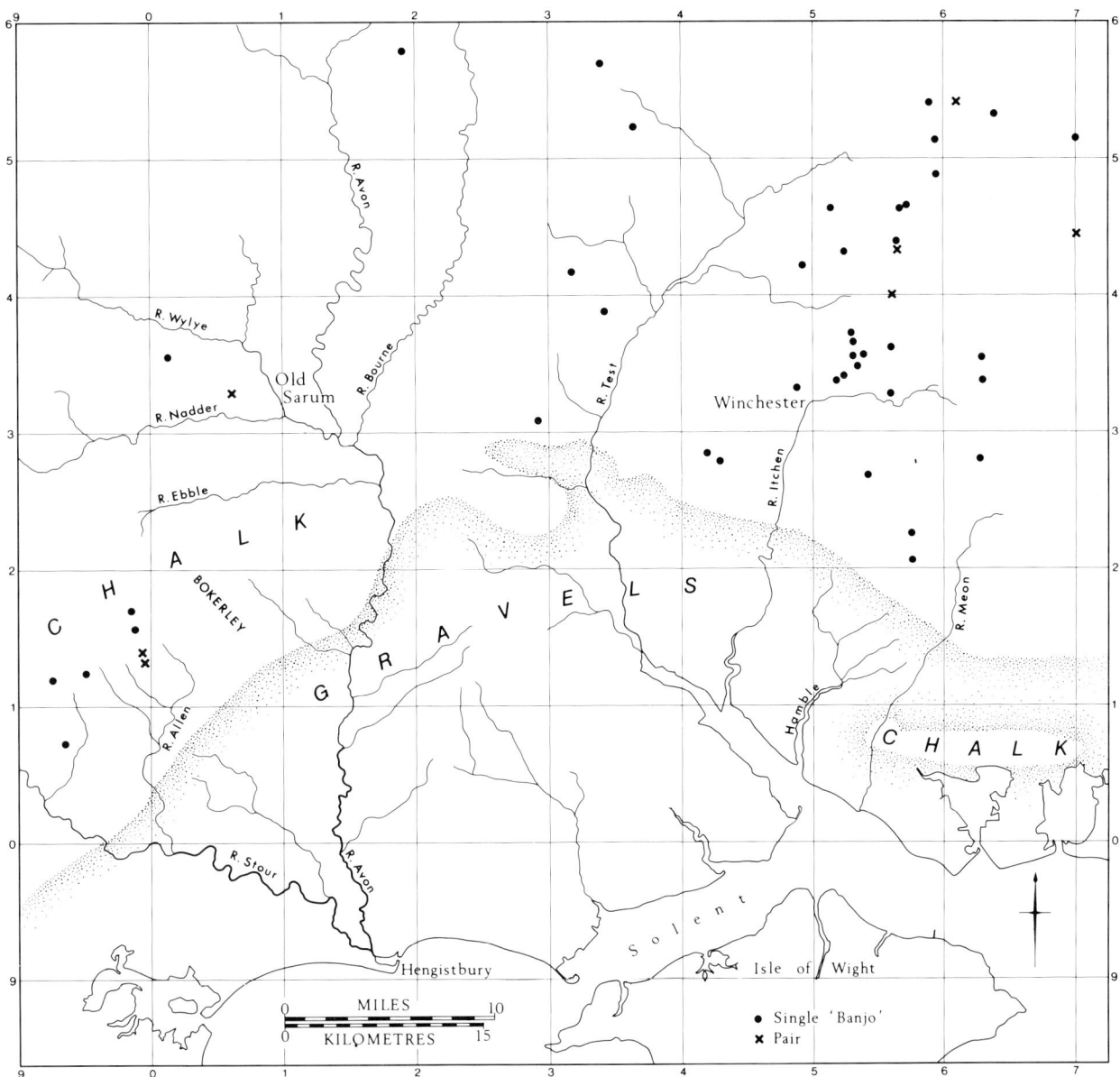

FIG 48   Distribution of 'banjo' enclosures in Hampshire, Dorset and Wiltshire (1:500,000)

Features and attributes found in 'settlements' and elsewhere

Some features of, or suggestive of, settlement recur in a variety of associations. They deserve noting and perhaps naming with a view to resolution of their nature and function and, in the context of this volume, whether they can be seen to occur on both sides of the Bokerley Line.

Bows

This term is applied to areas or segments of a circle with a chord of more than, say, 30 metres. Bows occur in settlements, for example, Gussage St Michael (7) (Area Plan 2); as deviations in the course of a linear, Martin (80) on Knoll Down (Area Plan 5); as part of a 'banjo' 'syndrome', Tarrant Monkton (a 36); in ditched runs among 'Celtic' fields (Plate 46: Nine Yews, Cranborne); or lynchetted among 'Celtic' fields (Oakley Down, Area Plan 3); or as discrete ditches close to settlement enclosures (Martin (68) or Rockbourne (47)). Even the rounded head of the category of 'tombstone-shaped' enclosures begs comparison. The so-called 'Church Barrow' by Woodcutts, Sixpenny Handley (19), re-illustrated here with necked enclosures (Fig 46g), surely a related form, remains unexplained despite partial excavation by Pitt-Rivers.

Within the scope of this volume the biggest and most obtrusive bow, with a chord of 350 metres, is that on Gussage Hill (Cow Down) in the Dorset parish of Gussage St Michael (Gussage St Michael (7)). Its purpose is not immediately

97

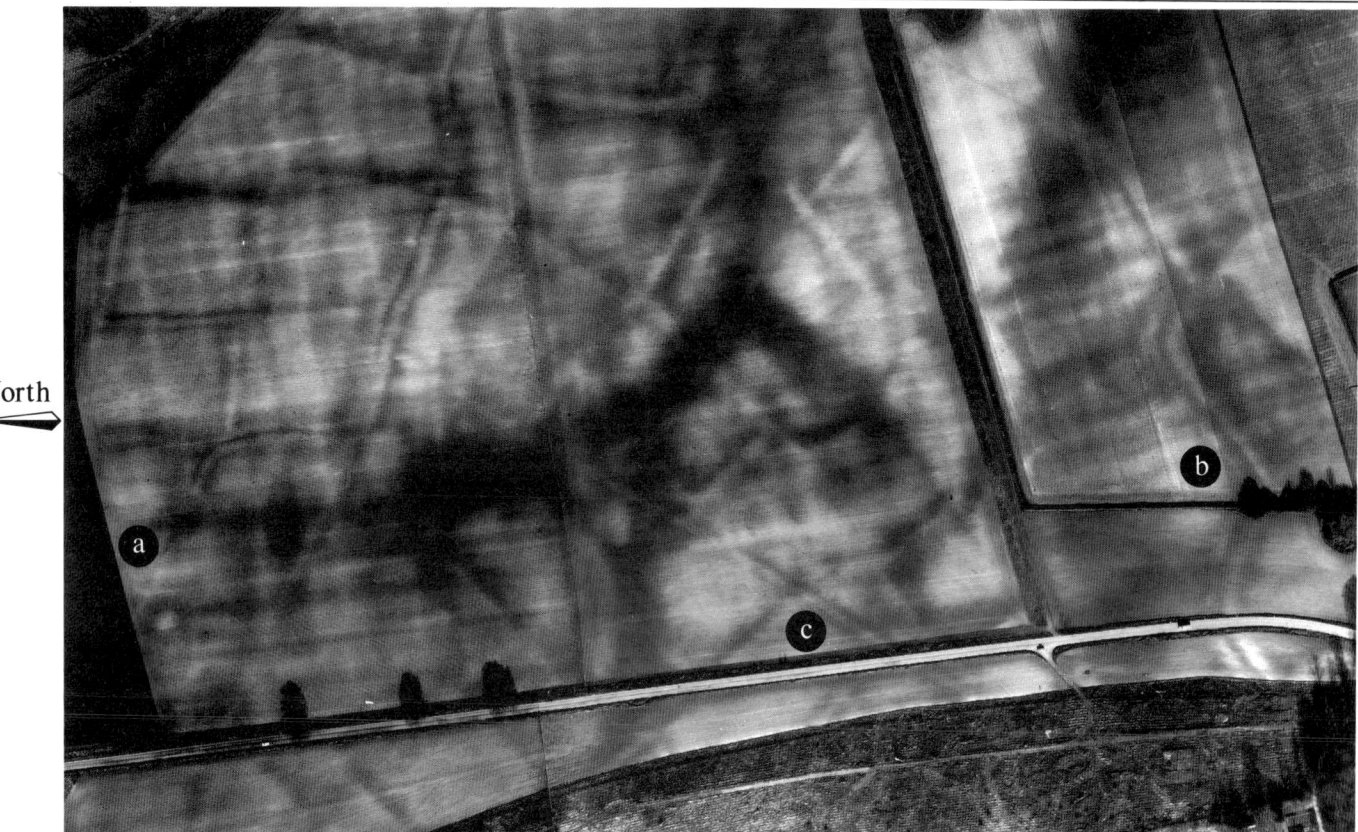

North

apparent but it is directly associated with one of the most extensive settlement areas, Bronze Age to Romano-British, in southern Britain (Area Plan 2). The ditches are multiple. The nearest comparison in terms of a single ditched bow is that on Knoll Down. Another abrupt change in line, but marking an angular loop towards a settlement (Iron Age and Romano-British), possibly giving entrance to it, is on Tidpit Common Down (Martin (63)) (*see* Fig 62).

Ditches following 'Celtic' field lynchets

Examples are found in 'Celtic' field group 85, around SU 0314 (*see* Plate 46), and at Winterborne Whitechurch (*see* Plate 39).

'Reserved' or 'blank' areas

These only suggest settlement if there are other reasons pointing to it, for example, tracks terminating abruptly or areas apparently free of 'Celtic' fields (as around Martin (56)), or a change in 'Celtic' field pattern (cf, Plate 46) and, occasionally,

apart from the ditched examples noted above, without a change in pattern. (On the south of Winterbourne Stoke Down, a 'Celtic' field surrounded a long barrow, again with 'open' side ditches that could never have been ploughed; cf, work in preparation on south Wiltshire by the Royal Commission.)

Parcels

Parcels of close-set parallel lines (cf, RCHM 1970b, 321; Bowen 1975, 109) are variable in form. The difference from 'normal' downland ridge-and-furrow is seen on Plate 21 (Oakley Down, Area Plan 3). Most are integrated with 'Celtic' fields or set tight by prehistoric or Roman settlement (eg, Rockbourne (47) on Area Plan 5). Occasionally the divisions are known to be, or have been, lynchetted. The little block within the complex arrangements on Tarrant Hinton Down (*see* Fig 47) is one such. Until individual examples can be closely examined, it is only possible to guess that at least some of these 'parcels' relate to special, small-volume, crops. Bundles of curved, roughly parallel lines are even less understood, for example, Pentridge (15) A.

Monument variations east and west of the Bokerley Line

This investigation of five Hampshire parishes east of Bokerley, together with the reinvestigation of a larger area of Dorset west of Bokerley in support of the current work on the Dyke, has confirmed that there are indeed major differences in ditched land allotment patterns on the two sides as well as a notable number of variations in other monumental forms.

Of all these differences the one displayed most clearly is the existence of very long linears widespread only east of the Line. These are not local (as some of the other differences may be) since there is a sufficient spread of them across Hampshire, into Berkshire and parts of Wiltshire to substantiate the assumption that a Wessex linear ditch system of a distinctive sort existed beyond the limits drawn by the Bokerley Line (cf, Bowen 1978, 122).

West of the Line there is only one complex — and that in an isolated though large area — to be considered as rivalling the very long ditches of the Wessex system (Area Plan 2). It is, however, essentially different from the Wessex system in that its ditches are largely multiple (or 'multi-stranded') and appear to be directly related to 'banjo' enclosures. Multiple ditches of a comparable sort and 'banjos' occur north of the exceptionally long Martin (69), on the Grovely ridge in Wiltshire (cf, Crawford and Keiller 1928, 97—9 and 120—2) and suggest, at the least, a Durotrigian influence in that area. (Little more is said of Wiltshire in this volume (except where Martin (69) and Whitsbury (22) enter that county) because of continuing Royal Commission field investigation in the county.)

Of other differences there are, among round barrows for instance, no disc barrows between Bokerley and the River Avon, but the only distinctive barrow arrangement so far found exclusively on one side of Bokerley (the east) is that here loosely described as 'ring-and-tongue' (see page 81).

What is most apparent, in the Iron Age, is that on the west side there is a display of monuments so totally absent on the other, east, side as to indicate a broad relationship between them and so, it seems reasonable to suppose, indicates at the least different working methods separated by the Bokerley Line. Specifically, there are 'banjo', other 'necked', concentric, large ovoid, and linked ('spectacle') enclosures on the Dorset side, as well as the 'banjo'-related multiple linears (Fig 46). Other local differences may be much less significant: thus, there are no small polygonal enclosures east of Bokerley, and, west of it, no clear parallel-sided, double round-ended enclosures.

Prominent and contrasting 'sports' among the enclosures, Wimborne St Giles (36) (Area Plan 3), on the west, and the great polygons, east of Bokerley, Soldier's Ring (Area Plan 4) and Rockbourne Down (Area Plan 6), to the east, were probably in contemporary use at least in the late Roman period.

On the Bokerley Line, and close up to it, there are marked differences, some of which, however, may be due to the chances of past land treatment and present management. The high number of substantial settlements on the east side, in Martin parish in particular, is in marked contrast to the few poor examples near on the west side. Pentridge (15), the area of Bokerley Junction investigated by Pitt-Rivers, provides the most challenging problems. It appears to be split by the Bokerley Line and this unusual aspect in itself may indicate the importance of a crossing point from one territory to the other, the 'necked' enclosure Pentridge (15) A perhaps reflecting the cultural separateness of the west right up to the frontier.

Work on artifacts and so on might contribute further to a view of cultural differences but the biggest progress would come from the discovery of major new settlements or, possibly, from new excavation. (For suggested economic excavation on the Bokerley Line itself, see page 41.)

99

SUMMARY

In the Neolithic period, the Dorset Cursus dominated much of the parts of Cranborne Chase discussed in this volume. Many long barrows are directly associated with the Cursus, within their general distribution between the Dorset Stour and the Hampshire Avon (Fig 1). In the Bronze Age, round barrows occur both beside and inside the Cursus, but notable concentrations lie away from it, as around the henges at Knowlton Circles (Fig 40) or on Oakley Down (Area Plan 3). The large round barrow cemetery on Rockbourne Down appears to be focussed upon Spring Pond (Area Plan 6).

The marked change in the pattern of distribution between the long and round barrows is further emphasised by the Bokerley Line, which passes beside the eastern end of the Cursus and cuts across and breaks the Neolithic cultural zone. This study has shown that, probably from the Middle Bronze Age, the earliest recognisable linear strands in the Bokerley Line served as the western boundary of the Wessex linear ditch system. Bokerley Dyke itself appears to encapsulate a Bronze Age predecessor, for the linear Martin (73), which appears to terminate at the Dyke, abuts another linear, Martin (72), from which General Pitt-Rivers excavated exclusively Deverel–Rimbury pottery. Additionally, Martin (73) is apparently continued by linear (74), whose ditch also contained only Deverel–Rimbury potsherds. Martin (72) at its north end meets a spinal linear, Martin (69), and this too, therefore, may have Bronze Age origins, at least near this junction. A second spinal linear (Martin (80) B), however, in its first phase apparently ended to the east of the Bokerley Line. Subsequently, when it was re-aligned (Martin (80) A), it terminated at Bokerley, on Blagdon Hill. In this secondary phase, Martin (80) A incorporated an elongated round barrow (Martin (24)), probably of the early Bronze Age.

The spinal linears appear to bear no relationship to the hill-forts and this too hints at the early origin of the partition of the land. The eastern end of Martin (80) is unknown but its alignment suggests that it was making for a point north of Whitsbury hill-fort (17). The linear, Whitsbury (22), which makes a butt-junction with Martin (69), passes to the west of Clearbury hill-fort (its relationship to Whitsbury (17) is not established (Area Plan 7)).

Some of these linear ditches (eg, Martin (72) and (80)) crossed, and presumably, at least to some degree, put out of use, areas of 'Celtic' fields. The marked variations in the size of the spinal linears, as seen both in their surface profiles and excavated sections, argues for their adaptation over a probably long period of time. Some linears certainly continued in use during the Iron Age when, for instance, the 'bow' was made in Martin (80) on Knoll Down and an entrance was set through the same linear beside the settlement on Tidpit Common, Martin (63). Another clear example of an original gap in a linear is that seen in Martin (80) C, east of Damerham Ridge (Knoll Down, Area Plan 5).

The spinal linears to the east of Bokerley Dyke contrast sharply with the shorter lengths of the linears to the west of it, in Dorset (Fig 3). This indicates a fundamental difference in the division and, therefore, presumably, also in the organisation, of the prehistoric landscape on either side of the Dyke. To the west, most linear ditches occur in distinct localities, as around Badbury Rings (Area Plan 1) and Gussage Cow Down (Area Plan 2). At Badbury, one linear originated in the Bronze Age (Shapwick (35)); none of the linears is linked to the hill-fort. On Gussage Cow Down multiple linears are in direct association with 'banjo' enclosures (Gussage St Michael (7)) and, apparently, an Iron Age square-ditched barrow (Sixpenny Handley (30)). One multiple linear (Long Crichel (7)) is remarkable in that it both utilised the north ditch of the Cursus and, it appears, incorporated a ring ditch (Gussage St Michael (a 36)). The same Area Plan (2) also shows several enclosures which are attached either at the side (Farnham (a 15) and Long Crichel (32)) or, probably, at the end (Long Crichel (6), (a 35)) of single-ditched linears.

Some other distinctions between the west and east sides of the Dyke are also clear in the archaeological record. Thus, 'ring-and-tongue' barrows appear only to the east of Bokerley. The types of enclosed settlements also vary, most notably since concentric ditches, 'spectacles' and 'banjos' are restricted very largely to Dorset (Fig 46). The large kite-shaped enclosure of Soldier's Ring (Damerham (19)), which lies over 'Celtic' fields, and another on Rockbourne Down (Rockbourne (54)), over a Romano-British settlement, are exceptional and unparalleled on the west side of Bokerley Dyke. Each of these has been set here in the context of its surrounding landscape (Area Plans 4 and 6).

This volume includes new plans of prehistoric and Romano-British settlement sites on the Hampshire side of the Dyke. Many sites are known almost entirely from crop and soil marks in arable, little or no ground relief still remaining. However, parch marks in grass allowed a detailed survey of Damerham (18) and indicated its several phases of use. The settlement and 'Celtic' fields on Tidpit Common (Martin (63)) are a rare survival as earthworks in old grassland. Attention has been drawn to various mounds and ditched features which are found associated with the settlements and which require investigation. Particular reference should be made to 'parcels' of short lengths of curved and straight ditches, which have been recorded on either side of Bokerley Dyke.

Bokerley Dyke itself, in its final form, was shown by Pitt-Rivers, where he excavated it, to belong to the late Roman period or later. The later possibilities have been argued in this volume. Pitt-Rivers' work, and that of Professor Rahtz, has now *inter alia* been amplified by information obtained from air photographs. In particular, these have revealed an Iron Age settlement on the west side of the Dyke, adjacent to the Roman one at Bokerley Junction (Pentridge (15)) (Fig 10), and they have shown the Rear Dyke to be a local and discrete enlargement of an early, slight linear. These new results, here together with a rigorous reappraisal of Pitt-Rivers' own work, and an evaluation of the changing landscape on either side of the Dyke, combine to indicate the role of Bokerley Dyke and its predecessors as a boundary in both the prehistoric and later periods. The importance of the Dyke was already clear to Pitt-Rivers, who saw it as a racial frontier. Its significance is in no way diminished by its reinterpretation as a cultural boundary since, apparently, the Middle Bronze Age. Today, Bokerley Dyke remains a boundary, part of that between the counties of Dorset and Hampshire.

PART V

INVENTORY

Linears and associated settlements and enclosures in five Hampshire parishes east of Bokerley Dyke

Note

Linears are numbered according to the westernmost parish in which they are seen. As with other monuments discussed in this volume, they are generally referred to by the initial letter of the parish name followed by the number of the monument:

B Breamore
D Damerham
M Martin
R Rockbourne
W Whitsbury

In Dorset, P refers to Pentridge.

Thus, for example, M (80) B is Martin (80), described under that parish though parts appear in other parishes, and B is a definable element within M (80). All are shown on Fig 3, with numbers. The inventory of Martin begins with M (69), a Hampshire designation though it is first detectable to the west in Wiltshire in an area under investigation at the time of writing by the Royal Commission where the numbering of monuments has yet to be made final. It was first mentioned under Pentridge (17) (RCHM 1975) but the detailed description thereunder related to the linear which, in this volume, is given revised consideration, under the same number, as a major 'strand in the Bokerley Line' (cf, pages 13 (short analysis of 'Grim's Ditch') and 36 (Bokerley Line)). Where appropriate, additional air photographic references are included at the end of entries.

Breamore

(13) *Linear* shows as 300 m of close-set parallel ditches N from NGR 13751955, a little uphill of, and parallel to, Long Steeple Lane, possibly a winter road lane and conceivably linked to Whitsbury (25) (Area Plan 7).

NMR OAP SU 1319/6/77; 1319/7/85

(14) *Linear* extends for at least 110 m NNE from abutting linear W (24) at 13792019. (Area Plan 7 and Plate 47 (NMR OAP SU 1320/15/341); cf, RCHM 1979, Plate 13.) Its sinuous shape is akin to that of W (24).

Damerham

A possibly ancient hollow-way associated with ditches is poorly indicated on air photographs for some 300 m, probably terminating at 107175 (NMR OAP SU 1017/4/106). The linear (22) may have been marked by a ditch before becoming hollowed as a track. Fragments of linear ditch, some sinuous, apparently associated with 'Celtic' fields, occur on Blackheath Down N of Boulsbury Down around 073174 (NMR OAP SU 0717/12). Another line stems from the SW point of a bow in the line. For monuments (22)–(24) discussed below, *see* Area Plan 4.

(22) *Linear*, variously double-lynchetted, hollowed, and ditched, climbs SSE from 07851810, just within Martin parish, to the top of the ridge of the former 'Top Down' curving SW, and making for settlement (18) where one ditch partly crosses enclosure (18) A.

Plate 22 (NMR OAP SU 0717/42/164)

The linear has been heavily ploughed except for a short distance N of the parish boundary where a disturbed double lynchet on scrubby ground falls steeply to modern arable now without any sign of continuation. 'Celtic' fields spring from the hollow-way, their lynchets still up to 1.3 m high. On the ridge top the linear hollow is seen to be about 0.3 m deep. (For detail near the settlement, *see* page 57.)

Dating and relationships are complex. The linear was sectioned in 1971–2, just S of the parish boundary, by Mr R A Hills and members of the South Wessex Archaeological Association (SWAA). A shallow linear hollow 3 m wide by 0.15 m deep lay at the foot of a negative lynchet, probably indicating that some ploughing ante-dated the formation of the linear hollow. It seems likely that the ditch crossing (18) A was earlier than that enclosure; the northern ditch parallel with it for a short distance preceded enclosure (18) C although it was apparently attached to the probable house ring within it. Finds from the SWAA excavation included a La Tène I brooch and some seventy struck flint flakes, regarded by Dr Isobel Smith as late Neolithic/Early Bronze Age.

CUCAP OAP PH 3 and 4

(23) *Linear*, hollow-way and probable ditch, enters settlement

enclosure (18) A at NW, a scarp flanking it on the S. It is seen otherwise on air photographs as a dark line curving irregularly among 'Celtic' fields for some 600 m SW of the settlement (Plate 22).

CUCAP OAP BHJ 84 and PM 3

(24) *Linear* extends for some 400 m from about 076172 ENE towards the SW angle of Soldier's Ring but seems to deviate sharply and end some 130 m short of that point. It is partly marked by parallel slight ditches some 6 m apart.

NMR OAP SU 0717/17/375–6

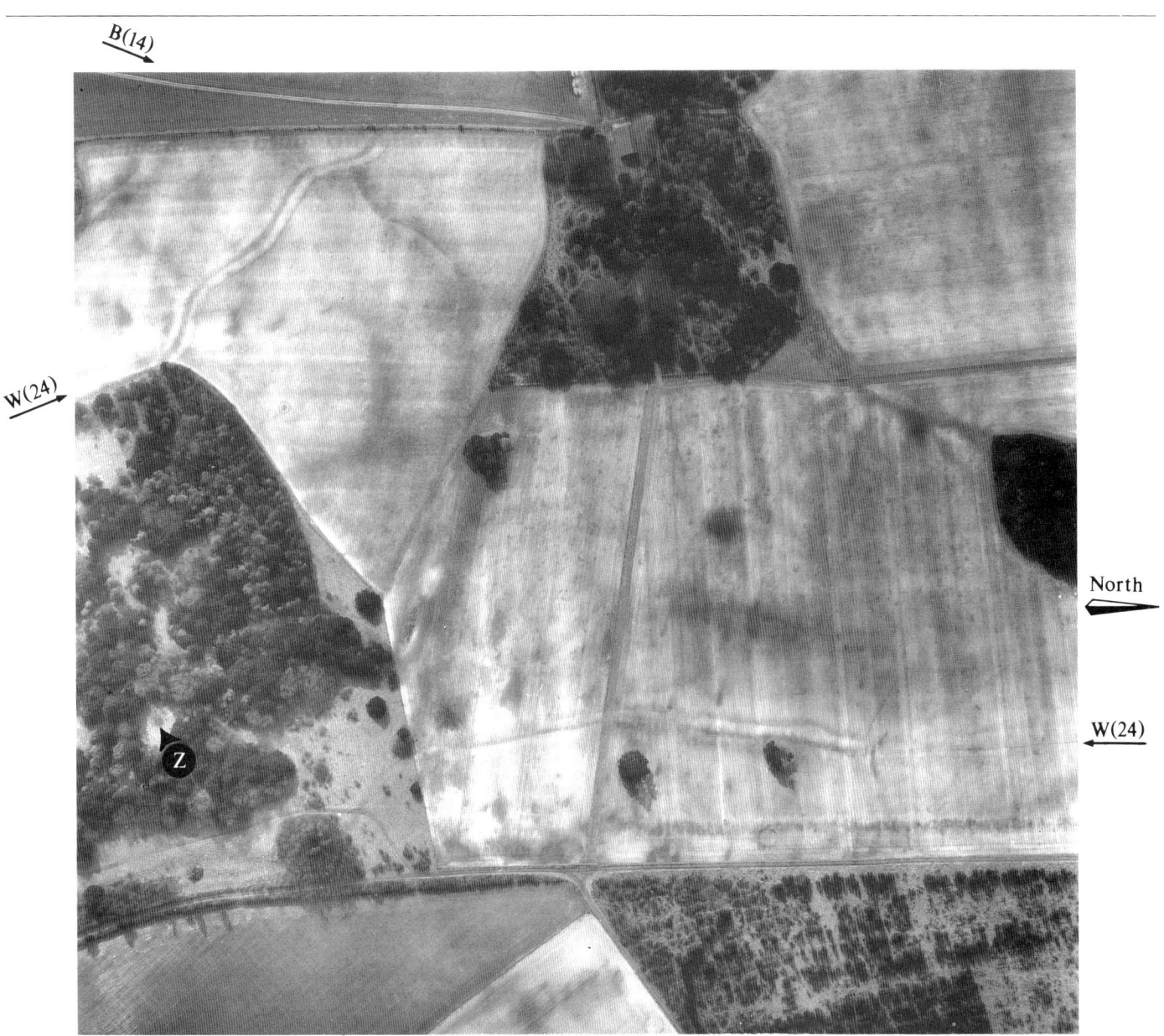

PLATE 47   Breamore, linears Whitsbury (**24**) and Breamore (**14**). A near-vertical air photograph centred about 140202, with north to the right, which complements Plate 13 in RCHM 1979. The apparent thin 'ditch' edging Whitsbury (24) on its north side is perhaps an accumulation of soil from uphill against the bank.
  The arrow labelled **Z** points to the Mizmaze on the hill encircled by Whitsbury (24) (Area Plan 7). (NMR OAP SU 1320/15/341)

(25) *Linear and other ditches* (101176) centred on the ridge SE of Knoll Farm consist of: first, a straight run of 300 m or more that ascends SW from the re-entrant N of the ridge to curve sharply W near the ridge top and probably (from less clear air photographic indications) continues on a parallel line downhill past ring ditches (10)–(14); second, a curved ditch line some 130 m long extending SE from a point 40 m SE from a sharp bend in the first line. These two curving lines would together form a rough semi-circle on the ridge top some 230 m across, suggesting the possibility of settlement.

NMR OAP SU 1017/4/102 and SU 0917/3/386

Martin

(69) *Linear* (00662025–14282320), the longest element of the traditionally so-called 'Grim's Ditch' (page 13), extends for about 14 km from near Middle Chase Farm in Bower Chalke, Wiltshire, to a junction with the linear Whitsbury (22) in Downton, Wiltshire, having otherwise passed through or bounded, in order from the west: Pentridge, Dorset; Broad Chalke, Wilts; Martin, Hants; Stratford Toney, Coombe Bissett and Odstock, Wilts; and Rockbourne and Whitsbury, Hants. Select detail is described by km squares below. About one third of its length is visible as an earthwork, relatively large as a linear but often much altered. The identity of the work as a single feature, suggested by its mean course, size, and the placing of any major bank usually on the N side, essentially depends, however, upon the assumption that it formerly continued unbroken for over 800 m under the Roman road, 'Ackling Dyke' (RCHM 1975, xxix–xxxv) (0421). Its apparent character

varies but this is partly due to its silted ditch having been used as a track (0421, 1022–1123). At the only point excavated the ditch was a relatively narrow 'V' (0922). West of the Roman road, the overall width tends to be less than that E of it. It is defined by double banks for part of its length, although both W of the Roman road (0220) and towards the E the original bank seems to have been on the N side. It crosses spurs and the heads of dry valleys in a variety of ways, rarely following a contour (cf, 0922). There are eight or nine near right angles in the run but no obviously consistent context for them. Other deviations and undulations, none of which can be safely explained but which challenge interpretation by excavation, are noted in the following select descriptions from west to east. (Cf, discussion of different 'behaviour', straight runs, right-angled bends, sharp angular or rounded or sinuous deviations, curved bows, flat bows, etc, page 11.)

(For 0020–0320 see Fig 1; VAP 58 RAF 3250, 0125–6; NMR OAP SU 0219/18 and 19)

DETAILED DESCRIPTION (BY KM SQUARE)

0020 Air photographs and the earliest large-scale OS maps show the ditch petering out at about 00662025 (Fig 49). Heywood Sumner drew it swinging NW from there to Middle Chase Farm (Sumner 1913, map after p 56). He says, however, that its course here, like most of that SW of Vernditch, is 'hardly discernible'. Colt Hoare indicated in his map for Fovant Station (1810, between pp 236 and 237, Station VIII) that this section of 'Grim's Ditch' did turn in a NW direction, but his plan of the work is otherwise demonstrably confused in this sector. The Ordnance Survey showed nothing of any curved section in its 1:2,500 survey of 1886.

0120 The short stretch in Denbose Wood is recorded as a shallow ditch 6 m wide (OS AM). The undulations in both the linear and Shire Rack E of this suggest a similar cause, possibly clumps of forest trees

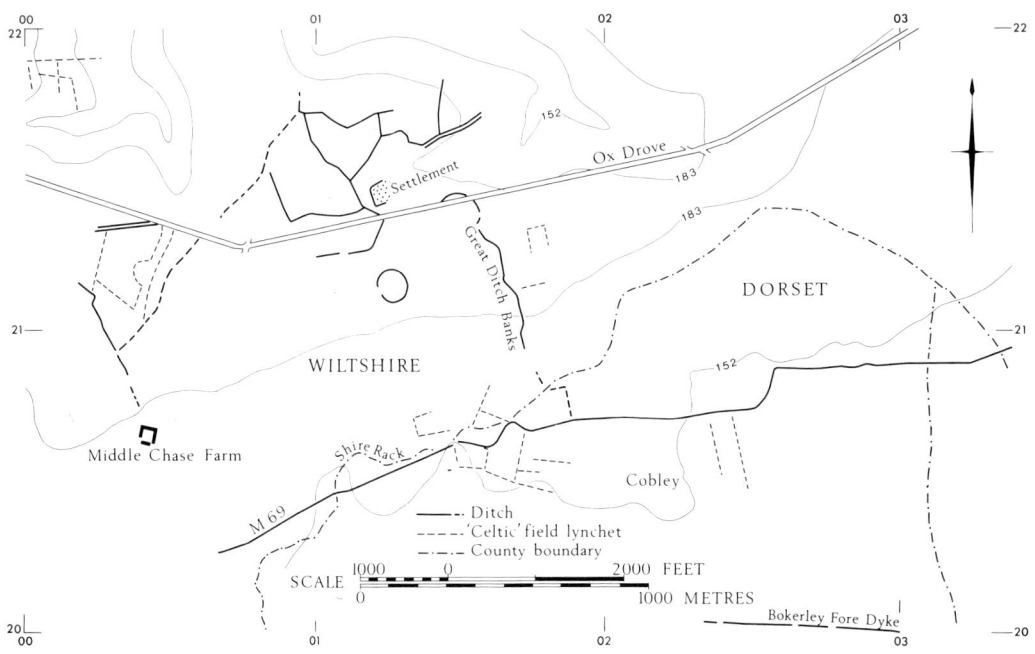

FIG 49   Plan of Martin (69) at its extreme west (1:25,000)

in an area with much clay over the chalk. A ditch, track or both spring from a gap in M (69) at 019207 to meet the Great Ditch Banks (Plate 48) where excavation revealed solely late Iron Age dating evidence (information from Professor Rahtz).

0220 Notably straight runs here, up to 600 m (cf, 0420) bank on N (cf, NMR OAP SU 0120/2/392).

0321 and 0421 Sumner shows double banks; OS emphasises the N bank W of Vernditch Chase. In the Chase OS and Sumner at first allow a N bank. The linear turns N at right angles where met by the much smaller M (72) (qv) and is there double (Fig 50). Dimensions W of the knuckle are strikingly large, the bigger bank on north 2 m above a ditch 2 m wide, the overall width being 17 m. North from the knuckle are two slight banks 1.5 m above a ditch. After 100 m it describes a sudden pronounced curve in a much disturbed area (Fig 51: profile R 1). At profile R 2 the ditch has certainly been used as a track. The overall width generally in this area of gentle slopes is about 13 m.

The ditch has been completely obscured about 15 m N of the Roman road. The ground dips down steeply NE from the shoulder close to this. There is a hollow-way (possibly the linear ditch recorded by C M Piggott (1944, 66)) flanking the *agger* of the Roman road on the S side. At Vitrell Gate, in the valley bottom, the area is much disturbed but a fragment of bank 8 m across and 0.3 m high can be seen on the county boundary where it diverges from the straight line otherwise

Great Ditch Banks ↓

Shire Rack →

M(69)

PLATE 48 Martin (69) near its west end, adjacent to the county boundary between Dorset and Wiltshire ('Shire Rack', here black with trees). A near-vertical air photograph taken *c*1924 in area SU 0120, with north to the top. A linear feature extends north from Martin (69), bending twice, once at **Shire Rack**, to join the ditch of **Great Ditch Banks**. 'Celtic' fields, clearest to the south, meet Martin (69) in an inconclusive sequence. The Shire Rack undulates in a very similar way to Martin (69). The white-edged long marl pits point both to a clay cap here over the chalk, favouring heavy tree growth, and to non-recent cultivation (Crawford collection of air photographs, ?1922) (*see* Fig 49). (NMR VAP SU 0120/1)

followed by the Roman road. This is a dimension more appropriate to the Roman road than to the linear it presumably in some sense incorporates. The straight run is some 800 m.

0520 The junction between Roman road and linear extending E from about 052221 has been destroyed (OS AM). A 13th-century perambulation notes this stretch as 'streteditch' to 'Wiltonweie' (Poole 1976, 53).

0722 Croucheston Down: the linear diverges N in a 'flat bow' over 350 m. Just E of this the bank is on the N side and the ditch 1.8 m below this, the overall width 11 m with no sign of a S bank. E of this Sumner showed 2 banks spanning 16.2 m above a ditch 2.4 m deep, more pointed than the deep but flat hollowed ditches in Vernditch, and the deepest recorded portion (Fig 51: profile SBA).

0822 The linear follows the W and N edge of Toyd Clump, its bank most unusually on the S or equivalent side. A bank on the other side could have been destroyed in arable.

0922 A linear, whether track, ditch or both, most probably a track but conceivably a continuation of M (74), met the linear at a knuckle near the valley head (Fig 52). The near-right angle just E of this was taken to run along a contour on the W shoulder of a spur.

At about 098228, near the E shoulder of the same spur, Mrs Piggott dug the only recorded cut across the line of the ditch (Piggott 1944, no 5 on accompanying map). This revealed a section with steep sides and narrow bottom which 'agreed exactly with the sections dug' by Sumner across M (80) (qv 0919) and Whitsbury (22). There was 0.6 m of silt over a turf line with gun-flint debitage (Piggott 1944, 67).

1022 main bank on N; ditch, on county boundary, flat-bottomed and used as a track. Sumner's profile (Fig 51: SCD) was at 10462287.

1023 and 1123 Bank on N up to 2 m above ditch.

1022–1123 include a straight section of about 8 m. Near the E end of this, bank is only a scarp, incorporated in a recent lynchet formation. Profile R 3 (Fig 51) shows bank at N. About 127235, E of Great Yews, Sumner noted the bank on S was the higher for a short stretch.

1323 At 13802345 the linear twists to N at 45° then bends at right angles, making a sharp triangular diversion before rejoining the course on a slightly different bearing after some 30 m (Fig 53). (Plate 49; cf, similar feature on Gussage Hill, Dorset, Plate 18.)

(NMR OAP SU 1323/11) (Fig 53, with grid square 1423)

1423 Colt Hoare noted the bank was on the N. He was also impressed by the irregularity of its course (Colt Hoare 1810, 232). There are sinuous curves immediately before the butt with Whitsbury (22) (qv). 'Celtic' fields, possibly incorporating a ditched enclosure, abut the ditch on the S (Crawford 1931, three plates of air photographs; cf, composite Plate 49 and Fig 53 in this volume, with grid square 1323).

(70) *Linear* (03441997–03951965), roughly parallel to Bokerley Dyke close on its NE side in Sector A 1 and into Sector A 2 (*see also* page 28), comprises two stretches not demonstrably connected and at the NW end difficult to entangle from tracks. It is possible that the two parts, described below, never did join and the southern section may, for instance, have been once linked to the 'Shoulder Angle' (Fig 6).

The more southerly section, certainly a bank with ditch visible in places on the W side 'facing' Bokerley Dyke, extends for at least 350 m, much of it poorly defined, petering out

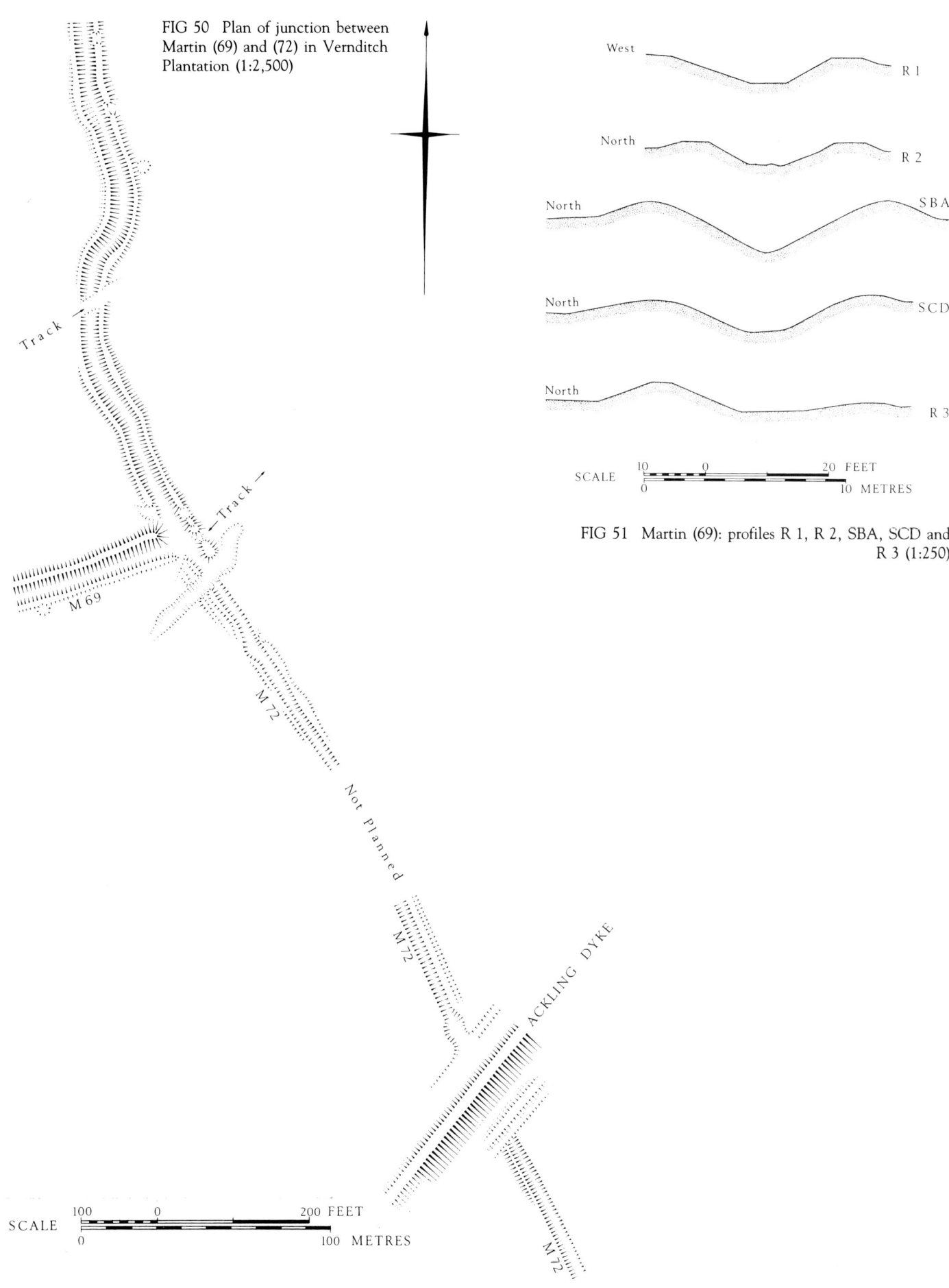

FIG 50 Plan of junction between Martin (69) and (72) in Vernditch Plantation (1:2,500)

Track

Track

M 69

M 72

Not Planned

M 72

ACKLING DYKE

M 72

West — R 1

North — R 2

North — SBA

North — SCD

North — R 3

SCALE 10 0 20 FEET
0 10 METRES

FIG 51 Martin (69): profiles R 1, R 2, SBA, SCD and R 3 (1:250)

SCALE 100 0 200 FEET
0 100 METRES

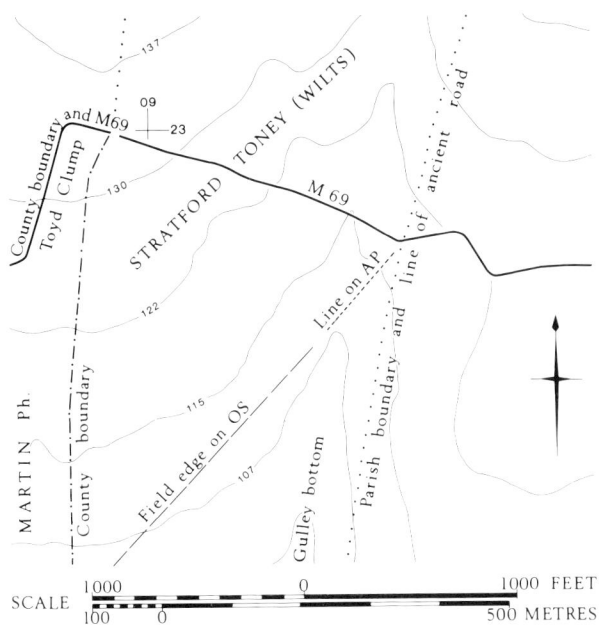

FIG 52 Plan of Martin (69) in SU 0922 (1:10,560)

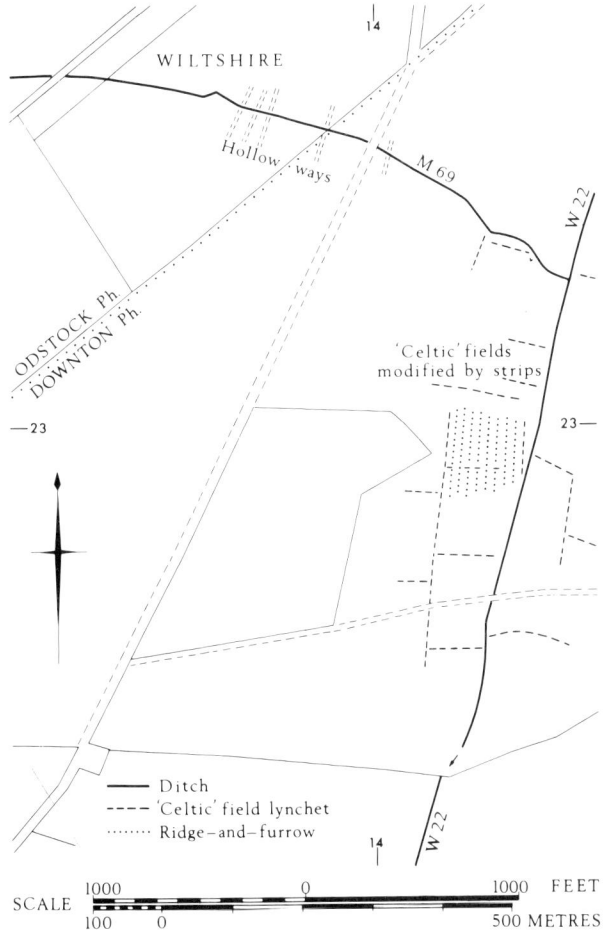

— Ditch
---- 'Celtic' field lynchet
······ Ridge-and-furrow

SCALE

FIG 53 Plan of junction between Martin (69) and Whitsbury (22) (1:10,560)

(probably levelled) at both ends. At best, the bank is up to 5 m across and 0.5 m high, its ditch being visible just N of the Epaulement. Opposite the Epaulement, NE of it, it is almost flattened, a condition it had apparently reached when Pitt-Rivers' plan showed it as a slight scarp, and it was given no mention in his text (cf, Pitt-Rivers 1892, Plate CLXIX, and Fig 13 in this volume).

A very low bank, (70) A, abuts this section at right angles. Its nature and former connections are, like that of the isolated fragment (70) B, again 3 m to 5 m wide, 100 m or so N of it, unknown. The obtuse angle in (70) B means that it is not part of a simple 'Celtic' field.

The northern stretch of the linear is for the most part a low bank some 4 m across, rising out of the combe bottom parallel with Bokerley Dyke until, at its NW end, it appears to diverge as a slight scarp which ends short of the A354.

(71) *Linear* (03981990–04202003) Martin Down West, flattened, extends in former arable for about 250 m from, at W, the edge of rough grassland in the area of the old rifle range (in which, at some time, it has been levelled) to a point some 100 m short of the W corner of (56), Martin Down 'Camp', described below, where it can also be seen on the ground as a depression in a track. It probably continued E from this point and there are faint suggestions on air photographs of an extension along the NW side of (56) (perhaps linked to the 'ledge' on Fig 54) and a return to NW short of the wide gap in that enclosure. 'Celtic' fields spring from either side of it (cf, Bowen 1961, Fig 3A).

NMR OAP SU 0420/1/250; CUCAP VAP RC8 BH 46; CPE/UK 1811, 1060; V 58/RAF, 3250, 0125

(56) *Enclosure and settlement* Martin Down 'Camp' (043201), Middle Bronze Age and Romano-British, lying on a site used in Beaker times, consists of an irregular, roughly rectangular, enclosure of just over 0.6 ha (1½ acres) defined by bank and external ditch interrupted by one very wide gap on the uphill, NW, side and by two slighter interruptions. Inconspicuously sited on a slight slope rising from the head of a narrow shallow combe from the east, the bank and ditch and about half of the interior were excavated by General Pitt-Rivers over the winter of 1895/6. The present earthwork, now under rough pasture, gorse and scrub, is his reconstruction. The W ditch was disturbed by ploughing in the 1950s (Figs 46a, 54) (Pitt-Rivers 1898, 185–214, and 8 pp unpaginated Relic Tables).

The enclosure ditch was relatively narrow and curiously deep in view of the large, but undoubtedly original, gap in its N side. Its mean depth, however, similar to the Section A reproduced here (Fig 54), was nearer to 7½ ft (just over 2 m) than to the 9½ ft (2.9 m) prominently presented by Pitt-Rivers in his 'average section' (Pitt-Rivers 1898, Plate 310) which included a short deeper portion (in which there were no finds and so just possibly dug by mistake into bedrock). The bank was higher at the corners, probably due to the greater length of ditch outside it.

The enclosure was with little doubt constructed in the Middle Bronze Age (though Pitt-Rivers shows a little pottery of 'number

107

PLATE 49 Linear Martin (**69**) at its east end, in grid squares 1323 and 1423, butting against the ditch of Whitsbury (**22**). The dark lines of north–south hollow-ways can be seen through Martin (69), but there are no breaks visible in Whitsbury (22). Probably superincumbent ridge-and-furrow suggests relatively early flattening of Whitsbury (22), formerly a boundary for 'Celtic' fields both west and east of it. Whitsbury (22) is notably straight in comparison with Martin (69), which has nearby marl pits indicating clay caps locally (and so a natural true cover?). (Two photographs: NMR VAP SU 1423/24 and 25)

2 and 4 quality', not normally thought of as Bronze Age, mixed with the preponderant 'no. 1 quality' (generally Deverel–Rimbury) under the bank). It was to some extent used in the Roman period but the published pottery distribution suggests that while there was twice as much Bronze Age pottery from the interior as from the ditch, there was eight times as much Romano-British pottery from the ditch as from the interior, perhaps pointing to settlement activity outside the enclosure.

Stratified finds came mainly from the ditch, which had silted to an almost level surface by the Roman period. Finds included very large quantities of flint flakes, about half from Roman levels. More elaborately worked flint seemed generally to belong to the Bronze Age or earlier. Other early material, apart from pottery, included a few bronze items including an awl and the possible stem of a razor. Animal remains, mostly from Bronze Age contexts, but none found in the interior, were preponderantly of oxen with some sheep, pig, red deer, horse, goat and dog.

Finds of the Romano-British period include decorated Samian and a variety of New Forest wares, an iron knife and nails, five fragments of Kimmeridge shale and a total of over 900 pieces of iron 'pyrites' (now thought to be a workable ore). A child, thought to be of this date, had been buried in the ditch. Ox bones were the most common animal remains but still only one-fifth the quantity of the early phases.

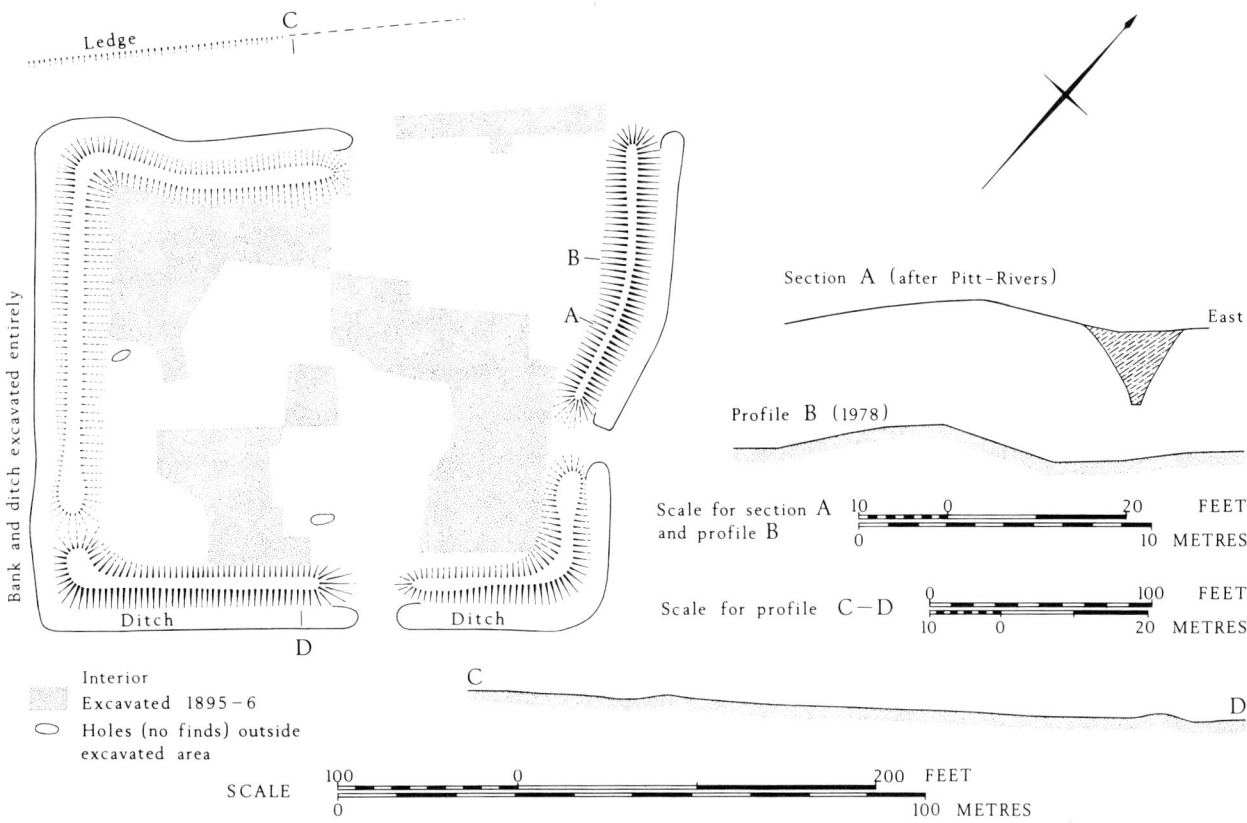

FIG 54 Plan of Martin (56) with section A and profiles B and C–D (1:1,250)

'Celtic' fields lie adjacent to the enclosure, but the pattern is unclear for 200 to 300 m N, an area including Roman pit (57), pointing to degradation conceivably related to settlement.

(72)–(74)

Martin (72) was formerly thought to continue direct to a junction with Bokerley Dyke. It is now known to abut M (73) at 04901943, and it is this linear which meets Bokerley Dyke. The linear M (74), apparently similar in date to M (72), is by reason of its course and form likely to be a continuation of M (73).

(72) *Linear* (04012108–04911935), Martin Down east, 2.2 m across, 1 m deep as excavated; at most, a spread bank on W side 3.5 m wide and 0.3 m high. Most has been flattened. Relatively straight stretches with angular turns. At N, it joins the very different M (69), having been cut by the Roman road at 04132086 (Fig 50).

Pitt-Rivers totally excavated a stretch 90 m long about 160 m E of his Martin Down 'Camp', RCHME Martin (56) (Pitt-Rivers 1898, 190). Middle Bronze Age sherds, superficially identical to those from Martin Down 'Camp' and in generally fresh condition, were found in the primary silting along the ditch. The ditch cuts 'Celtic' fields so the pottery could be derived from manure-spread rubbish, but the lack of other pottery at this level, and its condition, suggest it is a true indicator of the date of the first construction. Romano-British finds occurred in the upper fill.

A section 500 m further S was drawn by the Shaftesbury and District Archaeology Group (SDAG) across the line exposed by a gas-pipe trench (Catherall, Barnett and McClean 1984, 187). It is shallower than Pitt-Rivers' 'ideal' section (Fig 55: Pitt-Rivers' section with SDAG section superimposed), which conceivably includes a recut.

(73) *Linear,* from junction with Bokerley Dyke at 04831881 to 06652112. It is generally flattened, mostly in the area of the open fields of Martin, but survives as an earthwork at its SW end, S from Sillen Lane. Its form may vary. Plate 50 shows two ditches, the narrower on the S side at, and north of, the junction with M (72). The second disappears after the linear turns NE but reappears in other places. North east from 06052090 the spacing between the 2 m-wide ditch and the other, narrower, ditch is very variable, ranging from 4 m to 7 m (NMR OAP SU 0621/5/239). About 100 m NW of this section a short stretch of narrow ditch appears on a line which would continue the linear, but the double-ditched section almost certainly represents its main course. To S of Sillen Lane the earthwork remains display only one ditch. There is no room for a track *and* bank between the two ditches so the second, S, ditch must be assumed to be an addition flanking the bank and conceivably related to a track outside and along it, though any

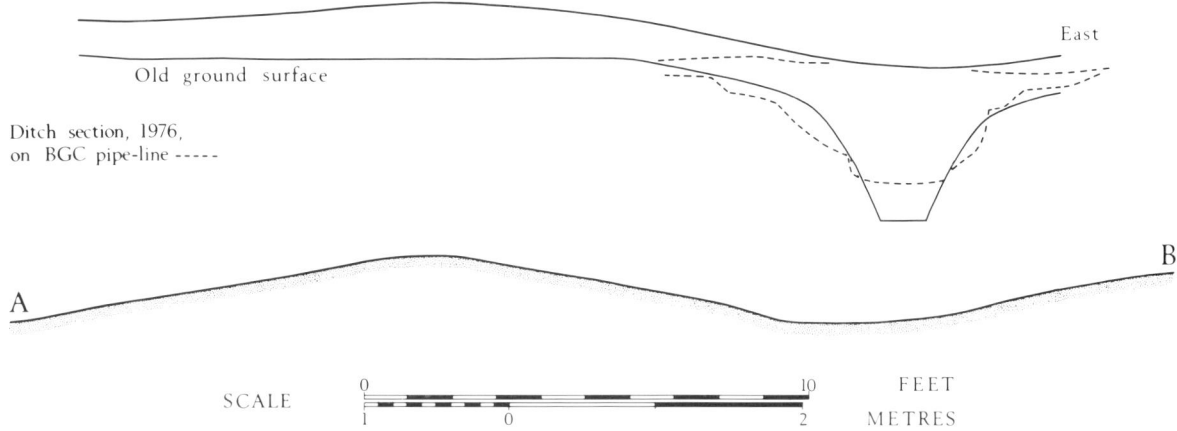

East

Old ground surface

Ditch section, 1976,
on BGC pipe-line -----

A

B

SCALE   0   10   FEET
          1   0   2   METRES

FIG 55   Martin (72): profiles and sections (1:50)

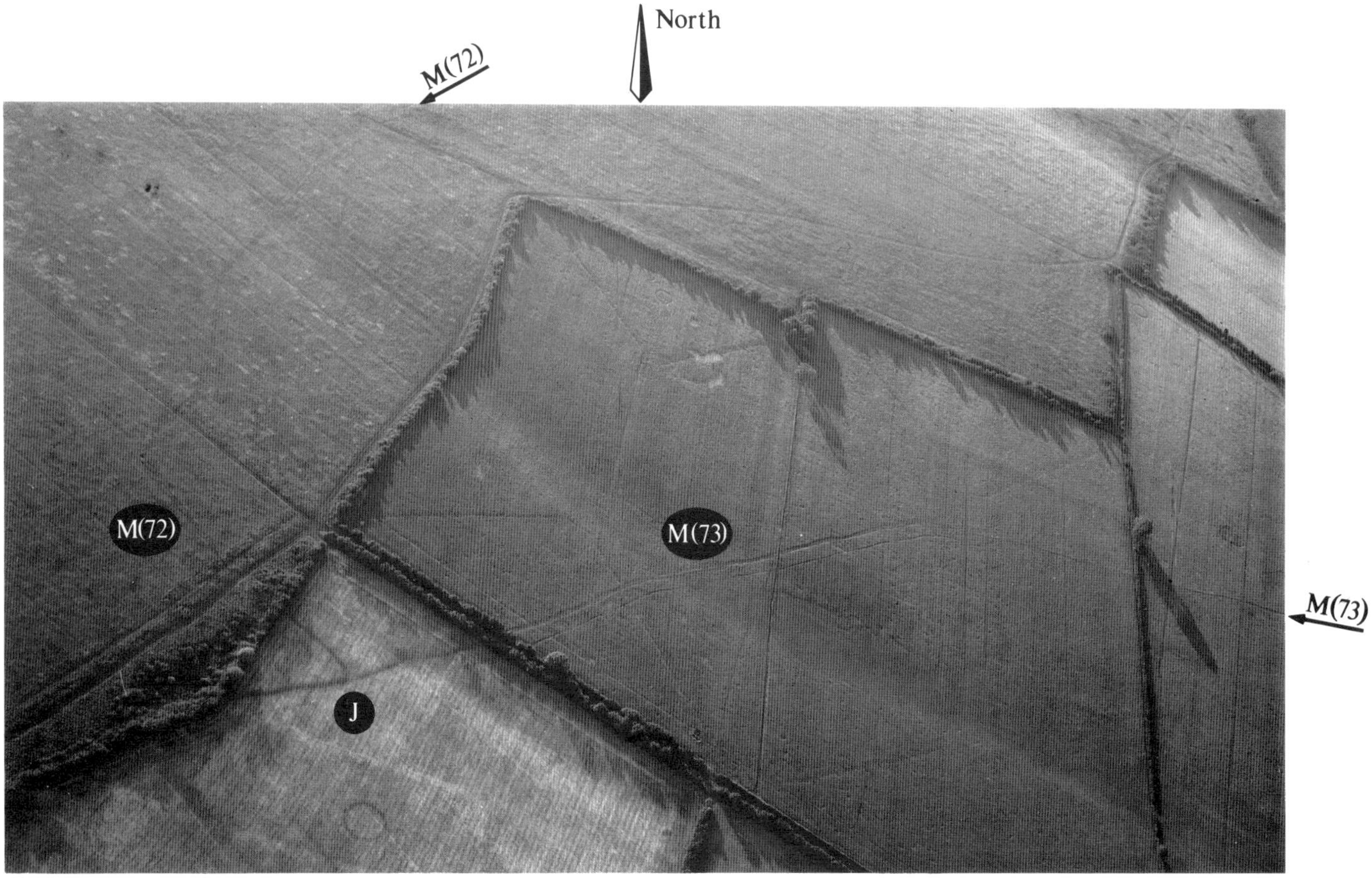

North

M(72)

M(72)

M(73)

J

M(73)

PLATE 50   Martin Down, showing the junction of Martin (72) and (73) at 049194 (J). An oblique air photograph with north to the top; Martin (73) extends here through former medieval fields. Its second, thin ditch is only just visible at J, is clearer to the north east and not apparent at all where labelled Martin (73). Martin (72) has suffered much relatively recent ploughing. (NMR OAP SU 0621/5/239)

such track would have been blocked by barrows Martin (7)−(9) S of Sillen Lane (Figs 20 (plan) and 21 (profiles at junction of M (73) and Bokerley Dyke)).

(74) *Linear* from 068213, E of the last sight of M (73), to 07372177, where it disappears in heavily ploughed ground; appears on air photographs as two parallel ditches, about 5 m apart, similar in disposition to M (73) N of Sillen Lane. The northern ditch was of V-section and the southern flat-bottomed. At 072216, just W of the E end, surface stripping and adjacent clear parch marks in grass enabled the ditches to be planned. Excavation by the Avon Valley Archaeological Society, near a sharp undulation in the line that suggested some contemporary activity, showed the northern ditch as the more substantial, which air photographs had already suggested both for this linear and for M (73) (Fig 56). The only pottery recovered was Middle Bronze Age, identical to that from Martin Down 'Camp', Martin (56) (Catherall, Barnett and McClean 1984, 172).

(75) *Linear* (07932148−08752180), narrow, partly on 'Burnbake' (Tithe map; ? formerly Bustard Down; cf, Poole 1976, 96) with divergent length 'A' turning SSE at right angles for 220 m almost to Paradise (formerly Upper Farm (OS 1871)); this latter may have continued to join (76). A number of narrow lines on air photographs, difficult to interpret but possibly 'Celtic' fields, stem from it at right angles; others appear to be intersected.

NMR OAP SU 0821/4/25; SU 0821/3/157; CUCAP OAP AVM 36; NMR VAP (BKS) SU 0818/18/911.

(76) *Linear* (08332122−08372080), disjointed but almost certainly continuous from just S of Paradise to area of settlement (66), described immediately below, where narrower ditches or hollows along its E side, as far as enclosure (f), relate

to an apparent road (Fig 57). Its alignment suggests a link with (75) A. (76) A, which makes a scissors intersection with it N of the settlement, extends NE for 400 m on a line continuing that of an extant track from SW; its course after it crosses (76) indicates, however, that it embodies more complex origins.

(66) *Settlement* (083206), just SW of formerly extra-parochial Toyd Farm in an area known as 'Barrow Field and Little Penning', Romano-British and, probably, prehistoric, covering 5 ha (12 acres) overall, is known, in arable, from air photographic marks and some surface finds. A long mound, (a), of uncertain origins, is the only element normally visible on the ground. The situation is almost level, on the shoulder of a slight spur facing SW (Figs 46c and f, 57).

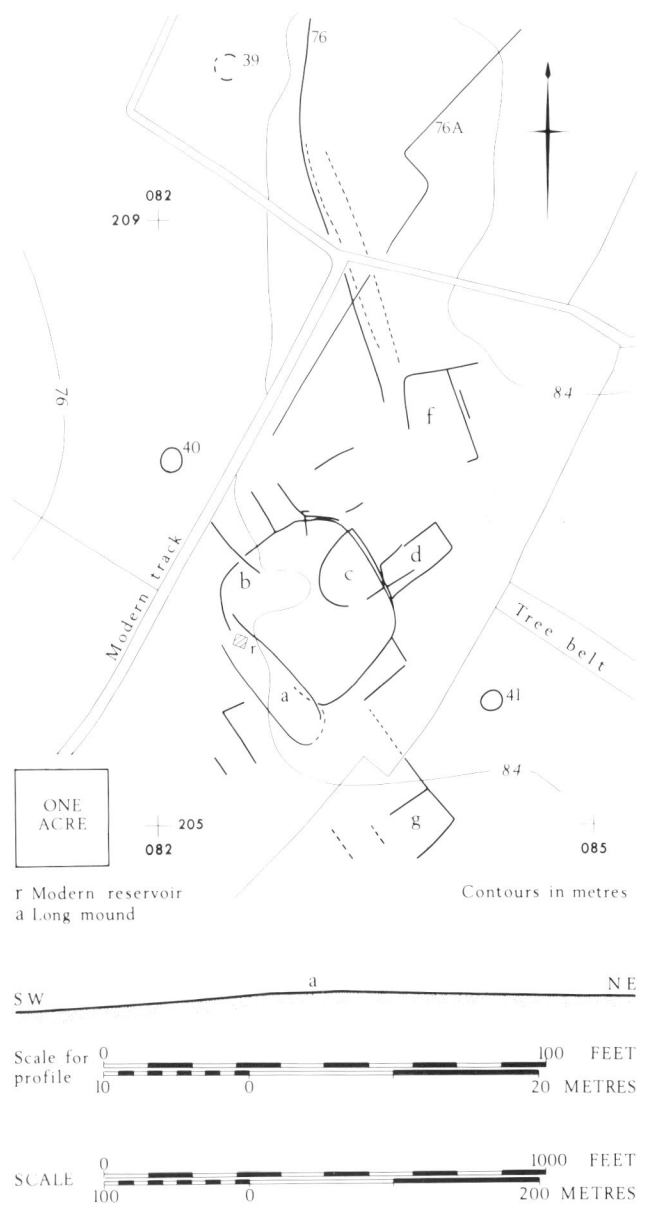

FIG 57 Plan of Martin (66) with linears (76) and (76) A and ring ditches (39), (40) and (41) (1:5,000)

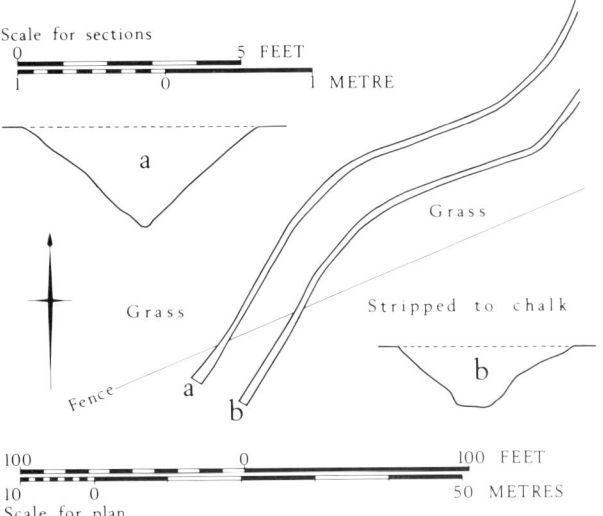

FIG 56 Martin (74): plan and sections (1:1,000)

Enclosure (b) about 1 ha (2½ acres) in area, contains many pits and signs of occupation. Its SW side corresponds with the mound (a), of chalk and flint with a broad dark line sometimes showing along its axis on air photographs, lying along a break of slope on the W edge of the spur. This mound is about 100 m long and, at its widest, 15 m from its E end, over 30 m across and just under 0.5 m high (Fig 57: cross profile at a). Air photographs suggest that it might have been flanked by insubstantial ditches and that a continuation of these ditches (otherwise to be explained as soil wash from the mound) carried around its E end. There is no clear evidence of how the SW ditch of enclosure (b) relates to the long mound. The only ascertainable entrance is a simple gap immediately above the (b) on plan. The half-hooped enclosure (c), with entrance gap facing S, intersects (b) and its NE side is immediately adjacent to that of (b). Enclosure (d), peripheral to the bounds of (b), has an irregularity central to its NW side which may be an entrance. The partial enclosure (g), 180 m SE of (b), is apparently connected to it by a series of ditches. Other enclosures are indicated by the incomplete trapezoid at (f), ditches between it and (b) and, again, S of (a).

Surface material found in the course of investigation includes part of a sarsen saddle quern or rubbing stone, from just N of enclosure (b); Romano-British pottery including New Forest wares, among them an indented beaker and a probably 4th-century storage jar; brick and tile fragments; unworked shale and other imported stone including oolitic limestone and sandstone. There are many flints, especially on mound (a), some of which are tabular fragments.

CUCAP OAP ARX 39 and 41; NMR OAP SU 0820/12/317−23; SU 0820/16/163 and SU 0821/3/149.

(77) *Linear* (05881927−05831936), probable fragment of track 100 m long directed towards settlement (58) 300 m to N. An associated ditch projects NE from it (Fig 6: overall plan of Bokerley Line).

NMR OAP SU 0519/25

(78) and (79)
Air photographs show a track clearly joining the E end of (78) to the W end of (79), 200 m NE of it, giving a strong but misleading impression of continuity (*see* Fig 6). It is unlikely, however, that either linear ended where it now seems to. Neither has appeared on modern maps, though (78) was shown by Colt Hoare in his map of Salisbury Station VII (1810, opposite p 223) (CUCAP VAP RC8 AC 287). The junction of (78) with Bokerley Dyke is very close to the apparent S end of the visible 'double ditch' along Bokerley.

(78) *Linear*, about 10 m in overall width with indeterminate bank arrangements, extends from junction with Bokerley Dyke at 05561809 NNE for 200 m to the edge of a steep slope where it apparently turns along the shoulder for some 30 m to 05711825 as a scarp and shelf only.

On the N, roughly following the contours on the less steep

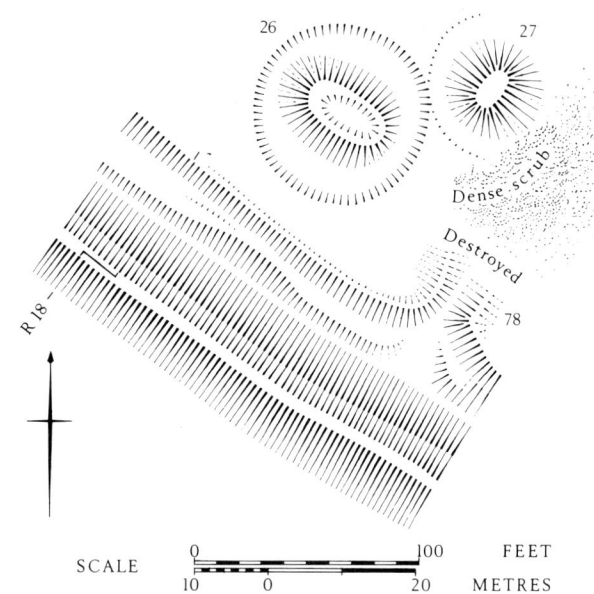

FIG 58 Plan of barrows Martin (26) and (27) with linear (78) and Bokerley Dyke adjacent (1:1,000)

shoulder of the hill, the linear is a very slight bank uphill of a scarp falling 0.5 m to ditch bottom with very spread slight bank beyond. The junction with Bokerley (Fig 58) is disturbed and the drawing should not be taken to indicate an elision of the bank with a counterscarp bank along the edge of Bokerley Dyke. A 'shelf' marking the 'outer ditch' of that work (cf, profile R 18 in Fig 22) extends for only 6 m SE of the junction. The linear ditch bottom appears to be at a higher level than the Bokerley 'shelf' ditch; just to NE it has been filled in to take the present track across it, and beyond that quarrying masked by scrub has destroyed any possibility of determining the exact relationship with barrow (27).

(79) *Linear banks and ditches*, in complex relationships, lie on the 400 m stretch between the foot of the slope from Blagdon Hill and settlement (61), described immediately below (Fig 59: plan and profile). Emerging W from the present field with settlement Martin (61) is a bank with S ditch, 9.6 m overall, the bank 0.4 m above the ditch recalling the proportions of (78). A slight depression, 4 m across, running along the S side suggests a flanking track. All this is crossed by a modern track after 25 m, while 15 m further on there is an abrupt change of character, superficially of trifurcation. The bank which swings W increasing in height to some 1.5 m, at first as an irregular mound, ends where the ground begins to drop in to a valley. The original alignment of the bank is continued SW, beyond a hollow, by a rough bank some 4 m across and 0.9 m high. Its line is continued uphill by a much less clear bank (not drawn) and thereafter a track which extends up to and past the end of (78). The third element is an ill-defined bank some 3 m across which appears to cut across the central line. It extends SSW to the foot of a steepening slope. E of these earthworks the central line, which is probably the primary feature, is continued as a

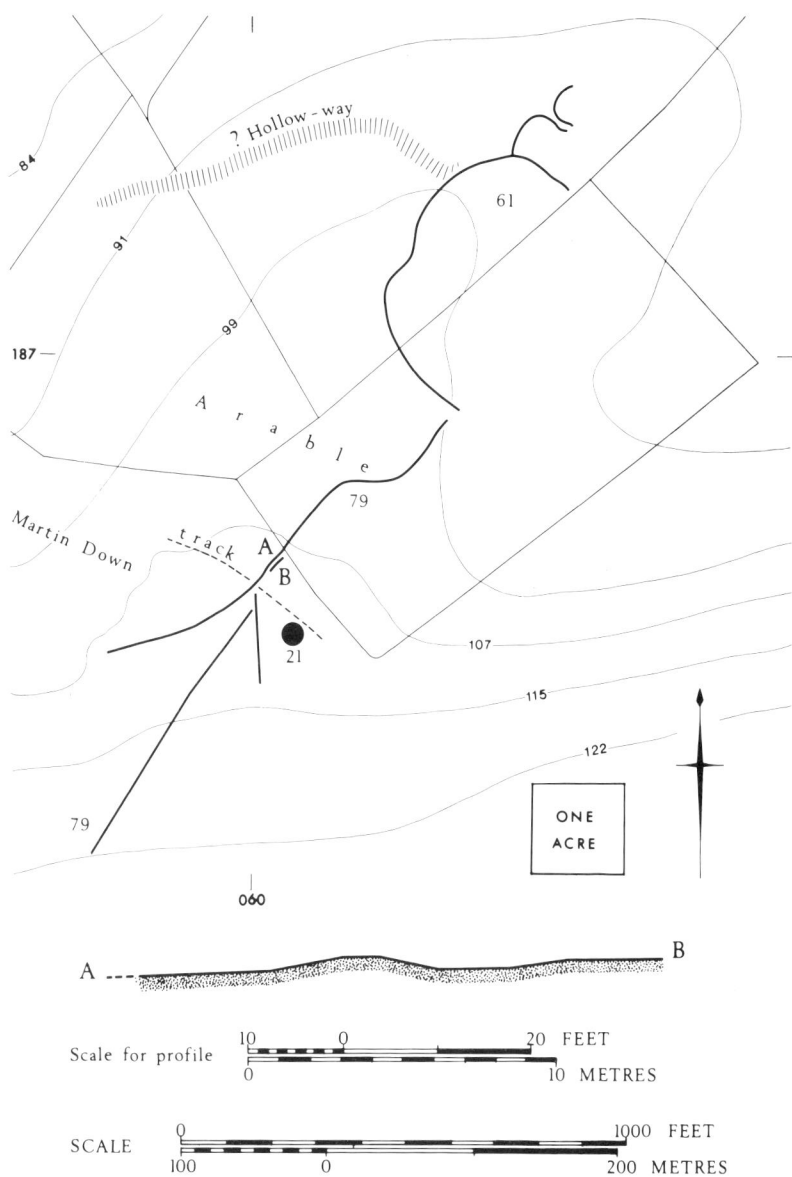

FIG 59 Plan of Martin (61) with linear (79) and round barrow (21), and profile A—B (1:5,000)

ditch crop mark apparently reaching enclosure (61). (Air photographic references are given under (61) below.)

(61) *Settlement* (061186—063188), prehistoric and Romano-British, in 'Well Field' (the local name), identified in aerial reconnaissance and from air photographs, occupies at least 2.4 ha (6 acres) of a spur of Upper Chalk. At SE the ground rises from it to 137 m above OD. At present, it lies in arable, formerly medieval open fields (Fig 59).

The settlement is marked, first, by an oval ditched enclosure of perhaps 2 ha (5 acres), containing many pits, the S side of which has not yet appeared on air photographs but has been seen from the air. Lesser enclosures immediately NE of it also contain pits. A track associated with linear (79) approaches it from pasture SW, while an apparent hollow-way winds towards the N side where there is a suggestion of settlement outside the limits of the enclosure. A fragment of spread bank under 0.3 m high is visible by the field fence about 06111864. Surface finds include a sestertius of Titus (AD 77—8), and abraded Romano-British pot sherds, none closely datable.

NMR OAP SU 0618/33—4; CUCAP VAP RC8 AC 287; NMR VAP (BKS) SU 0619/1/153925—6

(80) *Linear*, part of 'Grim's Ditch' (cf, pages 13—14 for discussion; extent on Fig 3 and on Area Plans located thereon), extending from Martin by Bokerley Dyke on Blagdon Hill across Damerham, Rockbourne and Whitsbury to a point NW of the hill-fort, at least 6.5 km long, incorporates three main elements, A—C (*see* Figs 60 and 61 for profiles). (The letters do not indicate chronological sequence, the stretch apparently originating furthest west being given priority for convenience. A select, detailed description is given by km square below.)

113

A: substantial bank and ditch, partly levelled, from Blagdon Hill (05651803) to Damerham Ridge (09461892): overall width around 13 m. Ditch 'V'-shaped. Maximum known height from ditch bottom to bank is almost 3 m (G–H on Damerham Ridge 0918 (Fig 60)).

B: a lesser bank and ditch largely obliterated by A but detectable as: a soil mark on Knoll Down, by Damerham (20), where A makes a bow N from the direct line; an almost flattened short earthwork, again on the direct line where A makes one brief angular diversion S to a gap by settlement Martin (63), described below (page 115); soil and texture mark and earthwork diverging entirely from A west from 066181. The sole well-preserved earthwork stretch is some 100 m long, dipping W to the valley bottom from the field edge at 06501796 (Fig 61). Excavated ditch on Knoll Down has a 'V' section 1.4 m across and 1.2 m deep (0818) (Fig 61).

C: a narrow ditch, entirely levelled, of at least two different widths but generally comparable with B and extending its line from Damerham Ridge ENE for a further 3.2 km, with certainty, to 11711997. Excavated section similar to B (0919) (Fig 61). There are hints of further elements, eg, on the former Tidpit Down just east of barrow Martin (24) (see 0618 below).

The work traverses almost all possible sorts of natural features, including two narrow river valleys, still with streams, and places where gravel and sands or clay-with-flints overlie the chalk. The course of A/B is approximately straight from Tidpit Common to

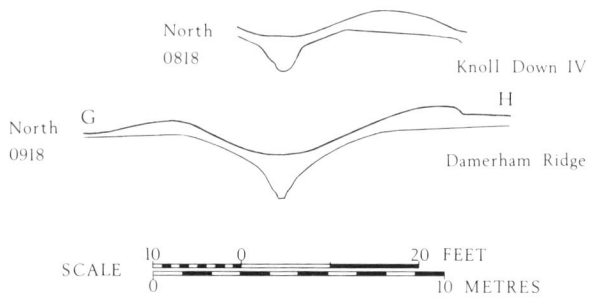

FIG 60 Martin (80) A: profiles and sections (1:250)

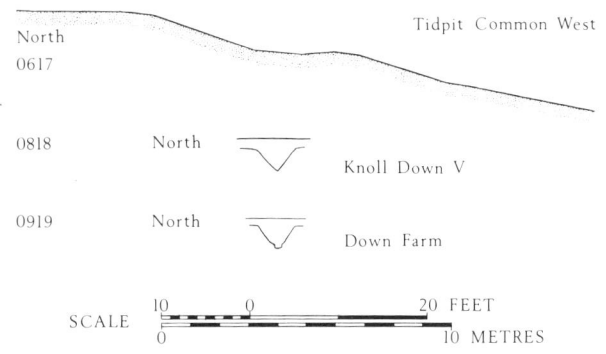

FIG 61 Martin (80) B: profile and sections (1:250)

114

Knoll Down, Damerham (08801865), where it changes direction and, prolonged by C, maintains a roughly straight alignment towards a point, not demonstrably reached, some 600 m N of Whitsbury hill-fort where it might have abutted or intersected W (22). Formerly it has been thought that A was continuous at W with Pentridge (17), also traditionally called 'Grim's Ditch', but there is nothing to support this assumption (cf, discussion on 'Grim's Ditch', page 14).

It seems likely that B/C was the first, relatively slight work, following for the most part a direct line but hingeing on Knoll Down by a settlement area, Damerham (20). Excavation has demonstrated prehistoric origins, Iron Age or earlier (0818 and 0919).

Circumstantial evidence for date is ambivalent. Line C, as noted above, is apparently unconnected with the hill-fort of Whitsbury; A incorporates in its line the elongated, probably Early Bronze Age, barrow Martin (24) (0618). The possible link with the likely Iron Age enclosure Rockbourne (46) on Damerham Ridge is very uncertain (0918). The linear mostly crosses over 'Celtic' fields as on Knoll Down (Plate 28), but occasionally makes angular turns, as on Tidpit Common and NW of it (Plate 51), suggesting that field edges were followed in places.

Only two ancient gaps, likely ways through, are known in the 6.5 km run: on Tidpit Common, by settlement Martin (63) (0618), and 400 m E of Damerham Ridge (0919). The latter is quite certainly contemporary, with primary arrangements, though also marking a further change in ditch widths (Fig 1; Plates 51 (Tidpit, Down) and 29 (E of Damerham Ridge)).

Bibliography: Bowen 1975, 106; Bowen, Evans and Race 1978; Evans and Vaughan 1985, incorporating details of test excavation of (80) C by Mr R T Schadla-Hall.

DETAILED DESCRIPTION (BY KM SQUARE FROM THE WEST)

0518 Blagdon Hill (see Figs 23 (plan) and 24 (profile R 21) with Bokerley Dyke and description on page 36): gravel partly overlies the chalk, the whole area scrubby pasture; A drops east gently along the almost flat top of a spur from the highest point where small quarrying and other disturbance have obliterated the link with Bokerley Dyke. The only banks to be seen extending W from Bokerley Dyke itself, in scrubby, wooded, ground, are the deer pale Cranborne (32) and parish boundary. These cross Pentridge (17) which probably continued SE past the point where it might have turned had it been a continuation of A; profile R 21 about 30 m E of Bokerley shows a counterscarp bank quite absent in Pentridge (17). The dimensions, 14.8 m across overall, and silted ditch still 1.5 m below bank top, suggest close similarity with those some 3 km to E (section and profile G–H in 0918 (see Fig 60)).

0617/0618 Tidpit Down, mostly arable where it falls towards Tidpit Common Down (cf, Fig 7), was formerly covered by a confusing sequence of 'Celtic' fields (Plate 51). The linear, having described a double right-angled turn, probably to integrate with a 'Celtic' field, is just detectable on the ridge top as a low scarp adjoining an elongated barrow (24) which it circumvents on the S side. Some 30 m further E a slight ditch continues E for a short way on the same line while the main ditch describes a clear obtuse turn away from it to SE, then makes another sharp obtuse bend to E where (80) B leaves it on an apparently earlier line. A profile of B (Fig 61 (0617)) was taken where it survives as a good earthwork for some 100 m after emerging from under a

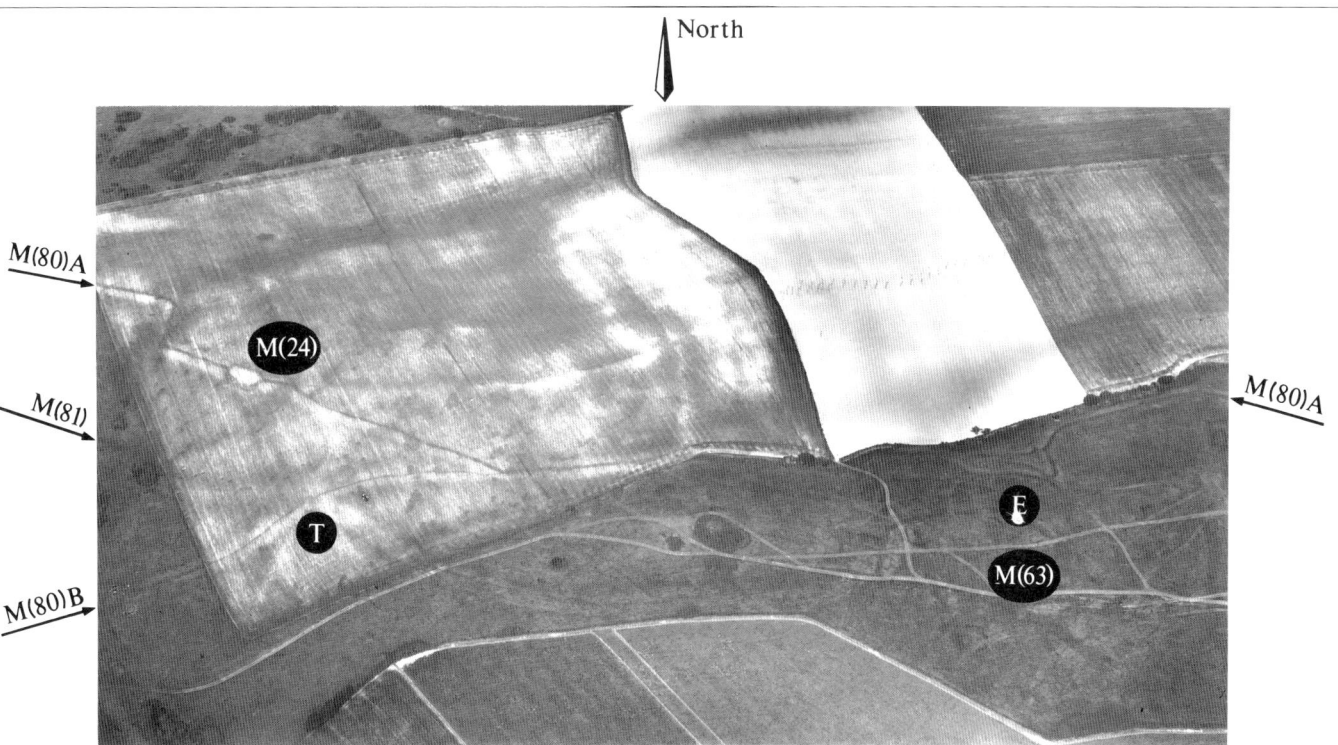

North

M(80)A

M(24)

M(81)

M(80)B

T

M(80)A

E

M(63)

PLATE 51 Tidpit Common, Martin. An oblique air photograph looking north. Settlement Martin (63) is adjacent to a gap E, possibly an original passage through linear Martin (80) A, here deviating from (80) B (cf, Figs 6 and 62). 80A, to the west, diverges north west from the probably early line (80) B, crosses 'Celtic' fields and incorporates elongated barrow Martin (24) in its course. At T, the linear, Martin (81), at least partly a double-lynchet track, intersects ditched linear Martin (80) B. (NMR OAP SU 0718/4/164)

'recent' lynchet nearly 1 m high, in the old pasture W of the arable clearly seen in Plate 51; point T, in the arable, shows double-lynchet track (Martin (81)) making a bend to W precisely where it intersects (80) B; it is not clear whether the ditch was interrupted here. The possible entrance in (80) A (E on Plate 51, by settlement (63)) is described and illustrated below with that settlement. The right-angled turn 130 m W of this seems determined by 'Celtic' field arrangements. The linear skirts this part of Tidpit Common below the N shoulder of the ridge (cf, profiles with (63) on Fig 62). It probably cut earlier 'Celtic' fields, but was on the edge of later cultivation.

(63) *Settlement* (070181), prehistoric and Romano-British, on the prominent spur to the E of Tidpit Common, survives as, and within, a broken pattern of earthworks deriving from changes and destruction begun long before the Roman period. The geology is Upper Chalk but there is a great deal of pebbly gravel evident in surface scrapes. The core of the earliest recognisable settlement, which is a partly flattened, roughly circular enclosure (A) of about 1 ha (2½ acres), is almost certainly Iron Age and lies on ground dipping slightly S but at its highest point achieving a dominant position at the edge of a short, steep fall N from the ridge. This was succeeded by an open Romano-British settlement of about 4 ha (10 acres) that overlay the enclosure and extended S and E from it (Figs 46f and 62, *loose*; Plate 51).

Enclosure (A) is defined, at NW and NE, by a spread inner bank, 7 m or so across and up to 0.4 m high, with beyond it the remains of a ditch some 6 m wide. The N side is seen as a steep scarp only (*see* profile A−B in Fig 62, *loose*); on the edge of this slope is a prominent and irregular 'long' mound up to 1.5 m high (*see* page 87). The original S arc of the enclosure seems entirely lacking. Later scarping, probably Romano-British, up to 1.7 m high, stands roughly on and partly across its probable original line. On this assumption the area enclosed would be about 1 ha (2½ acres). A hut circle about 9.5 m across stands just W of the enigmatic irregular mound. Platforms and slight depressions overall extend out of the enclosed area to SE and E, overlying the last discernible traces of 'Celtic' fields. Finds of Iron Age pottery have been reported in the past while Romano-British sherds were found during the Royal Commission survey on platform scarps at E, by (30), and SE of A, and uphill from the massive lynchet line (L), 1.7 m high. The unconformity of this line with the N−S strike of 'Celtic' fields beyond E of it strongly suggests a connection with the bounds of the settlement at some phase.

The linear (80) lies below the N shoulder of the Common here; opposite a point just E of the enclosure a former straight segment of the linear has been abandoned and a loop

115

constructed just S from it to take in a small local re-entrant dimpling the N side of the ridge. This loop rises to the level of the settlement area where it is pierced by a gap, plausibly an entrance contemporary with a phase of occupation, although the hollow-way entering it from NW owes much, at least, to more recent use. Enclosure A is probably later than some of the fields. Certainly, in the Romano-British phase, settlement which spread out over the fields nearest to it was surrounded by others. Double-lynchet track (81) extends W for some 0.75 km from the NW of enclosure A, whose ditch may have cut it. A gap in the enclosure bank opposite the present end of (81) and a slight bank crossing the filled ditch just N of this strongly suggests that the track was also used to enter the enclosed area at a later time. The curve of (81) in its approach to this point may relate to other settlement features but any ancient surface traces have been flattened by broad ridge-and-furrow. The low bank and ditch, (d), SW of the ridge-and-furrow, may be of relatively recent date.

CUCAP VAP RC8 AA 182; NMR OAP 0718/3/67–73; 0718/4/164 (Plate 51)

DETAILED DESCRIPTION (BY KM SQUARE)

0718 A straight course is maintained into, and presumably across, the flood plain of the little River Allen.

0818 The line continues, diverging slightly S, cutting diagonally across 'Celtic' fields (Plate 28) to Knoll Down and the settlement area Damerham (20). Here A is sent into a bow facing N, where the ground continues to rise gently, extending across the top of a ridge. The E half of the bow is well preserved as an earthwork though cut by hollow-ways passing through. B is totally flattened, visible only as a soil mark. Poor indications of enclosure ditches indicate the existence of settlement here (Damerham (20)), apparently built over former 'Celtic' fields. Both B and A also lie across 'Celtic' fields in such a way as to put them, at least locally, out of service. Recent excavation by Dr J G Evans has shown that the fields overlaid by A were cultivated in the Iron Age; that there were ploughed furrows (? ritual or for clearance) under the bank and that there was no evidence for any capping hedge. Ditch B was altogether smaller. It had been filled in deliberately but there was no indication of the position of an associated bank. In form and size (Fig 61) it was remarkably similar to a section dug in M (80) C by Mr R T Schadla-Hall 1100 m further E (0919). Measurements across A were closely comparable with others on the line (Evans and Vaughan 1985).

0918/0919 Sumner excavated A just W of the top of Damerham Ridge and showed it to be a formidable work with a ditch 3 m below the top of the bank (section G–H: Sumner 1913, on plan following p 56; Fig 60, this volume). The ridge here is certainly where the relatively large dyke A ended its eastward course. It seems reasonable to assume, however, that the probable original ditch C carried on (continuous with B) for some 3 km since there is no general change of direction after that made on Knoll Down (0818). For the elucidation of the course of C the Royal Commission is greatly indebted to Mr J R Boyden for active aerial search and to Dr A J Clark for arduous geophysical investigation.

It seems likely that A made junction on the ridge with Martin (83) or Rockbourne (61) (cf, Sumner 1913, plan following p 56) but the formidable effect of traffic N–S along the ridge top has both destroyed and created new earthworks to such an extent that their unravelling without excavation is rendered almost impossible. It seems probable,

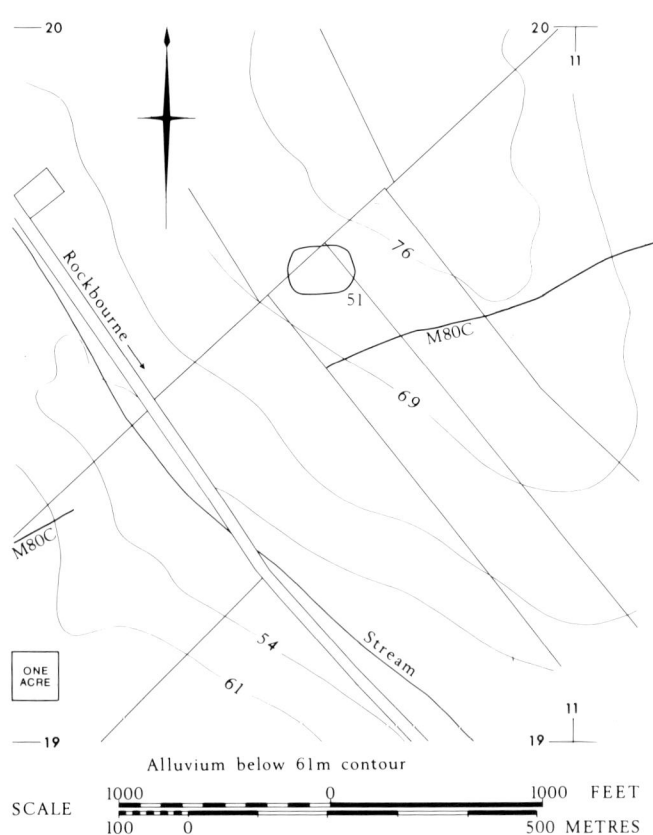

FIG 63   Plan of Rockbourne (51) with linear Martin (80) C (1:10,560)

however, that M (83) or R (61) embodies an Iron Age element which extended S and curved outside the almost certainly Iron Age enclosure Rockbourne (46) (cf, Area Plan 5).

The very rare gap in the linear (Plate 29) marks also a reduction in the present surface width of ditch C from about 1.5 m to 0.75 m. On the shoulder of a falling spur from Damerham Ridge, and in an area where former 'Celtic' fields can only just be detected, there is as yet no sign of track or settlement to associate with the gap.

Excavation by Mr R T Schadla-Hall at 098191 W of the 'entrance' gap showed a V-shaped ditch so similar to that excavated in B on Knoll Down (0818) (Fig 61: superimposed profiles) as strongly to suggest identity (Evans and Vaughan 1985). The line continues straight across the valley of the Rockbourne stream.

1019 It crosses a spur south of a likely Iron Age enclosure Rockbourne (51) (Fig 63).

1119 The vestiges in this area are extremely difficult to locate and none has been picked up E of the road running N from Whitsbury. It seems probable, however, that the line passed close to barrow Whitsbury (10).

(81) *Linear* double-lynchet track, Tidpit Common Down, 3 to 7 m wide with flanking lynchets up to 1 m high, survives as earthwork for 300 m W from settlement (63) and then for 220 m is flattened in arable; an earthwork stretch of 220 m or so emerges thereafter, extends to the valley bottom, rises up the W side in less clear form, cutting vestigial lynchets, and disappears in an area where former undated ploughing has almost destroyed widespread 'Celtic' fields. The placing of fragmentary lynchets abutting the track shows its contemporaneity with 'Celtic' fields E of the valley bottom (Fig 62).

The relationship with settlement (63) is less clear. The filled ditch of enclosure A intersects the track. An unexplained slight bank flanks a continuation of the track across the ditch fill and there is a break in the enclosure bank beyond. An abrupt bend in the track immediately W of (63) is unexplained. Any features in the gently rising ground N of it have been finally destroyed by broad ridge-and-furrow ploughing. Air photographs over the arable section show both track and linear (80) B changing direction where they intersect (Plate 51).

(82)–(85)
See Area Plan 5 (Knoll Down) and Plate 26 (NMR OAP SU 0819/23/153)

(82) *Linear*, SE for 600 m from indeterminate point in arable about 083195 to barrow Damerham (3), against which it appears to end. At most a hollow between two banks up to 13 m across, overall it cut deeply through 'Celtic' field lynchets and was at some time used as a road contained by the line of M (83).

(83) *Linear*, overlaps (82) extending SE from 08611926 through Damerham into Rockbourne where it intersects Martin (80) on Damerham Ridge. It appears on air photographs as a ditch which skirts barrows Damerham (3), (6) and (8) on S.

NMR OAP SU 0819/11/348–9; CUCAP VAP RC8 X 106; NMR VAP (BKS) SU 0818/18/153908

(84) *Linear*, extending in an unusually irregular fashion from around Beggars Bush (08621930) to about 08832037, appears on air photographs of arable as a ditch between spread banks, overall width some 13 m, cutting across some 'Celtic' fields, following one field side (08751985) at least, and bending round probable Iron Age enclosure (67). It elides with M (85) about 08751945.

(85) *Linear* (08651930 on Windmill Hill to around 09581985 in Rockbourne) extends from at least intersection with M (82) at SW (but may have continued further SW), leaves (84) and sweeps past settlement Rockbourne (47), opposite which it delimits 'Celtic' fields and other features. Thereafter it curves NE almost to meet linear Rockbourne (62) curving SE, plausibly related to a track system which lay along (85).

NMR OAP SU 0819/11/348–9 and 50

NOTE
There is a pattern of narrow ditches on the hill rising from North Allenford 084184 (NMR OAP SU 0818/29 and SU 0918/8/122; cf, Plate 40). These include an incomplete polygonal arrangement with one long straight side, covering about 0.8 ha (2 acres), and, above, a sharply angular zig-zag of

indeterminate age or function. There is documentary evidence in AD 1518 (Poole 1976, 175) for a large sheep fold, 'Lordescroft', at Allenford, to which these features could perhaps relate.

Rockbourne

(60)–(62)
These monuments are shown on Area Plan 5.

(60) (SE from 094189) is a *linear* feature with multiple strands, most of which may be due to traffic, continuous in some sense with both Martin (83) and Rockbourne (61). Two parallel scarps 15 m apart falling as much as 1.5 m to NE, with slight linear hollows and ridges running between them appear in rough pasture just SE of intersection with M (80) (09451891), which is here cut up and ploughed over. These features have been destroyed some 250 m SE by digging but a diagonal scarp thereafter reappears, drops from the ridge shoulder which it has otherwise followed and, looking like a much-disturbed bank with ditch on its SW side, it loops round outside and below enclosure (46), petering out shortly beyond (*see* Fig 32: plan with (46)).

(61) *Linear*, apparent ditch on air photographs, springs from Rockbourne (60) N of intersection with Martin (80) and extends for some 650 m N towards, but not visibly reaching, settlement (47).

NMR OAP SU 0918/6/483; CUCAP VAP RC8 X 106

(62) *Linear* extends 200 m ESE from about 09551987, on ground falling towards Down Farm, possibly flanking the opposite side of a route following along linear Martin (85).

(63) *?Linear*, possibly part of a very large enclosure W of Rockbourne Down (10202096–10152150), shaped roughly like a parenthesis open to the east with bracket tips 500 m apart (cf, Area Plan 6). It lies for the most part on a shoulder with gulley W of it. To SE it disappears under farm buildings. Some air photographs suggest a broad bank with dark soil E of it and light-coloured soil to W, perhaps, therefore, separating two different types of land use. There are other curving lines to E (around 103213) probably linked to 'Celtic' fields and overlaid by vestiges of broad ridge-and-furrow.

NMR OAP SU 1021/3/26

Whitsbury

Two linears described under Martin relate to the parish: M (69), its N boundary, and M (80), making for a point N of Whitsbury (17). The former OS Archaeological Division (LIN 74) noted that a line could be faintly seen, on some air photographs and in distant ground observation, as shown with a broken line on Fig 64 leading SW from the hill-fort. This, it suggested,

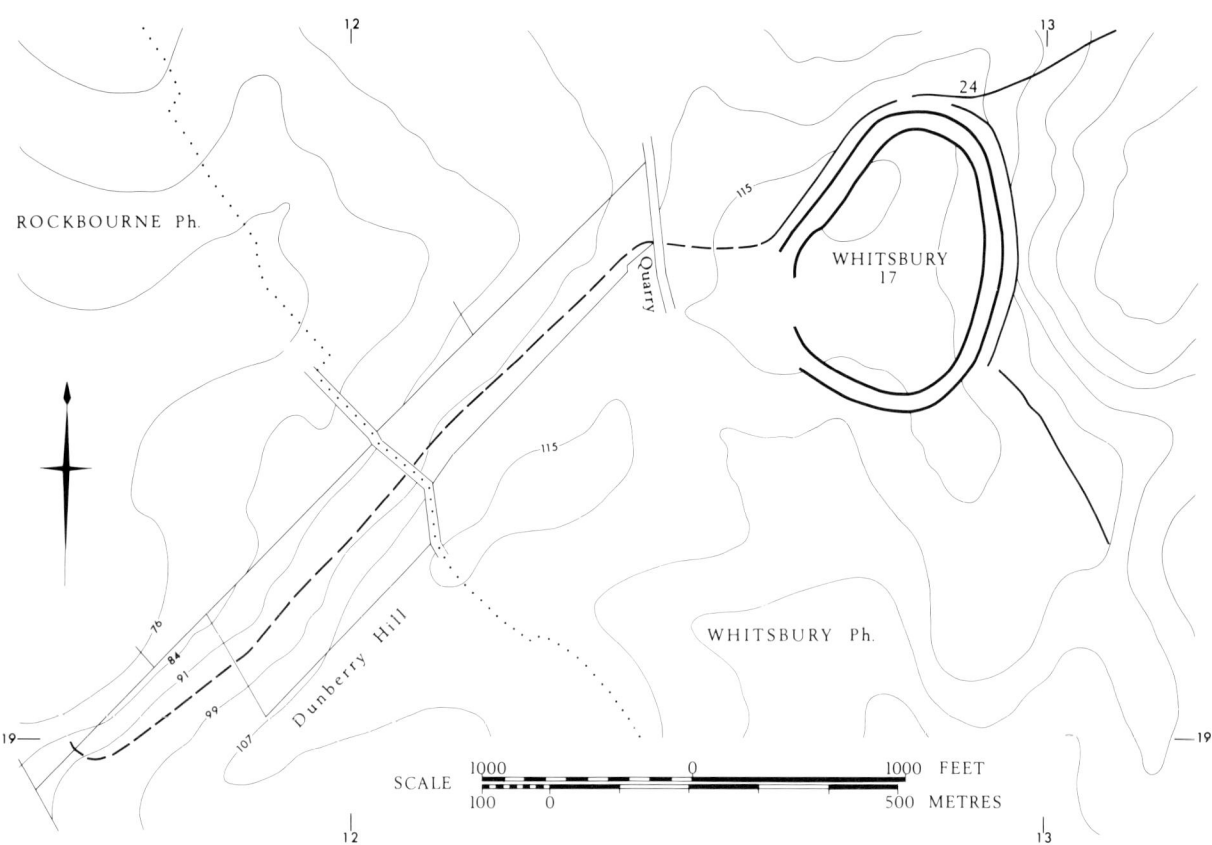

FIG 64   Plan of linear feature south west of Whitsbury hill-fort (suggested by former OS Archaeological Division) (1:10,560)

continued the counterscarp bank, itself notionally incorporating an extension of linear W (24). There was also the possibility then, now known to be not so, that this linked with M (80). No sign of it could be picked up at the time of the Royal Commission's investigation and since it might be, for instance, a track, possibly associated with open field arrangements, it has been omitted from the overall archaeological plan (Fig 1). On Whitsbury Down at 113218 a sinuous dark line about 14 m across, edged with white, is almost certainly part of a hollowed track.

(19) *Linear* (10832244–10822298), single ditch, ?about 3 m across, NW of Whitsbury Down, 550 m long and gently sinuous, rises diagonally from valley bottom to ridge top. It passes close to probable barrow (4) and crosses the angle of a 'Celtic' field at 10832255.

NMR VAP (BKS) SU 1107/1/154070

(20) *Linear* (10952222–11212255), single ditch about 2.5 m across, 370 m long, gently sinuous SE of (19), rises from valley bottom probably cutting 'Celtic' fields. It 'ends' N of Long Plantation at a point where there is a change in arable treatment.

NMR OAP SU 0921/8/192

(21) *Linear bank* N of Whitsbury Down, with possible ditch on its E side (11772278–11902235), straight for 450 m, ? over-riding 'Celtic' fields; of uncertain date. Two or more possible barrows (not inventorised) on its W side.

(22)–(26)
These linear monuments appear on Area Plan 7.

(22) *Linear*, spinal bank and ditch, at least 5 km long, can be traced mostly on air photographs, from a point N of the hill-fort Whitsbury (17) (12852008) in generally straight runs NNE (Area Plan 7; Fig 53; Plate 49: junction with linear Martin (69)). It marks the county boundary NW of Breamore and extends into Wiltshire across Downton parish where it is recorded on OS maps, and seen on air photographs, as far as the border with Odstock parish, 0.8 km south west of Clearbury 'Camp' (14502387). Colt Hoare saw it continuing further north 'leaving Clearbury Ring to the right'. His 'Salisbury station map' takes it to about 140253, another 1200 m (Colt Hoare 1810, map VII and p 231). There is no visible gap or 'entrance'; the bank is consistently E of the ditch, whatever the slope. It remains a substantial, though variously disturbed, earthwork along the county boundary – profiles at 131208 and 133211 – but even in this area parts have been entirely quarried away. Heywood Sumner excavated it between these two points (13202096) and

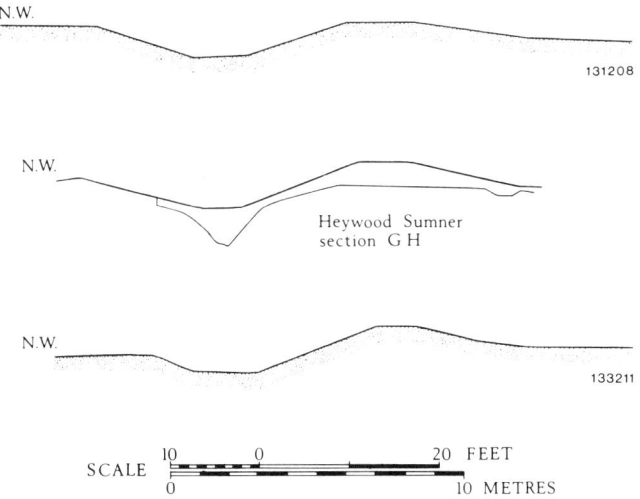

FIG 65   Whitsbury (22): profiles (1:250)

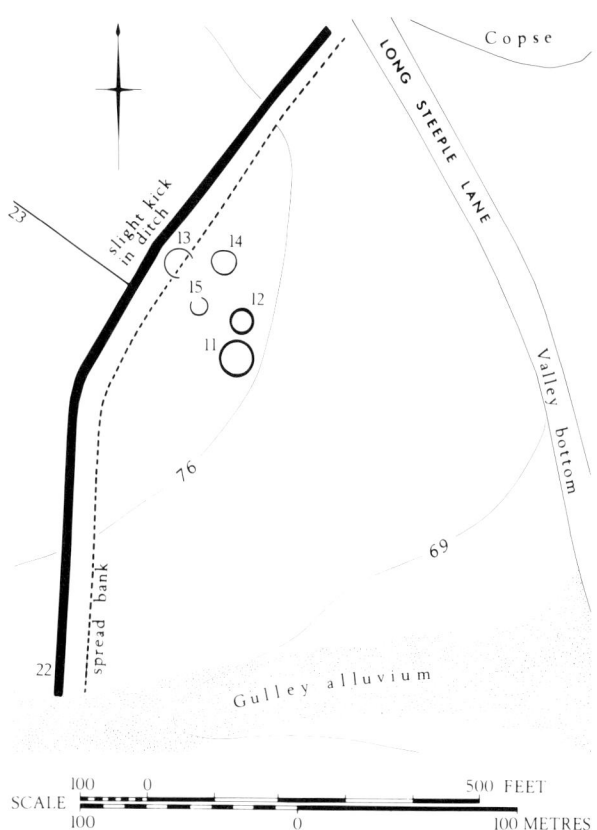

FIG 66   Plan of Whitsbury (22) and (23) with ring barrows (11) to (15) (1:3,333)

his section, G−H, is here reproduced at the same scale as the Royal Commission profiles, the overall width about 14.5 m and ditch 2.5 m below bank (Fig 65). There were no finds. The sides of the ditch were 'unbroken', the bottom 'smooth, and water-worn − owing to the fall of the ground', put at 1:15 (Sumner 1913, 61 and Fig XXXIV). It only survives otherwise for a short length on Wick Down around 139220. The direct course of this linear takes it across valleys, up slopes directly or diagonally, evincing no obvious preference for topographical placing. The relationship with Whitsbury hill-fort is unknown. The ditch is not visible on present air photographs S of 12852008 but at that point has crept towards the hedge which at 12881995 makes a bend of the sort found repeated in the linear's run. It skirts clusters of barrows at three points: Whitsbury (11)−(15), Breamore (2)−(3) and a possible group of five apparently noted by Colt Hoare (1810, 231) just NE of the junction with M (69) but of which no sign remains. It seems that barrow Whitsbury (13) was actually incorporated in the bank which certainly changed direction by 7° at that precise point (Fig 66; Plate 52). A narrow ditch (Whitsbury (23)) joins it at right angles opposite the barrows (11)−(15). On Wick Down a linear, unnumbered, is seen on air photographs (CUCAP VAP RC8 W 44) approaching close (13752183) as if to make a butt junction. N of Whitsbury, about 128202, 'b' on Area Plan 7, an undated parcel of three, possibly four, narrow dark lines, make a junction at an obtuse angle. These lines are about 22 m apart and 90 m long (cf, page 98).

A small boundary bank, about 30 cm high, corresponding with the county boundary from NW, crosses the ditch of this linear beside Long Steeple Lane at 13052074. On the bank where it lies over the ditch is a Shaftesbury estate boundary stone inscribed with 'S' under an Earl's coronet. A boundary stone, uninscribed except for an OS bench mark, is set on top of a compound mound, on Gallows Hill, 2.5 m high above the ditch bottom, piled up on top of a fragment of the linear that had become isolated by tracks and other disturbance.

O G S Crawford took this linear in its developed form in Wiltshire to be a 'military' work associated with the advance of Cerdic and Cynric into Wessex. Air photographs, which he published, seemed to him to show it cutting through 'Celtic' fields (Crawford 1931, 454, Plates I, II; cf, Plate 49 in this volume). Mrs C M Piggott, later insisting on the prehistoric origin of the linear, took the air photographs to mean that it had been used as a boundary for a 'Celtic' field system (Piggott 1944, 68). The evidence is confused by the imposition of strip fields into and over the 'Celtic' field pattern. Some 'Celtic' fields are laid out from the linear; others E of Charlton Furze are probably crossed by it, while strips lying on these same 'Celtic' fields appear also to lie over a flattened section of the linear.

(N of Whitsbury) CUCAP VAP RC8 BM 192−3; NMR OAP SU 1220/7/89−90; SU 1220/8/91; SU 1221/4/333 (Plate 52)
(In Wilts) CUCAP VAP RC8, W 42−4; RAF VAP CPE UK 1811 4140−1; NMR OAP 1423/11

(23) *Linear ditch*, under 0.9 m wide, seen on air photographs, probably prehistoric, extends NW for 250 m from a butt junction with (22) at 12922057. It bends slightly westward at 160 m from (22) (*see* Area Plan 7).

NMR OAP SU 1221/4/333 (Plate 52)

(24) *Linear*, largely destroyed, with bank where detectable

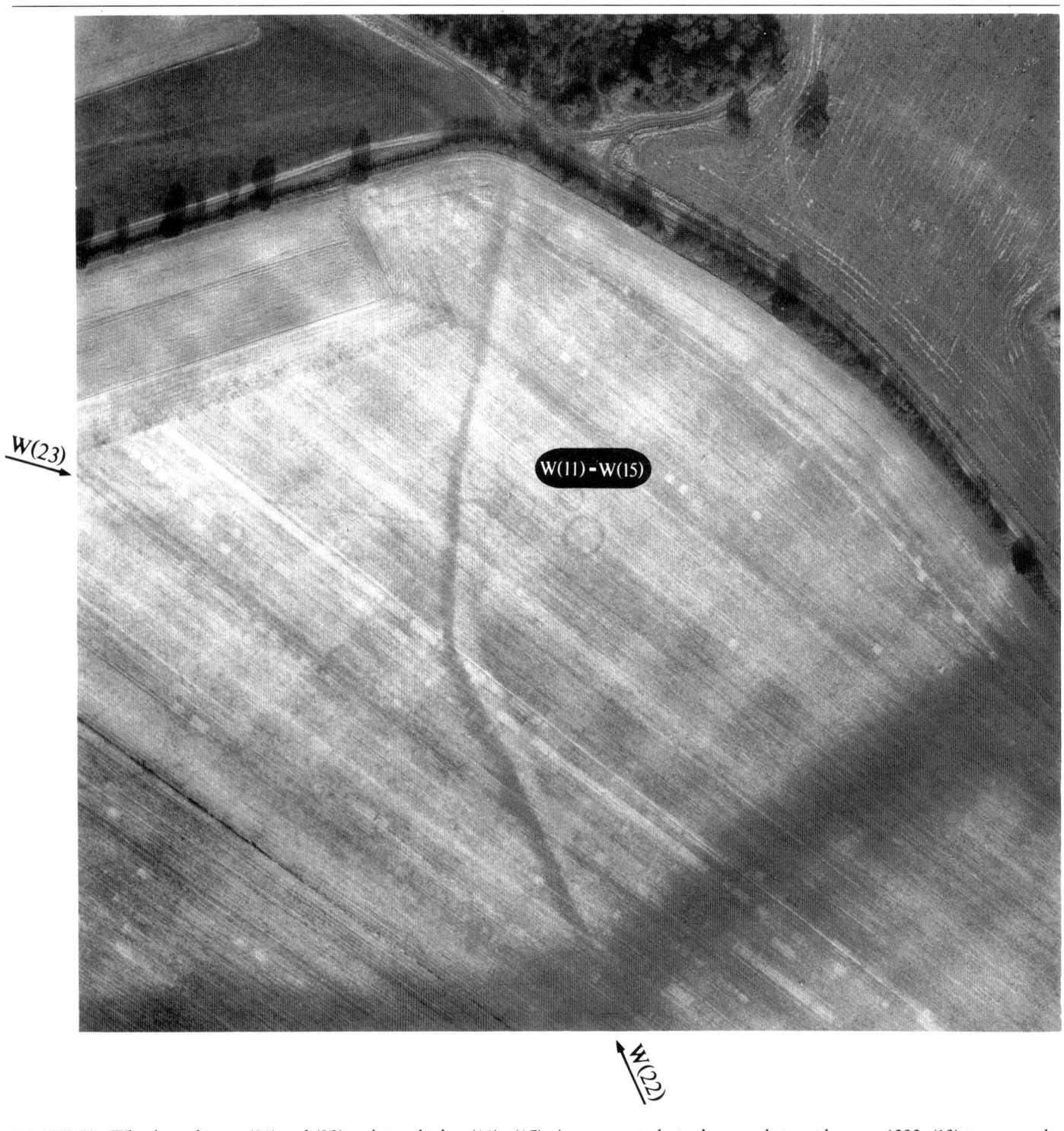

W(23)

W(11) - W(15)

W(22)

PLATE 52   Whitsbury, linears **(22)** and **(23)** and ring ditches **(11)**−**(15)**. A near-vertical air photograph in grid square 1220; (13) intersects the bank of (22) just north east of the point where narrow ditch (23) meets the ditch of (22) (*see* Fig 66, a trace of the air photograph, and Area Plan 7). (NMR OAP SU 1221/4/333)

consistently on the north side, undated, extends E about 2 km from the N of Whitsbury hill-fort (12861994) to and round the S side of Mizmaze Hill, thence N to disappear in arable around 13922065 (Area Plan 7; Fig 38).

The relationship with the hill-fort is uncertain because of disturbance and the existence of additional fragmentary banks of unknown attribution (Fig 37). It appears to change direction opposite the large mound, probable barrow (16), where the ditch would have intersected the skirt of the mound. E of this the bank, just discernible, is some 4 m across and a terrace S of this corresponds with the ditch. Some 45 m W of the valley bottom the bank is some 3.5 m wide and 0.3 m high. A lynchet under 1 m high touches its ditch on S. It drops into and crosses the valley bottom (Long Steeple Lane) without a break, and then, markedly sinuous, it climbs E to the base of Mizmaze Hill and curves round it at this level before meeting hollowed tracks of South Charford Drove which make identification difficult.

Some air photographs show a dark line along the uphill edge of the bank W of Mizmaze Hill (cf, Plate 47). This is possibly due to lynchet accumulation rather than to a ditch. The bank is seen as a scarp up to some 1.5 m high. 'Celtic' fields were eventually laid off it in this area but its sinuous shape, and that of Breamore (14), a fragment of sinuous linear abutting it, strongly suggests that this was not a primary intention and that trees presented obstacles to be avoided in this naturally wooded area.

Bibliography: Sumner 1913, 21

(25) *Linear* of uncertain nature, partly twin, partly single ditched, is seen on air photographs W for at least 320 m from 13322007 where it meets linear (24) in quite unknown relationship. The narrow twin ditches maintain a spacing of some 8 m for most of the distance; thereafter the lower, N ditch, crosses over to take up the line of the upper ditch. In this area there is a sharp distinction in the colour of the soil on either side, suggesting that it proved an effective boundary for some considerable time. It is conceivable that this linear linked with Breamore (13), similar in its twin and single ditch pattern and from its position arguably a road.

NMR OAP SU 1220/8/94

(26) *Linear*, bank and ditch, with bank on E side, extends SSE from 12961948 just S of Whitsbury hill-fort for about 1.3 km, in a belt of trees formerly known as 'Rowditch' (Sumner 1913, 21). The bank is there about 3.5 m across and 0.6 m high. Further S it is less than 1 m across above a ditch of similar width. It runs into the clayey soils and gravel of the Reading Beds, bends E about 13401868 where its ditch is briefly incorporated in hollowed track dropping to the valley, then returns to a southerly course but now somewhat sinuous, disappearing at the parish boundary (13641844). It is not known what relationship there might be between this linear and the hill-fort (17).

Williams-Freeman claimed that this work was on the line of the old county boundary (Williams-Freeman 1915, 178) (cf, page 72 above for discussion about position of county boundary on Rockbourne Down).

(27) *Linear*, double ditched on air photographs, rising from the valley bottom at Long Steeple Lane (13941896) running W, curving slightly N, for some 400 m.

NMR OAP SU 1418/1

Bibliography

Alcock, L 1971. *Arthur's Britain: History and Archaeology AD 367–634.* Allen Lane The Penguin Press, London
  1987. *Economy, Society and Warfare among the Britons and Saxons.* University of Wales Press, Cardiff

Andrews and Dury 1773. *Andrews' and Dury's Map of Wiltshire 1773. A Reduced Facsimile.* Wiltshire Archaeological and Natural History Society, Records Branch, vol VIII (1952). Devizes

Barrett, J C and Bradley, R J 1978. Trial excavation at South Lodge Camp 1977. *Antiquity* LII, 223–7

Bowden, M C B and Tingle, M 1984. Hand-in-Hand flint cairn, Tollard Farnham. *Proc Dorset Natur Hist Archaeol Soc* 106, 109–10

Bowen, H C 1961. *Ancient Fields: A Tentative Analysis of Vanishing Earthworks and Landscapes.* British Association for the Advancement of Science, London
  1975. Air photography and the development of the landscape in central parts of southern England. In *Aerial Reconnaissance for Archaeology*, ed D R Wilson, CBA Research Report 12, 103–18
  1978. 'Celtic' fields and 'ranch' boundaries in Wessex. In *The Effect of Man on the Landscape: the Lowland Zone*, ed S Limbrey and J G Evans, CBA Research Report 21, 115–23
  1979. Gussage in its Setting. In G J Wainwright, *Gussage All Saints. An Iron Age settlement in Dorset*, DoE Archaeological Reports 10, 179–83

Bowen, H C, Evans, J G and Race, E 1978. An Investigation of the Wessex Linear Ditch System. In *Early Land Allotment*, ed H C Bowen and P J Fowler, British Archaeological Reports 48, 149–53

Bradley, R J 1983. Archaeology, Evolution and the Public Good: the intellectual development of General Pitt-Rivers (Proceedings of the Summer Meeting of the Royal Archaeological Institute at Weymouth in 1983). *Archaeol J* 140, 1–9
  1986. *The Dorset Cursus: the Archaeology of the Enigmatic* (Wessex Lecture III). CBA Group 12

Calkin, J B 1962. The Bournemouth Area in the Middle and Late Bronze Age, with the 'Deverel–Rimbury' problem reconsidered. *Archaeol J* CXIX, 1–65

Catherall, P D, Barnett, M and McClean, H 1984. *The Southern Feeder: The Archaeology of a Gas Pipeline.* The British Gas Corporation

Colt Hoare, Sir R 1810. *Ancient Wiltshire*, Vol I. London
  1821. *Ancient Wiltshire*, Vol II. London

Cotton, M 1961. Robin Hood's Arbour and rectilinear enclosures in Berkshire. *Berkshire Archaeol J* 59, 1–35

Crawford, O G S 1924. *Air Survey and Archaeology.* Ordnance Survey Professional Paper No 7, HMSO, London
  1931. Cerdic and the Cloven Way. *Antiquity* V, 441–58

Crawford, O G S and Keiller, A 1928. *Wessex from the Air.* Clarendon Press, Oxford

Current Archaeology 1984. Milton Keynes. *Current Archaeology* 90, 199–208

Ellison, A 1980. Settlements and regional exchange: a case study. In *Settlement and Society in the British Later Bronze Age*, ed J C Barrett and R J Bradley, British Archaeological Reports 83, 127–40

Ellison, A and Rahtz, P 1987. Excavations at Whitsbury Castle Ditches, Hampshire, 1960. *Proc Hampshire Fld Club Archaeol Soc* 43, 63–81

Evans, J G and Vaughan, M P 1985. An Investigation into the Environment and Archaeology of the Wessex Linear Ditch System. *Antiq J* LXV, 11–38

Evison, V I 1965. *The Fifth-Century Invasions South of the Thames.* Athlone Press, University of London

Fasham, P J 1979. Excavations on Bridget's and Burntwood Farms, Itchen Valley parish, Hampshire, 1974. MARC 3 sites R5 and R6. *Proc Hampshire Fld Club Archaeol Soc* 36, 37–86

Ford, S 1981–2. Linear earthworks on the Berkshire Downs. *Berkshire Archaeol J* 71, 1–20

Green, M T 1979. Note in 'Dorset Archaeology in 1979'. *Proc Dorset Natur Hist Archaeol Soc* 101, 135–7
  1981. Interim Report on the excavation of an unrecorded pond barrow at Down Farm, Gussage St Michael. *Proc Dorset Natur Hist Archaeol Soc* 103, 117
  1982. A recently discovered Iron Age settlement at Farnham. *Proc Dorset Natur Hist Archaeol Soc* 104, 179–80

Grinsell, L V 1940. Hampshire Barrows. *Proc Hampshire Fld Club Archaeol Soc* XIV, 9–40, 195–229, 346–65
  1982. *Dorset Barrows Supplement.* Dorset Natural History and Archaeological Society, Dorchester

Hawkes, C F C 1940. The excavations at Quarley Hill. *Proc Hampshire Fld Club Archaeol Soc* XIV, 136–94
  1947. Britons, Romans and Saxons round Salisbury and in Cranborne Chase: Reviewing the Excavations of General Pitt-Rivers, 1881–1898. *Archaeol J* CIV, 27–81

Hewitt, A T Morley 1972. *The Story of Fordingbridge* 2nd edn (privately printed)

Hoade, W H 1975. Ring ditches near the Dorset Cursus at Pentridge. *Proc Dorset Natur Hist Archaeol Soc* 97, 48–9

Johnston, D E 1982. *The Excavation of the Roman Crossroads at Batt's Bed. An Interim Report.* Wimborne

Kinnes, I A and Longworth, I H 1985. *Catalogue of the Excavated Prehistoric and Romano-British material in the Greenwell Collection.* British Museum Publications Ltd, London

Lewis, B and Green, M 1980. Excavation of a ring ditch at Down Farm, Gussage St Michael: Interim Report. *Proc Dorset Natur Hist Archaeol Soc* 102, 85

Light, T 1983. A Romano-British waster heap at Allen's Farm, Rockbourne. *Proc Hampshire Fld Club Archaeol Soc* 39, 69–75

Mercer, R 1980. *Hambledon Hill: A Neolithic Landscape.* Edinburgh University Press, Edinburgh

Mills, A D 1980. *The Place-Names of Dorset, Part Two.* English Place-Name Society vol LIII

Piggott, C M 1944. The Grim's Ditch Complex in Cranborne Chase. *Antiquity* XVIII, 65–71

Piggott, S 1931. Ladle Hill – an unfinished Hill-fort. *Antiquity* V, 474–85
  1941. An unrecorded Iron Age enclosure on Rockbourne Down, Hants. *Proc Hampshire Fld Club Archaeol Soc* XV, 53–5

Piggott, S and Piggott, C M 1945. The excavation of a barrow on Rockbourne Down. *Proc Hampshire Fld Club Archaeol Soc* XVI, 156–62

Pitt-Rivers, A 1887. *Excavations in Cranborne Chase near Rushmore on the borders of Dorset and Wiltshire. Volume I. Excavations in the Romano-British village on Woodcutts Common and Romano-British antiquities in Rushmore Park.* London (privately printed)
  1888. *Excavations in Cranborne Chase near Rushmore on the borders of Dorset and Wiltshire 1880–1888. Volume II. Excavations in barrows near Rushmore. Excavations in Romano-British village, Rotherley. Excavations in Winkelbury Camp. Excavations in British Barrows and Anglo-Saxon cemetery, Winkelbury Hill.* London (privately printed)
  1890. *King John's House, Tollard Royal, Wiltshire.* London (privately printed)

1892. *Excavations in Bokerly and Wansdyke, Dorset and Wiltshire 1888–1891, with observations on the human remains. Volume III.* London (privately printed)

1898. *Excavations in Cranborne Chase near Rushmore on the borders of Dorset and Wiltshire 1893–1896. Volume IV. With Address to the Archaeological Institute of Great Britain and Ireland by General Pitt-Rivers enlarged to serve as a guide to the Bronze and Stone Age models in the Museum, Farnham, Dorset.* London (privately printed)

Pitt-Rivers, A and Gray, H St George 1905. *Excavations in Cranborne Chase. Volume V. Index to Excavations in Cranborne Chase and 'King John's House, Tollard Royal'.* Taunton Castle

Poole, E H 1976. *Damerham and Martin: A Study in Local History.* Compton Russell Press, Tisbury

Rahtz, P A 1961. An excavation on Bokerley Dyke, 1958. *Archaeol J* **CXVIII**, 65–99

Ross, A 1967. *Pagan Celtic Britain: Studies in Iconography and Tradition.* Routledge and Kegan Paul, London

RCHM, 1960. *A Matter of Time: An Archaeological Survey of the River Gravels of England.* HMSO, London

1970a. *An Inventory of Historical Monuments in the County of Dorset. Volume Two. South-East. Part I.* HMSO, London

1970b. *An Inventory of Historical Monuments in the County of Dorset. Volume Three. Central Dorset. Part I.* HMSO, London

1972. *An Inventory of Historical Monuments in the County of Dorset. Volume Four. North Dorset.* HMSO, London

1975. *An Inventory of Historical Monuments in the County of Dorset. Volume Five. East Dorset.* HMSO, London

1976. *Ancient and Historical Monuments in the County of Gloucester. Volume One: Iron Age and Romano-British Monuments in the Gloucestershire Cotswolds.* HMSO, London

1979. *Long Barrows in Hampshire and the Isle of Wight.* HMSO, London

1983. West Park Roman Villa, Rockbourne, Hampshire. *Archaeol J* **140**, 129–50

Saunders, E 1980. A prehistoric skull burial and post circle at Rockbourne, Hampshire. *Proc Hampshire Fld Club Archaeol Soc* **36**, 87–90

Smith, C R 1848. *Collectanea Antiqua,* Vol I. J R Smith, London

Sumner, H 1913. *Ancient Earthworks of Cranborne Chase.* Chiswick Press, London

1914. *Excavations on Rockbourne Down, Hampshire.* Chiswick Press, London

Thomas, A C 1981. *Christianity in Roman Britain to AD 500.* Batsford, London

Thompson, M W 1977. *General Pitt-Rivers, Evolution and Archaeology in the Nineteenth Century.* Moonraker Press, Bradford on Avon

Toms, H S 1925. Bronze Age, or earlier, Lynchets. *Proc Dorset Natur Hist Archaeol Soc* **46**, 87–100

Vatcher, F de M and H L 1965. An excavation of an earthwork near Badbury Rings, Dorset. *Proc Dorset Natur Hist Archaeol Soc* **87**, 101–2

Wainwright, G J, 1979. *Gussage All Saints. An Iron Age Settlement in Dorset.* DoE Archaeological Reports **10**. HMSO, London

Warne, C 1872. *Ancient Dorset.* D Sydenham, Bournemouth (privately printed)

West, W 1816. *A History of the Forest or Chace Known by the Name of Cranborn Chace, collected from authentic early Records, and continued to a late period: with a brief Description of its present State.* Gillingham

White, D A 1970. The Excavation of an Iron Age round barrow near Handley, Dorset, 1969. *Antiq J* **L**, 26–36

Williams-Freeman, J P 1915. *An Introduction to Field Archaeology as Illustrated by Hampshire*

Index